Kill Your
Mortgage &
Sort Your
Retirement

HANNAH McQUEEN

Kill Your Mortgage & Sort Your Retirement

**TAKE CONTROL OF
YOUR MONEY & MAKE
IT WORK FOR YOU**

ALLEN&UNWIN
AUCKLAND · SYDNEY · MELBOURNE · LONDON

First published in 2015
This revised edition published in 2024

Allen & Unwin
Level 2, 10 College Hill, Freemans Bay
Auckland 1011, New Zealand
+64 (9) 377 3800
auckland@allenandunwin.com
www.allenandunwin.co.nz

83 Alexander Street
Crows Nest NSW 2065, Australia
+61 (2) 8425 0100

A catalogue record for this book is available from the
National Library of New Zealand.

ISBN 978 1 99100 678 3

Design by Kate Barraclough
Set in Minion Pro and Montserrat
Printed and bound in Australia by the Opus Group

10 9 8 7 6 5 4 3 2 1

MIX
Paper | Supporting
responsible forestry
FSC
www.fsc.org
FSC® C001695

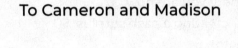

To Cameron and Madison

Contents

Introduction

Back in the day, provided you spent less than you earned and were prepared to delay gratification, you could be sure you would drift towards a comfortable retirement. This is no longer the case.

Even so, financial success isn't solely reserved for high-income earners, or those who start saving for retirement early. Success follows progress, not income. When it comes to financial success, your money habits are more important than your income level, and self-awareness is more powerful than financial literacy.

Financial success is about consistently getting two things right:
1. Mastering your money psychology (habits, beliefs, mindset) so you can save more.
2. Applying the science of wealth creation, so your money works hard and grows faster.

The art of wealth creation is how you go about doing this. The best wealth-creation strategy differs based on where you are starting from, where you want to go and the time you can take to get there. Your strategy needs to consider your money tendencies and your strength of financial character. It must understand your trump cards, and your blind spots. Yes, conditions are harder than before. Be better. Get help. Never hide from hard.

In this book, I will show you how to set financial goals, and find your North Star. You will learn the science of growing wealth and how to determine which wealth strategy is right for you.

The first pillar of financial success is your ability to save well. I'll teach you how to maximise your rate of saving by changing your money behaviours and your environment. This is the engine room of wealth creation, so let's master it.

The second pillar of success is about maximising your forward momentum, or rate of progress. This means focusing on getting your money working harder for you. Time, or your length of runway, plays a big part in wealth creation. How much time do you have before retirement? Depending on the length of runway, different levers will need to be pulled.

These two pillars create a sound structure for a financial plan.

Success lies in your ability to execute the plan well. This is the third pillar of success: mastering the art of execution, and strengthening your financial resilience and character. I'll explain the guardrails and methodologies my clients use to achieve success, no matter their financial situation.

Most people find financial success hard to achieve. And heaven forbid if you've started your run late, you've been a shopper or you've gone through a divorce or a financial setback that forces you to start again! We don't all start from an equal financial footing. Some of us seem financially favoured, others are financially challenged. Many of us are starting on the back foot, and as a result will need to punch above our weight.

Financial success is not a rite of passage, but it does tend to favour the self-aware and it rewards bravery. Success shines on people who have a well-thought-out plan and who are able to clinically execute this plan. Irrespective of where you are starting from, you must diagnose your situation accurately, understand your psychology of spending and money behaviours, learn how to budget effectively and save for a property, and navigate the many financial roadblocks life will throw at you. If you have a mortgage, you must learn how to attack it, to kill it as quickly as possible while also growing wealth. For many, running parallel strategies will be key to reaching the destination in time.

Do not be naïve enough to think the bank is your friend. Do not be silly enough to think that a celebrity endorsing an investment makes it a good one. You must learn the art of financial warfare.

Paying off your mortgage is a strategic step towards financial success, but this alone will not achieve a comfortable retirement. You need to understand how much time you have and the investment constraints you must work within. What suits one person may not suit another. Keep your head, understand your options and move forward. Being the underdog simply means you have to take a less traditional route to reach your goals.

In this book I will teach you the rules of the game, depending on the hand of cards you have been dealt. I will show you how to play your hand to win.

Many a book and movie has been written about ordinary people facing opponents or ideas bigger than themselves. We call it a *David-and-Goliath situation,* when you come up against something seemingly insurmountable.

For a lot of baby boomers, and now Gen X as well, staring down the barrel of retirement can feel as if you are up against a powerful opponent — time, or the lack of it — and that you may have left your run too late.

But whether time is on your side or not is irrelevant. Anyone approaching retirement has a financial place to be and a deadline to get there by. Some of you will be ready to push forward and take more purposeful steps on an already well-thought-out journey, but many of you will be starting off on the back foot.

I have written this book to help people from right across the spectrum of financial confidence and retirement readiness. Even if you are a financial underdog, I hope you will realise that isn't a reason not to try. You may have been dealt a different hand to some, but all that means is we must play your hand differently. We will most likely need to cover more ground, faster and with less wriggle room, but financial success is still achievable. It's the route you take to get there that differs, not the actual destination.

I will show you how to spot opportunities. I will teach you that money is not bigger than you, retirement is not impossible to achieve, but also that success doesn't wait for anyone. Depending on where you're starting from, it may be a lot easier than you realise. Financial success is equal parts psychology (your money behaviours) and strategy (the science of wealth creation). This book will teach you the theory, provide real client stories and share proven methodologies to nudge you forward. In showing you the impact of your choices, it will hopefully motivate you to confront yourself and take the required action to achieve a better financial outcome. Your money psychology may initially work against you, but as you start to understand your money beliefs, natural tendencies and shortcomings, you can develop the plan that will work for you.

Many financial books assume you are already in control of your finances. For the vast majority of people, this is simply not the case. This book starts at the beginning, showing you how to diagnose your starting point in order to better determine the route you need to take to get your money working harder. It then builds on this diagnosis and shows examples of how you can change your money personality and do better. It openly discusses money and relationships. Poor negotiation skills may mean you are not paid what you are worth, and a lack of confidence may be holding you back from tackling this head-on. This book also discusses how to teach your children what they need to know to get ahead in today's harder conditions. Most importantly, this book breaks down the jargon and challenges your previous beliefs about achieving financial success and saving for your retirement.

I am the founder of a business called enable.me. We call ourselves financial personal trainers. We specialise in setting financial strategy and executing on the plan. We are a team of chartered accountants, financial advisors and money coaches who work with our clients to get them ahead faster.

We are not aligned to any particular investment product or bank, and we provide impartial, expert and astute advice. We determine the right strategy for a client based on their money tendencies and goals, and set about improving behaviours, mindset and savings rates, strengthening their financial foundations so we can then apply the right wealth strategy. We work with our clients at the coalface, understanding the nuances of each situation and determining the best plan of attack to bridge the gap between where our clients are going to end up if they change nothing and where they need to be in order to achieve their financial goals.

My team and I have worked with over 10,000 clients. We've learnt that people can sabotage their efforts to get ahead, through a lack of knowledge, a lack of confidence and a lack of action.

This book tells you all you need to know to dramatically change your financial landscape and propel yourself to the financial conclusion you deserve. So get ready: it's time that retirement met its match.

**Change is hard at first, messy in the middle
and gorgeous at the end. —Robin Sharma**

A note from the author

I am a financial advisor and a chartered accountant with a master's degree in tax. I understand money psychology and how to change money behaviours and build a wealth mindset. I specialise in designing the right strategy to get my clients ahead faster, and am experienced at executing these plans. One of my favourite sayings is from boxer Mike Tyson: 'Everyone has a plan until they are punched in the face.' Never a truer word spoken. Executing a plan well when you are ducking and diving is exhausting, and trying to land a couple of knockout blows is sheer hard work.

My job is to get a better financial outcome for my clients, to help them maximise their progress, and to get them in control of their money, saving more, paying down their mortgage faster and growing wealth for retirement. For most clients we have to do all four things at the same time, because their situation requires it (we don't have time to dilly-dally), or their money psychology needs to see big improvements to keep them engaged for longer.

At the time of writing this book, I've had over 20,000 client meetings — so I've seen it all. When it comes to money, nothing frightens me. When I cut through the noise, 'doing better' has a face. So when I say I 'do better', I want to create measurable improvements. As a starter, I aim for the following client outcomes:

- Increase saving rates by up to 500 per cent.
- Save no less than 20 per cent of their income if they have a mortgage.
- Save no less than 50 per cent of their income if they don't have a mortgage.
- Grow wealth to become mortgage-free in less than 10 years.
- Grow wealth to fund retirement. Typically, a client will need an additional $750,000 of wealth to fund their retirement (that's $1.5 million for a couple). This is in addition to being mortgage-free.
- If a client wants to retire earlier than age 65, my job is to have helped them grow enough wealth for this to be possible.

- If a client wants to help their kids onto the property ladder, we need to do this as well as sorting the client's retirement.

Of course there is more science behind working out your retirement number than this rough estimate — but we want to start with the broad concepts of how we are going to get you ahead faster. I call these key concepts 'pidgin economics'.

I have a couple of guiding principles with finances and in life. If I am going to put effort in to something, or expect my client to put in effort, then by jingo I want to see a result. Progress is the key to everything. I am going to track effort and payback, progress and return to make sure we have the right inputs to create the right outputs. Because we don't have unlimited capacity for effort, we'll adopt the Pareto Principle, more commonly called the 80/20 rule, where we focus on the 20 per cent of actions that will unlock 80 per cent of results.

Despite being a financial force, I love to shop. I'm married to a Scotsman, who is tight with everything apart from art supplies and his weekly trip to Bunnings. I have two children, which makes me worry about the financial mess they are going to inherit — not from me, but from the wider economy. I am nervous that the Covid pandemic saw some of the largest economies in the world start printing money, and no one seems to care. I worry that in trying to protect the market, we have caused it to fail. I am disappointed that we don't tax foreigners who invest in our country, and I am also a bit disappointed we don't tax capital. I believe to be financially responsible is to be socially responsible. Most importantly, when it comes to your own finances, I believe that your past behaviour does not translate to your future capability.

My money story

After I graduated from the University of Auckland in 1998, I worked at accounting firm KPMG for a time. My husband and I had a combined salary of $32,000 and we thought we were doing just fine. Fast-forward a few years and we were earning much more than our graduate incomes, yet we'd failed to make any great progress. Sure, we were earning good money, but we felt that we had to keep earning at this level in order to maintain our lifestyle. In fact, despite earning almost five times the level of our graduate income, we were not five times happier and our wealth wasn't five times higher. We were caught on a treadmill of our own making that required us to run faster and harder to simply hold our line.

I didn't think that we were outrageous with our spending. Sure, we enjoyed buying coffees, and I tended to buy my lunch instead of packing it, and OK, I did like buying clothes. But who's judging? We didn't have really expensive hobbies, although as our incomes increased, I found it easier to spend money without much thought. At enable.me we call this 'lifestyle creep', where your living costs slowly increase, usually at the same pace (or slightly faster) than your income. The harder I worked, the more I felt justified in my spending. I enjoyed holidays — I still enjoy holidays — and I have always loved clothes. I felt we worked hard and I wanted us both to be able to enjoy the fruits of our labours. At the time, though, I didn't have a reason to question my spending behaviour. We never argued about money — neither of us seemed to care enough to argue, as there was always money when we needed it to do what we wanted to do.

Reality began to catch up with us when we wanted to buy our first property. The property cost $350,000 and we needed a mortgage of $300,000. (This was almost 25 years ago; again, don't judge.) We had to save our deposit, which was around 15 per cent of the purchase price.

When it came to raising the mortgage, we did what everyone does: we played the banks off against each other to get the best interest rate. We did get a good rate, but the interest saving achieved from the discounted rate was comparably low. Sure, we'd save $20,000 over the life of our mortgage, and of course we preferred having this money in our pocket as opposed to the bank's. However, the $20,000 we were going to save was small fry when compared to the $490,000 in interest that we were going to pay to the bank over the next 30 years.

For some reason, I became fixated on how I could lower this interest cost. I kind of understood that compound interest was making it so high, but I didn't *really* understand how compound interest worked, nor did I have an appreciation of how to reduce it. I recognised that the longer I had the mortgage, the more money I would pay to the bank in interest. On a conceptual level it was clear that to save myself interest I would have to repay the loan faster. Of course. But I didn't want to compromise my lifestyle to achieve this outcome. I also understood that the concepts of repaying my mortgage faster and living a life I enjoyed were not necessarily mutually exclusive but that it would require a precise point of balance if I were to achieve both.

I wanted to understand how I could optimise the structure of my mortgage in order to repay it as quickly as possible. It was at this point that I reached out to Dr Jamie Sneddon, then a mathematics tutor at the University of Auckland. I met with Sneddon over the coming months, and after a few pages of calculus we found we had written a formula for structuring debt to repay it as fast as one's circumstances allow while also living the lifestyle one enjoys. I called this Mortgage Optimisation, and I then patented the formula.

This formula makes one key assumption: that you will have money left over at the end of each week, month and year that can be used to repay your debt faster. This seems a reasonable assumption. However, when trying to apply the formula to my personal situation, I soon realised that, despite earning the most we had ever earned, we had no money left at the end of the month. We were living pay day to pay day. Sure, we were living well — but there was absolutely no money left over. So, even though I had a powerful formula for debt reduction, it was of no value until I found out where my money was going and why I wasn't in control of it.

And this is where it got interesting. Being an accountant, I helped clients to manage their money. I could write a budget — I could even colour-code it (which only an accountant would find exciting) — but writing a budget for myself and sticking to it were two completely different things. When I spoke to my friends about it, they acknowledged that, as their incomes increased, they cared less and less about their finances because there was always enough money to do what they wanted to do. While it was reassuring to not be alone in my financial conundrum, it was equally disturbing to realise that my money personality or psychology of spending could be more of a driver of my financial outcome than my qualifications and income level.

Personally, I was and continue to be a shopper. Telling me to go without something is more likely to cause me to want it more. Telling me to spend less than I earn if I want a shot at getting ahead doesn't motivate me. Asking me to spend less than I earn in the hope of future rewards does nothing to excite or encourage me to even try. Because I work hard I tend to think I should be able to spend what I want, when I want and how I want.

This was my predicament. I questioned whether being a shopper, not a saver, meant that I was destined to financial mediocrity.

I may be a shopper, but I am not financially stupid. I did not accept that just because I was predisposed towards enjoying my lifestyle it meant I wouldn't get ahead. I simply needed to understand how to achieve both a lifestyle I enjoyed and financial progress.

I needed a good reason to try, and an accurate diagnosis of where I was starting from, what I wanted to achieve and whether I was on track to achieve it. I needed a methodology to follow, a better structure to work within, clear expectations, guardrails and accountability. I also needed to identify how much money I frittered away.

I respond well to impartial and intelligent advice. I work better with clear goals, good structures and accountability. To keep me engaged I need to see results, fast. I learned that life inevitably throws curve balls and I needed to learn how to navigate around these.

Slowly but surely I determined a way to keep myself on track. I started to understand my financial pressure points and how to overcome them . . . and very quickly momentum started to build. Best of all, I achieved results and sustained them.

When talking to friends and peers, it seemed I was not alone. The more people I shared my story with, the more fascinated people became. I talked about money and my experience with it openly and honestly, and shared the lessons I had learned with candour. People reacted to this and got on board. I was able to keep testing and fine-tuning the different paths people needed to take depending on their starting point, money tendencies, end goal and time remaining to get there to increase their odds of success.

Early on, I formed the company enable.me to help people get in control of their finances. We describe ourselves as financial personal trainers. We want to help Kiwis get ahead faster, by providing a constructive solution for people who want to become financially successful, whether they are shoppers or savers, with a mortgage or without, on track to retirement or too scared to even think about getting old! Everyone can get ahead faster. If I can do it, surely anyone can.

Money is an emotive topic. Our relationship with money can be sensitive. It's intrinsically linked to our self-worth and self-esteem, yet the tools for getting ahead too often deal with the science of finance, not the behaviours behind it.

When clients work with enable.me, they work to a plan, with a clear framework, support, guardrails and accountability. They know when to expect results and achieve their outcomes. We have worked with thousands of clients throughout New Zealand and the world (including Dubai, the UK, Europe, the US and Australia).

In my role as founder and head coach at enable.me, I have been exposed to many varied and interesting client situations. Some clients are just starting out, others want to retire, many are somewhere in between. Some couples are financially compatible with each other; many aren't. Everyone has obstacles, and it's usually these obstacles that upset their momentum. Most clients aren't bad with their money, but rather 'comfortably inefficient'. Most aren't making the progress their income suggests they could, and almost all could get their money working harder. No matter where you're starting from, you're undoubtedly capable of getting ahead faster. The question to ask is whether the trade-off is worth it. And if it is, are you ready to start?

I am good at diagnosing situations quickly and spotting the problem that needs to be solved. I will share my tricks with you and help you understand the hand you have been dealt, what the trump cards are, and how to play your hand to win.

Money is a complex subject, and it's not discussed honestly. It plays a critical but often unspoken role in relationships, and is connected to our general wellbeing. Yet many of us fail to grasp the basics of money management, preferring instead to do nothing, or drift — maybe because it all seems too hard, or maybe because we just never get around to it. If this sounds familiar, this book is for you.

To be in control of your money means you have choices, options and confidence in your future, even though you may not be quite sure how to get there.

Getting ahead is not easy, but it can be done. Sure, making financial progress would be infinitely easier if we didn't have the continual knockbacks that life throws at us — but that's life. So the plan we develop needs to be flexible enough to absorb the aftershock of these setbacks and still push forward, instead of pretending knockbacks don't happen. In this book I will share with you my tips for overcoming the many challenges to making financial progress.

Remember, no matter what financial life stage you are at, the rules of the game are the same. It's time you learned the rules. Let's go!

PART ONE
Money and you

1.   Money behaviours

Every day I see smart people earning good incomes, yet failing to get ahead. Why is that?

Surely the more money you earn, the easier it is to get ahead? This assumption, like many things connected to money, is a myth. For many, earning more money makes it easier to go nowhere in particular, because money is no longer a concern. Instead, the security of a higher income gives you permission to disengage from your finances.

What you do with your money will always be more important than how much money you earn.

Layers to money decisions

Every financial decision is underpinned by a set of layers. The outside layer, the one we tend to see, is the financial impact of an action or inaction, the financial detail of how the money being earned or spent fits into your overall financial plan. This layer is the quantifiable impact of a choice. We usually focus on this layer because it is visible.

The second, less visible layer is the 'how and why' supporting those financial decisions. These are the reasons sitting underneath every financial choice. These reasons are not always obvious, and they can stem from assumptions or the value you place on money.

To understand these assumptions, you need to look closely at the third, almost invisible layer: your relationship with money. Your relationship with money is driven by your money personality, your environment (both now and in your early years) and even genetics.

A lot of people don't make the right money calls because money seems mysterious to them. They feel that way because they don't 'look under the hood' at their financial decisions.

Money beliefs

How we feel about money shapes how we behave with money. After all, our behaviour is not governed by models of logical thinking; instead it is governed by feelings, which in turn shape our thoughts and actions. Our beliefs about money include our mindset around money and our money scripts.

We all think about money differently, depending on our upbringing, our friends and family, and our community. Most of us blindly follow our families' ideas and attitudes to money. You absorb what you are taught or have observed and then you interpret it, forming your attitude towards money. Researchers call this inherited mindset your 'money script'.

In *Wired for Wealth*, the authors have this to say about money scripts: 'A money script is not necessarily wrong, but neither is it necessarily right. Our scripts are often skewed, exaggerated or one-dimensional, consisting of incomplete or partial truths. They are usually highly contextual, true in one circumstance but false in many others. Since our money scripts are mostly unconscious, we don't question their accuracy or examine the degree to which they are true and work for us, yet we continue to act on them as if they were entirely true.'

These scripts or beliefs form your attitude towards money — which in turn impacts your relationship with money and how you behave with money, including how you think you can and cannot use it. Your money script shapes how much you think you can earn, how much you think you can spend on yourself, your family and your friends. It dictates how you use debt in your life and whether you choose to invest or give all your money to charity.

These beliefs can be limiting or empowering — but you need to take time to reflect on what your money beliefs might be. Unless you reflect on your beliefs, you won't be aware how they influence your behaviour, which can leave you open to missed opportunities and questionable choices.

How do you figure out your beliefs around money?

The first step is to observe yourself. Pay attention to your thoughts, actions and behaviours around money. Do any of the points below resonate with you?

- My parents tried to teach me how to budget, but when I see them spending willy-nilly, I think that spending when you feel like it is OK.
- My parents spent money they didn't have as a stress release, so I tend to do this too.
- My parents argued about money, so I associate any discussions

about money as being linked to a blow-up, and I have negative emotions towards money as a result.

- I think that rich people are entitled idiots, so I am less inclined to want to be financially successful.
- My parents don't earn much money so I don't think that I can either.
- People like me will never be wealthy.
- More money, more problems.
- I deserve to be wealthy.
- I don't deserve to be wealthy.
- My parents never discussed money so it mustn't be important.
- The universe will provide, so there is no point trying.
- It will be okay in the end, so I don't need a plan.

Each script can have a significant impact on your behaviour. For example, if you think that money is bad or it makes you unhappy, you might sabotage yourself financially. If you don't think you deserve money, you are more likely to earn below your potential. If you think you deserve money, you are more likely to overspend. If you think there will always be enough money because the universe will provide, you are likely to never take action. If you think money is unimportant, you might excuse your poor financial decisions. Beliefs matter.

Become aware of your thoughts, because your thoughts impact your feelings, and your feelings impact your behaviour, and your behaviour impacts your thoughts, and round we go again. Without self-awareness, you'll mindlessly get caught in this cycle.

You are not your parents. You can be wealthy. You can design the life you want. Start believing it, then accompany this belief with a strategy, then action it — which changes your attitude, which changes your thoughts, which changes what you believe is possible.

The good news is it's possible to change the way you think about money. First, it's important to identify and understand which money beliefs may be stunting your ability to get ahead. The next step is adopting new ways of thinking, and that often means learning more about your money tendencies in order to understand which strategy will be the most effective for you. Are you a shopper or a saver? Do you find it easier to grow wealth or hold wealth? Are you ambitious or nervous with your money? You will lean in a direction. This direction is neither good nor bad, but each point has a slightly different way of engaging you to make it easier to make better choices, which leads to more wealth.

The way you think about money does influence how you manage your finances. But once you've identified the factors behind how you think about money, you can work on improving your relationship with money and start making better financial choices.

I discuss your psychology of money in more detail in the next chapter.

Money myths

Money myths also influence what you think is possible, which feeds your beliefs. Here are the most common myths I encounter (which I then disprove):

- I need to earn more money, and then it will be easier.
- I need to have a lot of money if I want to work on a financial plan.
- I can't start unless the conditions are perfect.
- It's easier to get ahead if I am in a relationship.
- A man is a financial plan. (As if!)
- I need to be financially literate and confident before I can make progress.
- I haven't achieved financial success before, so I probably won't now.
- I'm too old to get started; opportunity has already passed me by.
- Financial progress is outside of my control.
- Willpower is the key to achieving my goals.

Money habits

What we do with our money is more important than how much money we earn and our level of financial literacy. Behaviour trumps knowledge every day of the week. Or as Morpheus said in *The Matrix*, 'There is a difference between knowing the path and walking the path.' It's been proven that teaching someone a financial concept doesn't necessarily translate to them applying that concept in real life. In fact, in a recent piece of research, lifting financial literacy translated to a minuscule 0.1 per cent improvement in financial outcomes within three months of teaching. So while financial literacy programmes are popular, there's limited evidence that they lead to significant changes in savings behaviour. Learning about something doesn't mean that you will act on your new knowledge.

Simply giving information to people isn't a good recipe for changing behaviour. Social science tells us that if we want to change behaviour, we have to change the structure we're working within (the system) and our environment. Wherever possible, we want to align the desired outcome with the easiest behaviour, and make the invisible visible. Aerodynamics tells us that if you want to get maximum propulsion you need to reduce friction. In the same way, your money habits can create the biggest friction to your ability to save.

> Your money behaviours are your money habits or tendencies. They are what you would do if left unchecked. To get a quick gauge on how good your money habits are, ask yourself how much you've saved in the past 12 months, or take a look at your bank balance. Both quickly indicate the health of your habits.
>
> If you don't save, your money habits are weak. If you save 50 per cent of your income, your habits are awesome. Most people will be somewhere in between.

The science of habits

Habit science tells us that making conscious decisions repeatedly can be hard. The harder something is, the less likely you will continue to do it, so anything that takes a lot of willpower and discipline is less likely to be sustainable. The easier a habit is to adopt, or the more enjoyable it is, the more likely you'll stick to it. Making a habit easy requires hard-to-miss cues and a plan of action.

James Clear, author of *Atomic Habits* and one of the world's leading experts on habit formation, says that in setting new habits we do not rise to the level of our goals, but we fall to the level of our systems. So even if you can dream big, if the system you are working with is inefficient or ineffective, you aren't likely to make any progress.

When it comes to changing habits, seeing really is believing. Getting quick, measurable wins is usually the most direct way of influencing your mindset and making new habits stick.

In their book *Dollars and Sense*, behavioural economist Dan Ariely and writer Jeff Kreisler delve into how vision impacts our financial choices. Two thousand years ago, people saved their income in goats, cattle or chickens. Debt wasn't really a thing, and it certainly wasn't easily accessed. Looking at your neighbour reminded you daily of how well they were doing. This visual reminder created a benchmark to measure yourself against. With the invention of money, then digital money, then consumerism and debt (buy now, pay later), this benchmark is gone, meaning that you don't know how you are doing relative to others. Now you can only see what people spend their money on. Savings remain invisible, while spending is visible.

Making progress visible is the key to building momentum.

Why is it so hard to save?

The key to habit change is to make the desired outcome easy to achieve, and to create pain around the actions you are trying to discourage. Therefore, any system that makes it easier to spend also makes it harder to save. Using digital currency and digital payments removes friction from the process of paying. It's a lot easier than swiping a card, which is easier than making a bank transfer, which is easier than having to write a cheque (remember them?), which is easier than withdrawing the money in cash from a bank teller during bank hours. Banks and suppliers have made it easier for you to spend your money. If it is easy to spend, then it's disproportionately harder to save. The system is literally wired against us. We also know that one of the challenges with saving for long periods of time is the concept of hyperbolic discounting, which concludes the further out in time we get the reward, the less motivating the reward will be for our behaviour.

This is why clever goal-setting and introducing payment friction, as well as visible progress that creates momentum when it's correctly tracked, goes a long way to overcoming the system that tilts us towards overspending.

Goal-setting

Goals are exciting because they provide focus for our lives and a target to aim for. They cause us to stretch and grow in new ways. In order to reach our goals, we must become better. We must change and grow.

One of the first things that I ask my clients to do is to list their financial goals. Often this request is met with a slightly embarrassed, 'I don't really have any'. We might have a vague notion of what we would like to achieve, but nothing defined in detail, and certainly nothing that can be broken down into smaller digestible milestones that are easily tracked. Ambiguous goals produce ambiguous results. Incomplete goals produce incomplete futures.

When I ask a few more questions, the answers tend to be along the lines of: I want to get ahead faster. I want to feel more in control of my money. I want to pay off my mortgage faster. I want to be able to retire. I want to help my kids onto the property ladder. Or, I just want to grow wealth and get my money working harder.

Yes, these statements could be the start of a financial goal, but robust goals need to be specific, measurable, attainable within your timeframe and realistic, and they need to have an end point.

You want to make sure that the greatest pull on your life is the pull of the future. Some people live in the past, re-affirming the money scripts they have written for themselves. Yes, you must remember and learn from the past, but your future must be your focus. If you are skinny on your dreams, or skimp on your objectives and your financial purpose, then that ain't going to pull you forwards. You're more likely to be pulled backwards or pulled apart by distractions. But to be pulled forwards, you need to have your future planned. To design your future, you must have well-considered goals that can act like a magnet towards your objective. The better you define and describe the goal and the harder you work on it, the stronger the pull.

Of course, it's easier to achieve great things when you have a reason. That's the key to it all, according to Jim Rohn in his book *The Art of Exceptional Living*. Rohn discusses the science of goal-setting and believes 'that you have to have enough reasons' to aim higher. The major reason for setting a goal is for what it makes you do to accomplish it. This will always be of far greater value than what you get at the end. Goal-setting provides focus, shapes our dreams and gives us the ability to hone in on the exact actions we need to take in order to get everything in life we desire.

Reasons first, answers second

Rohn maintains that when you know what you want and want it badly enough, you will find a way to get it done. The answers will become evident to you, but you have to want it badly enough. Necessity drives us to find solutions.

What are some reasons for doing well, or wanting more? This will vary from person to person. For some, their reason to do well is for their family, or to be able to help others. For some, their reason is to achieve recognition, and for others, it's about how it makes them feel about themselves.

There is a science to goal-setting and it is profoundly simple. Decide what you want, and write it down. In a study conducted by Dr Gail Matthews, a psychology professor at the Dominican University of California, participants who wrote down their goals were 42 per cent more likely to achieve them than those who didn't. By writing down your goals you engage your brain in a different way. Writing down goals forces you to clarify what you want. Writing on paper also gives you a physical reminder of what you are aiming for.

Not everyone knows what they want to achieve. If this is you, answer some of the questions below to help open your mind to your financial dreams.

Looking out five or 10 years from now:
- What do I want to have?
- What do I want to share?
- How much do I want to earn?
- What projects do I want to support?
- What do I want to be known for?
- What extraordinary things do I want to do?
- What ordinary things do I want to do?
- What silly things do I want to do?
- What important things do I want to do?
- When do I want to retire?
- What do I want to be able to do in retirement?

Decide your answers, and write them down. This is your list of what you want your future to look like. Now, let's work out how to get you there.

Powerful goals have three components:
- They must be inspiring.
- They must be believable.
- They must be goals you can act on.

A client may start out by saying, 'I want to get rid of my mortgage.' I will ask how quickly they want it gone; often they don't have an answer for this. So I set about determining how quickly the mortgage could be repaid if the client stuck to a plan with everything working as it should (including a lift and shift of their money habits and mindset). Once I've done some quick number-crunching, I get a pretty good idea of what's possible.

This is when I set our first goals. Some clients know what they want to achieve — e.g., I want to be mortgage-free in seven years. If they have a plan to achieve it, then all power to them. But if they have a goal without a plan, I need to first assess whether the goal is achievable based on saving improvements that could be unlocked, and wealth creation strategies that could be applied. The more efficiencies they can unlock by managing their money smarter and saving faster, the less reliant they are on achieving a wealth-creation strategy. We have greater control over our spending, saving and mortgage repayments than we have on the markets. This means that the more progress we can unlock ourselves, the lower the wealth-creation goal will need to be, and the more likely it will be achieved within the required timeframe.

Let's say we can get this person mortgage-free in seven years (compared to the 30 years that the bank would prefer). For the client to believe this timeframe is possible, I need to believe it is possible, and I need them to understand how it's done. I work backwards in the explanation: let's say you have a mortgage of $500,000 that you are currently on track to pay off over 30 years. You are already saving $10,000 per annum, although this money is sitting in a savings account, rather than working for you. To get you mortgage-free in seven years, I would need to lift your savings rate to $50,000 (from $10,000), so we need to close the gap by $40,000. Whether that saving improvement is likely will depend on how inefficient your financial foundation is. Normally I can unlock 60 per cent of the savings targets from working to a carefully designed budget, supported by a better structure, clear targets, guardrails and a hefty dose of accountability. The other 40 per cent comes from getting everything structured correctly (your KiwiSaver, insurances and mortgages), which I facilitate for my clients.

To increase your savings rate, I will show you how to change your money habits, improve your money-management system, and introduce friction in certain places to tilt you towards the right behaviours. I am going to help you to be as efficient as possible, so saving money will be easier. I will break your seven-year goal into annual actions, and break each year down into quarterly targets: a saving target, a spending target, a mortgage-reduction target and a stretch goal. We will measure progress every 12 weeks. The quarterly target will be broken down into monthly milestones and weekly actions.

In this example, your savings rate is unlikely to lift to $50,000 per annum, then we need to think about how we can get your money working harder, rather than you working harder. This is where the right wealth-creation strategy can help close out any gap we couldn't naturally achieve ourselves.

I recommend setting goals that will stretch you, both for what it will make of you and the skills you will learn. With the achievement of each financial goal, you are becoming more disciplined, considered and deliberate with your money. With financial goals, you prove to yourself that you value your future instead of sleepwalking towards it. Set the type of goals that will make something of you by achieving them.

Never set your goals too low or surround yourself with people without financial aspiration. Go where expectations are high. Go where the pressure is on to perform, so that you will grow, change and develop new skills and get better results.

Achieving your goals

To increase the odds of achieving a goal, you first need to believe the goal is possible. If you are not sure whether it's possible, enlist experts who can confirm that your strategy will work, or refine your strategy to unlock greater potential. Having an expert in your corner gives you confidence, and confidence helps you to move forward.

Next, write the goal down. It doesn't matter where; on a Post-it Note or the back of an envelope, who cares? But write it down.

Stick the goal to your fridge. Look at the goal every day. Commit it to memory. Feel yourself focus. Visualise what success will look and feel like.

Next, it's about getting to the nuts and bolts of progress. Know what inputs will lead to the output you're after. What three actions do you need to do to get you there? Understand the rhythm you need to work to. Be nimble, because the winds of change get gusty as soon as you set off.

To achieve your goals, you're going to need:
- Clarity on where you are going and why.
- An understanding of what you are about to encounter (over the next 12 weeks) and why you are doing things in a particular way.
- Clear systems to work within — ones that insert guardrails and friction to discourage bad habits.
- Accountability.
- An ability to track progress in real time.
- Preset check-ins to measure progress and reset the plan.

Never sleepwalk towards your goals. For my clients, every 12 weeks religiously, we meet and determine how well they've gone against the goals we set 12 weeks prior. We take time to understand what went right and wrong. We set the next 90 days of goals based on expected spending commitments and known opportunities. We can see where it's going to get hard, and we prepare for it early.

Focus is key for goal achievement. People who focus on their goals achieve them 23 per cent more quickly and report 17 per cent less effort in reaching their goal. Knowing where you are going makes it faster and easier to get there.

Getting started

When providing advice, many financial experts assume you are already in control of your money and that you are good at saving. But most people don't save anything at all, and don't know how to start. To get ahead, you need to first understand where you are starting from. For example, if you are wanting to lose weight, you hop on the scales. If you are reading a map, you need to know where you are, relative to your destination. In the same way, if you are serious about making financial progress, you need to hop on the financial scales, look in the mirror and become self-aware.

To get ahead, you need a plan. Not a budget; a plan. A budget is static; a plan is fluid and dynamic. A plan can be tailored to the nuances of any situation, recognising opportunities and obstacles and, most importantly, changing as life changes and resetting quickly.

The first step in creating a financial plan is to take a high-resolution snapshot of your current situation. You need to determine where you measure up, what your financial body mass index (BMI) is and identify some of the wider issues affecting your financial health. I won't lie, getting to know the financial you can be a confronting process, one you might be scared to attempt — but, as I tell my clients, if we are going to get ahead as quickly as possible we need to understand where you are at now, what you are up against, what tools you have in your arsenal (some you might not even realise you have, or don't yet know how to use properly) and what you want to achieve.

It's a necessary but possibly uncomfortable first step — much like the moment you hop on the bathroom scales after a holiday. You may already know that you are financially overweight or fiscally unfit. What you don't know, though, is your financial BMI, which is a detailed analysis of where you are starting from with a focus on your money tendencies, beliefs and mindset.

To create a financial plan, and before you can diagnose your financial aptitude, you need to understand your money story and starting point, by answering the following five questions:

- What are your money habits, beliefs and mindset? Understanding your money story helps you to understand why you do things the way you do.
- What is your current financial life stage? (See opposite.)
- What is your cash position on a day-to-day basis? (See Chapter 2.)
- What is your goal and what motivates you to achieve it?
- How much time do you have to achieve your goal?

Your financial life stage

The number of life stages differs depending on whether you are a devotee of Shakespeare, who thought seven, or psychologist Erik Erikson, who thought eight. Financially speaking, though, you will fit into one of three life stages, depending on your financial position. You will either be 'Starting Out', 'Building Up' or 'Sitting Back'. There is a traditional route most people take when working through each of these stages, although life tends to wreak havoc when it comes to 'traditional' financial progress.

Despite each person's situation being specific to them, within each stage patterns arise relating to income levels, family dynamics, spending priorities, curve balls and areas of financial concern. While this might give you some comfort — in the sense that you may be experiencing similar problems to other people at the same life stage as you — this is of little benefit, as the average person is also making financial mistakes.

Financial life stage	Traditional life events	Financial events	Most common investment options
Starting Out (Stage 1)	Enter workforce Get married / live with a partner Go on OE	Start earning Develop financial habits Purchase car Pay off student loan Start saving	Savings KiwiSaver Term deposits Managed funds Shares
Building Up (Stage 2)	Start a family Career advancement Divorce Career change Inheritance	Purchase home Upgrade home Accumulation of wealth (savings, KiwiSaver, investment property, business, shares) Pay off mortgage	Residential property investment Leverage KiwiSaver Own a business
Sitting Back (Stage 3)	Retirement Grandchildren Death of spouse	Greater cashflow sensitivity Liquidating assets (KiwiSaver, downsizing home) Preserving wealth Estate planning	Residential property investment (with reduced leverage) Commercial property Managed funds, unit trusts Art, gold, term deposits Shares

My objective is to help my clients move through each financial stage as quickly as possible, while still living a life they enjoy. If they are not living an enjoyable life, their plan will be unsustainable, resulting in financial bingeing, general frustration or worsening of relationship dynamics. All these things lead to financial backsliding. Most financial plans do not have tolerance for slippage.

It's not a case of going hard out. Clarity and consistency are the two key components of progress, supported by sustainability. If the plan is too tight, you won't be able to stick with it, and you'll fall off the wagon. The science behind behavioural change requires minimum change for maximum outcome. We apply the same philosophy to our financial plans, and spend time on actions that provide maximum 'bang for your buck'.

Stage 1: Starting Out — building a financial foundation

People in the Starting Out phase are usually in their mid- to late twenties or early thirties. At this age, you don't have much in the way of net worth, but you do have time — and some would argue this is a more precious commodity. The sooner you start working on a plan, the better off you'll be.

While historically most people at this stage are young, in recent times more mature people are finding themselves still in, or catapulted back to, their financial beginnings, perhaps after a divorce or relationship breakdown or after experiencing a financial Mack Truck event.

If you are Starting Out, your net worth will be less than $100,000 (lower if you live outside Auckland). This represents a typical deposit needed to secure a basic property. The only exception to this is if you already own a property, even if you have less than $100,000 equity in it. (Property ownership moves you into the next financial stage, Building Up.) Keeping it simple, your net worth or net wealth is the total value of your saleable assets (excluding the value of your vehicle and furniture) after deducting everything you owe. (See Appendix III for an example of a Net Worth Statement, or Statement of Financial Position.) Or, even more simply, if you cashed everything up today and repaid all debts in full, what would you have left?

When you are Starting Out, you are developing your financial habits and starting to become familiar with your natural tendencies around money (your money personality). If you are re-entering the Starting Out phase due to a relationship breakdown or financial catastrophe, then you will need time to put yourself back together, both financially and mentally.

Much like first-time Starting Outers, it is during this readjustment that you will need to create better financial habits to ensure you can still achieve financial success and a comfortable retirement, despite your setback and shortened timeframe. The difference for a second-time Starting Outer is that your income should be a lot higher than when you were first in this stage, making it easier to move up faster. If your income is *not* higher, then you will have to focus on increasing your cash surplus despite income constraints.

Because income tends to be at its lowest when you enter the workforce, when you are Starting Out you face the task of learning how to manage spending and saving within the constraints of your income level. Developing sound financial habits is critical, although often ignored. This is the time when you need to focus on the following things:

- Understand your psychology of spending (see page 41).
- Learn how to set financial goals (see page 25).
- Understand the structure, habits and disciplines needed to save more easily.
- Calculate your financial resilience and have a plan to improve it.
- Learn how to prepare a household budget (see Chapter 3).
- Don't borrow unless it is for things that provide long-term value (like an education that will result in a job or pay rise).
- Avoid the use of credit cards.
- Save at least 20 per cent of what you earn.
- Join KiwiSaver.
- Set some savings goals (like saving for a car or a deposit for a property).
- Make sure you have adequate insurance.
- Take advantage of employee benefit plans at work.
- Understand what's needed to get a payrise.

For those under 30, you should aim to be in this phase for no more than five years. For those over 30, you should be here for no more than three years. If you don't have a plan to move through this stage, then you will need an experienced financial advisor to help you. Doing nothing is actually doing something — you have made a decision to do nothing. Burying your head in the sand is a waste of energy. Get help. Move forward.

Use the worksheets in Appendix III to calculate your annual cash surplus, then divide $100,000 by this number to determine how long it will take you to get out of this stage. Can you move on within the recommended timeframe? If not, what will you need to do to move forward faster?

To achieve your financial goals, you need a clear strategy to reach the prescribed net-worth threshold and/or property ownership within the specified number of years (see Chapter 3). Your strategy will depend on whether you have taken the traditional route of spending less than you earn, investing wisely and starting early, or if you are on the more common leave-it-till-the-last-minute path. Regardless, all strategies start with creating a cash surplus and making it as big as possible.

Note: When I work with my clients, we reduce the target for completing Stage 1 from five years to two years, and often to just 12 months. If you are likely to take longer than the maximum five-year duration then you need to rethink your strategy or speak with an experienced financial advisor. Taking your time won't help you when you're trying to propel yourself forward; taking action is where it's at.

Stage 2: Building Up — your prime earning years

This stage begins once you have purchased a property or your net worth exceeds $100,000. This is often a time when your income is rising as well as your expenses. You are likely to start a family and want to upgrade your home. Nicer homes, nicer cars and raising children can easily consume your increasing income. In fact, the more money you earn, the harder it often is to get ahead.

This is also the time when the financial decisions you make will have the greatest impact on the lifestyle you will enjoy during retirement. By now, you should have accumulated some savings and developed the expertise to make sound choices.

Plan ahead for your big-ticket costs. Children's secondary and tertiary expenses often grind family budgets to a halt.

During this stage, focus on the following:

- Maximise your cash surplus through budgeting (see Chapter 3).
- Have a clear strategy to kill your mortgage — ideally by the age of 50 (see Chapter 16).
- Take full advantage of employer-offered retirement plans and KiwiSaver. Contribute enough to earn the maximum contribution from your employer. If you are self-employed, contribute the minimum amount to earn the government tax credit.
- Determine how much you will need in order to retire (see Chapter 26).

- Determine if you are likely to reach your retirement number within your timeframe (see Chapter 26).
- Depending on how much risk you can take in financial matters (due to the number of years you have before retirement), develop a wealth-creation plan to reduce the shortfall and provide a measure of progress (see Chapter 11).
- Invest wisely. Do your homework.
- Measure your progress towards your retirement plan annually.
- Adjust your wants as needed.
- Be sure your insurance requirements have kept pace with your needs. Having adequate personal insurances (life, income and trauma) to protect your family in case of your untimely death or serious illness is critical. However, as your wealth increases, your need for insurance should be reducing.
- Prepare an estate plan to ensure that your custodial, financial and medical wishes are carried out (see Chapter 31).

Ideally, the above points would be actioned in a timely manner to ensure you're on track for retirement. In reality, however, this doesn't happen.

Kiwis seem to take a relaxed view of their lack of retirement savings, and often do not take their head out of the sand until they are staring down the barrel of a questionable or non-existent retirement and only have a limited number of years left to work and save. We know that 62 per cent of Kiwis are not on track to be mortgage-free by retirement; 79 per cent don't know how much they will need in retirement; and 90 per cent run out of money within the first 10 years of retirement. A million Kiwi parents are still financially helping their adult kids get by, which also puts pressure on retirement. Although your late forties and early fifties are traditionally the years of highest income-earning potential, it is not until earnings start to wane that many people become aware of the limited number of years they have left to work. Not surprisingly, every year we have an influx of fifty-somethings visiting our offices, burdened with mortgages but with no real plan for how to repay them by retirement and no savings to combat the financial hole they will most certainly fall into.

In this situation, the time left on the working-age clock determines what options you have available and whether there is any room for further delay or inertia.

Clearly the longer you delay planning for your retirement, the shorter your runway and the more urgent your situation becomes. This in turn necessitates the need for a clear strategy and action, because we don't have the luxury of getting it wrong.

The great thing about mature clients is that they are highly motivated to change their situation and are committed to taking action promptly. These attributes can help them to achieve staggering results which surprise even themselves — and also lead to the three most common pieces of feedback I receive.

1. 'I am sleeping so much better.'
2. 'I wish I had done this 10 years ago.'
3. 'I can't believe you got away with saying that to my spouse.'

Stage 3: Sitting Back — arriving at retirement

This is the destination at which you have 'arrived'. You have a mortgage-free home and sufficient money in the bank to fund your retirement. Because of this, your retirement years are supposed to be the most enjoyable and fulfilling time of your life. You have worked hard, have followed your plan and have enough money squirrelled away to live a lifestyle you enjoy. If children and grandchildren are part of your life, having the financial ability to help them can be rewarding.

Having a cash surplus is the key to moving through the first two life stages as quickly as possible. Maximising your cash surplus requires you to understand your psychology of spending and is the building block for determining the structure of your spending plan.

Remember, your investment options change as you move through each life stage. Most asset types will feature in your financial plan at some stage, but the timing of when you introduce different types of investment is important to get right. If you invest in the wrong asset too early or late, you will slow down your progress and destabilise your plan.

2. Assessing where you are now

Before you can work out where you need to go, and how you are going to get there, you need to know where you are now.

What's your cash position on a day-to-day basis?

The idea of doing a budget can scare people, and while a spending plan is a necessary component of any financial plan, you should be able to diagnose your cash position without completing a full budget spreadsheet. Your cash position can be split into one of three categories:

- sinking — slowly taking on water, with short-term debt
- floating — cruising and comfortable
- flying — plenty of income and some savings, and wanting to maximise.

Your financial resilience describes your ability to 'hold on' if your income stops, before you have to do something drastic. Your financial resilience is measured by the size of your rainy-day fund. Your rainy day fund doesn't need to be available cash, and could include available funds on your credit card or access to lines of credit on your mortgage. The more money you can access during this time, the longer you can hold on without having to sell down non-liquid assets or adjust your wealth strategy. The longer you can last, the more likely you can reinstate or replace your income without having to sell an asset at the wrong time (when its value has dropped).

Being able to weather negative events without having to sacrifice your wealth strategy to survive is a key component of wealth creation. This is also described as a defensive play, as it serves to protect your financial flank. Selling an asset isn't always a bad thing, but selling an asset at the 'wrong time' usually means you are forced to sell when the market is low, which translates to you taking a financial hit, and this can leave a scar. The higher your financial resilience, the more likely you can endure bad times without suffering a major blow.

How long could you survive if your income stopped?	Financial resilience
Less than 3 months	Low
3–6 months	Moderate
6–12 months	High
>12 months	Target

Sinking: Financial resilience = low

If you are sinking, you're on the back foot and quite probably going backwards on a day-to-day basis. There is insufficient money coming in to cover your living costs and this is resulting in you slowly incurring more debt or using credit cards when life throws you a curve ball. You are unable to consistently repay your credit cards in full each month. Your back is up against the wall and, no matter how you try, things always feel tight. The accumulation of debt has a servicing cost (repayment), which in turn puts more pressure on an already stretched cashflow.

Weirdly (in my opinion), some people like to have money in a savings account while they have credit-card debt. While this is illogical, they feel the savings account gives them some form of comfort or buffer for a rainy day, despite a similar amount being owed on the credit card.

> **Tip:** Use savings to repay debt, then work on a plan to rebuild your savings balance. It makes more financial sense to use your savings to pay off your credit card, as it will save you more interest than you would earn.

Not surprisingly, people who are sinking do not set out to be in this situation. It usually starts slowly, with being slightly on the back foot. Then a curve ball throws you further backwards, and, before you know it, you are picking up momentum in the wrong direction. Many self-employed people or people with commissioned or irregular income sit constantly on the cusp of sinking as their fluctuating income can play havoc with their finances.

> **Tip:** If you are sinking, you have to focus on stabilising your situation quickly. You will need to make drastic cutbacks immediately. I call this a financial detox. You aren't supposed to stay on a detox forever, but the length of your detox will depend on how desperate your situation is.

Floating: Financial resilience = low to moderate

The most common cash category is 'floating'. You're not going backwards, but you're not getting ahead particularly fast either. You may be earning the most money you have ever earned, but you don't feel any better off. You're living a lifestyle you enjoy, and you can repay your credit cards in full each month, but at the same time you are not proactively saving or consciously improving your financial situation. If you receive a pay rise it doesn't make much of a difference, as it seems to be absorbed by your lifestyle. If you were to lose your job tomorrow, you could probably survive for a few months with your available cash before using credit or equity in a property.

When you are floating, you are saving less than 20 per cent of your income. The objective is to optimise your situation, removing all inefficiencies so you can start to make faster progress.

Flying: Financial resilience = high to target

Flying means you have no money worries. There is enough cash going around the system to maintain your lifestyle plus you are making regular savings or paying off your mortgage faster. Technically we would want you saving at least 20 per cent of your income before you are categorised as 'flying', but when your income is high, this shouldn't be a problem. Some clients on a high income describe their position as 'flying blind', or 'good income but chaos'. There's an awareness that you should have more to show for your income and usually a desire to start maximising your savings rate and get your money working harder.

Once we understand your cash position and life stage, an appreciation of your natural tendencies around money will help to determine the level of detail required in drafting your financial plan.

Cash position	Sinking	Floating	Flying
Savings rate	Not saving, and short-term debt	Saving 0–20% of income	Saving at least 20% of income
Objective	Stabilise	Optimise	Maximise

Genetics

It's true, some of us are predisposed to save or spend the money we have, regardless of our wealth, gender or upbringing. This isn't to say you can't overcome this tendency, because you can — but it needs to be actively overcome, which requires a degree of effort or discipline.

A study published in the *Journal of Consumer Research* in 2008 indicated that around 41 per cent of us sit at the extreme ends of the spectrum: 25 per cent of us are tightwads and 16 per cent are shopaholics, with the masses sitting somewhere in between. (A tightwad finds it painful to spend, and spends less than they should on their own wellbeing because of the 'pain of spending' or the anxiety that comes from spending.) George Loewenstein, a professor of economics and psychology at Carnegie Mellon University in Australia who conducted the study, explained that researchers would first show the study participant a product. If they liked it, the reward centres of the brain (called the nucleus accumbens) would 'light up' through the release of dopamine, when the brain benefits from a natural high. Dopamine is a compound in the brain that helps control reward and pleasure centres and is a precursor to adrenaline. It helps regulate movement and emotional responses to stimuli, and enables us not only to recognise rewards, but also to take action and start to move towards them.

The researchers would then show the subject the product's price, which triggered the area of the brain (called the anterior insula) that acts as a 'handbrake'. In the people with tightwad or saver tendencies, activity in the handbrake area of the brain was more pronounced when they viewed the item's price. This braking system is the angst centre of our brain. Through the release of noradrenaline and other neurochemicals, it creates a sense of gnawing anxiety that causes us to slow down and tread carefully. In extreme cases it can evoke disgust.

These findings suggest that, for a tightwad, the emotional pain or anxiety of actually having to pay for an item works to keep their pleasure-seeking in check. The researchers concluded that the mental anguish is so strong that it overrides rational deliberation; these people don't buy something even when they know they should.

For shopaholics, the opposite is true. The pain of throwing money around does not register in the brain like it does for other people. They experience little to no pain when spending money and thereby part with their money more easily.

What the research shows is that some of us are genetically more likely to behave a certain way when it comes to money. For shoppers this is a bit of a concern, because this means that your wiring is not to your financial advantage. Delayed gratification does not come as easily to the shopper as it does the saver. Your anterior insula is off on holiday, or at the very least not firing on all cylinders, so you are going to have to consciously train your brain to recognise that forgoing pleasure now can bring a greater pay-off later.

Neuroeconomist Paul Zak of Claremont Graduate University in California claims that it's possible to increase the number or strength of the calming signals your brain produces to delay impulsiveness, but this skill needs to be learned. As an extension of his research, he further comments that when 'people are happier and have greater social support' they save more. According to Zak, the happier you are, the more patient you can be and the more likely it is that you will make decisions that are better for you.

This rings true for me, because it's part of my job to help shoppers achieve their financial goals, despite their natural tendencies. Accountability and support are precursors to a better result with regard to most things in life, but especially with the things that you find hard to do.

Money personalities

We all have a natural tendency, or series of traits, when it comes to our relationship with money. Theories differ as to how many personality traits there are, although most agree that they can be slotted into two broad categories — your money personality and your strategic personality — with a weighting then given to which of the two categories is more dominant in influencing your financial behaviour.

When it comes to money, most of us have a natural tendency to either spend or save, and to be strategically adventurous or risk-averse, although some people fall in the middle. The three cashflow personalities — how we spend our money — are shopper, plodder and saver. The strategic personalities — how much we are prepared to plan and take on risk — are adventurer (risk-taker), dreamer (whatever goes) and safekeeper (consistent).

Money personality	Strategic personality
Shopper	Adventurer (risk-taker / daredevil / outgoing)
Plodder	Dreamer (no plan / laid back)
Saver	Safekeeper (safety warden / worrier)

Your personality has nothing to do with your budget, your net worth, level of debt or retirement savings balance. It is not linked to your level of financial literacy or gender. Financially literate people can have trouble sticking to a budget. In fact, people who manage money as part of their day job (accountants, managers, CEOs) tend to be terrible with money in their personal life. They get it, they can do it as part of their job, but in their own time it's not a priority. It's almost as if they have an allergic reaction to it, or get decision fatigue, because financial decisions fill so much of their week already.

There's no correlation between being rational in your everyday life and being rational with money. Builders don't finish their homes, accountants are late filing their own tax returns and the mechanic's car still needs to be fixed. Knowing and doing are two very different things.

Each personality has its strengths and its challenges. Each can help you make great decisions, and each has the potential to get you into financial trouble. There is no right or wrong personality, but understanding your personality helps you understand how you deal with money. When you understand the cons of each personality trait, you can better identify the tools and the skills you need to learn to mitigate against the risks of your financial tendencies.

Shoppers

Shoppers find it easier to spend money than to save. They are neither stupid nor irrational, but they need a reason not to spend, as opposed to a reason to spend. They derive emotional satisfaction from spending money. They like to shop and are usually good at it.

Some shoppers spend little amounts often; others can be tight on a day-to-day basis, but when they find something they really want, they'll buy it. They may be an infrequent shopper, or a controlled shopper, or a bargain shopper, but they are still a shopper.

Some shoppers will shop because they feel good; others may shop because they simply do not have a reason not to. If you find it difficult to save, you simply haven't been given a compelling enough reason to do so.

Subcategories of the shopper include the comfort shopper and the binger. A comfort shopper spends money as a way of celebration or distraction. If they are happy, they spend money, or if they are feeling sad or out of control, they spend money. The extreme comfort shopper does both. The binger can be quite frugal on a day-to-day basis, but will spend up big when the occasion calls for it. They can budget for a time, then they blow out.

Not everyone is a shopper all the time, and not all shoppers spend money on themselves. Many shoppers are big-hearted and tend to be generous. Simply, shoppers find it easier to spend than others.

Plodders

Plodders are ambivalent about spending and saving. They take things as they come and have an expectation that if they keep doing what they are currently doing then everything should be OK. Disappointingly, a plodder doesn't have much to show for what they have spent, in contrast to the shopper, which can be a frustration.

Savers

Savers derive more satisfaction from saving than from spending. Some savers are conditioned by their social, cultural or economic circumstances; for instance, people brought up during the Depression or during wartime are more likely to have been savers.

Savers will rarely buy impulsively. They will turn the light off when they leave the room, reuse plastic bags, and prefer to keep something even if it is broken rather than throw it away. Savers can have hoarder tendencies. They are happy to recycle and buy second-hand rather than new. If they don't have an immediate use for something, they will store it until they need it.

Not all savers save in the same way, and not every saver objects to buying something new. Some wear designer clothes, but buy them at a discount. Some drive nice cars and go on great holidays. The difference between a saver and a shopper is the saver is more likely to have saved before spending the money, often paying for things in cash and spending more consciously, rather than relying on credit.

Savers are usually more organised with their finances. The most extreme saver will save at someone else's expense, a trait I deplore. Every friend group has a friend who is a little too tight or cheap.

Savers find it easier to set savings goals, which gives them an advantage over spenders. But this advantage can come with a lack of strategy, as savers typically don't want to part with their money.

Outliers

There is a spectrum within the three money personalities. For example, a shopper is someone who enjoys spending money. If they can't control this urge then they are considered a shopaholic or a spendthrift. Similarly, a saver is happy to go without, but some savers, again at the extreme, have great difficulty spending money. It physically pains them to do so.

Males are three times more likely than females to be tightwads, who show no bias to either end of the spectrum. The use of credit cards can be the financial equaliser, as credit cards weaken impulse control, particularly for people who would normally be very careful with their money, whether male or female. Not giving up anything tangible seems to cure tightwads of their affliction.

For spendthrifts, the medium of purchasing doesn't really matter. That said, spendthrifts who use credit cards are three times more likely to have debt than tightwads who also swiped the plastic.

Income levels don't vary much between the two personalities, which suggests that spending decisions arise not from the size of one's bank balance, but from ingrained spending behaviours.

Knowing your money personality

Some people can easily identify their financial personality, while some of us have tendencies from across the board. If you can't easily identify your spending habits, ask your partner or a friend — they'll be able to spot it right away. To help you quickly identify your money personality, ask yourself the following questions:

- Do I find it easier to save or spend money?
- Do I enjoy spending money?
- Am I rational with my spending?
- Am I more generous than my peers or partner?

When I interview my clients, I ask them to describe both their own money personality and their partner's. I then ask their partner to answer the same question. Most people are more forthright when diagnosing their partner than themselves. If you are in a relationship, have a go at diagnosing their spending personality. Also, ask yourself the following questions:

- Does my partner agree with me around money matters?
- Are we financially compatible?
- Do we share the same financial goals?
- Do we value money the same way?

You and your partner's money personalities need to be incorporated into your financial plan.

Calculate your financial BMI

To determine your financial starting point and therefore how serious and urgent it is to develop and stick to a plan, work through the Financial BMI

Matrix below. Answer each of the five questions by circling your response and adding up your score. This will give you an idea of where you're at, and where you need to go.

Financial BMI Matrix

Value	What financial life stage are you at (see page 31)?	What is your cash position on a day-to-day basis (see page 37)?	What is your money personality (see page 41)?	How motivated are you?	How many years until your retirement?
1	Starting Out	Sinking	Shopper	Not very	Less than 10
2	Building Up	Floating	Plodder	Semi	10–15
3	Sitting Back	Flying	Saver	Very	16 or more

Results

	Commentary	Tip
Total: 12–15	Your financial future looks bright. With an overarching retirement plan you should be able to comfortably sit back and enjoy your retirement, possibly even before retirement age.	Don't let your favourable financial situation lull you into inaction. Small, sustainable steps are all that's needed to achieve and maintain financial success.
Total: 8–12	With a considered financial plan and by taking action you should be able to achieve your financial goal of being mortgage-free and having funds available for retirement.	You have some obstacles working against you, but with consistent and purposeful steps towards your financial goals and by keeping your spending in check, you should be able to reach a comfortable retirement.
Total: 7 or less	Your situation is tight, but with an overhaul of your finances and a willingness to be brave and move forward, you could start to bridge the gap between where you are now and a comfortable retirement.	Getting control of your finances and creating a plan will be confronting, but ultimately empowering as you take back control. Money is not bigger than you and a comfortable retirement is achievable, but you will need to work hard.

Strategic personalities

Once you understand your spending tendencies, we need to think about which strategies are going to be most effective at engaging you, based on who you are and what you aren't.

At this stage I encourage you to think about how ambitious you naturally are when thinking about your financial future. Do you dream big, or do you feel more comfortable thinking small? If you had your way, would you prefer to deliberately grow your wealth, or drift towards your financial future? There's no wrong or right way to think about this, but knowing what you are will help to determine which wealth strategy you should adopt and which obstacles you are going to face.

Let's start by thinking about how financially ambitious you are. What is your stomach for reward and risk? Everyone sits somewhere within these three categories: adventurers, safety wardens, dreamers.

Adventurers

The adventurer is the risk-taker, the financial daredevil. Where others might see risk, adventurers tend to see opportunity. I love risk-takers, because I'm one myself. Adventurers are big-picture people. They like to move fast, and get excited by possibility. They create opportunity instead of waiting for it to arrive.

If something doesn't feel right, a risk-taker walks away. They accept that some deals will go wrong. They're not afraid of failing; if they do fail, they tend to fail fast, picking themselves up quickly and moving on to the next thing. They can make decisions quickly, which can scare the living daylights out of someone who isn't a risk-taker. They don't like feeling constrained and resent being held back, preferring to move forward, even if they don't have the full picture; they use intuition and their 'gut' to fill in the gaps. The flip side is they can be blinded by an idea, impatient to execute it and slow to compromise (for example, booking a holiday without researching it).

Adventurers can be careless about details. It's not that they don't appreciate detail, but they don't get excited by it. They can make plans, but don't consider all the facts. At times, they can be perceived as insensitive, because they are on a mission and are not particularly interested in the views of people who are not on board with what they are trying to accomplish. They expose themselves, and can be hurt or misinterpreted at times.

Adventurers want to get mortgage-free quickly and grow their wealth. If they can see how that is possible, then they are more than happy to pay attention to their spending, but you have to make it worth their while.

Wherever possible, I try and use my clients' personalities to their advantage, and let this shape the right strategy for them. One adventurer/shopper client, on a great income, still had $50,000 of short-term debt and wasn't yet on the property ladder. She knew she should pay off the debt, but she wasn't that interested in doing so, even knowing she'd save interest in paying the debt off faster and most likely feel better in herself. But still, this didn't excite her. What excited her, however, was getting into a property within nine months of working with us. This was a big enough goal for her to do what was needed to get there. This meant she was happy to stick to a savings plan, which paid off her debts faster, but she saw this as a side-effect of the real plan to get her onto the property ladder.

Safety wardens

The safety warden needs financial security and consistency. They are not boring, but they are predictable and prefer little to no risk. They can worry and be indecisive. Safety wardens are happy to spend money, and will invest, but they want to make sure they are spending their money wisely — the safer the investment, the better. They don't usually enjoy the process of investing.

Adventurers scare them, which can cause pressure in a relationship if their partner is one. Even if they believe in their partner, they may still struggle to accept the risk that the partner wants to take on, which the adventurer typically interprets as not having faith in them.

Safety wardens want to know that the future is settled and safe. While gender is not a significant factor in risk personalities, I do have a lot of older female clients who have ended long-standing relationships because they can no longer abide the risk tendencies or lack of action of their partner. They deem it safer to go it alone than to rely on someone who they no longer trust financially.

Safety wardens investigate and research. They are prepared to invest, but they do their homework. They do a lot of homework, sometimes to the point of paralysis. They tend to prefer traditional investments, like a term deposit. They are willing to sacrifice and are prepared for the worst. They tend to be more negative than positive about investments, sticking to the certainties rather than the possibilities, and making decisions out of fear. That said, they can make good partners because their careful planning and steady approach to money can help a couple avoid disaster.

Typically, safety wardens are savers. This initially gives them an advantage, because they are better at building and maintaining a cash surplus — but they fall short when it comes to getting the cash surplus invested and working hard. At this point they nervously retreat. Safety wardens need more support than shoppers when implementing a wealth-creation strategy.

Dreamers

Whatever happens, happens. The universe will provide. We will end up where we end up. These are all mottos of the dreamer.

Dreamers (also called no-planners) can be creative, easily adaptable and at times unconventional. They are simply not fussed about money. They make great friends, and tend to be content with their life. They usually have less than most, but they're OK with this. They are happy to let their partner take care of their finances. They usually love their job and are not motivated by money — which is just as well, because following your passion tends to be a sure way to lower your income-earning potential.

While they don't think about money, a no-planner can only continue with this attitude if someone else is managing things, otherwise it eventually catches up with them. When it comes to money they can be easy-going, but this quickly turns into being disorganised. Money issues simply don't register on their radar; their partner might consider this irresponsible, but this isn't their intention.

Typically, dreamers aren't in any rush to do anything, which is fine while their runway is long and opportunities are rife. As their runway shortens, they don't feel as sure of their future, which is an unfamiliar feeling. I tend to see dreamers a little later than most when it comes time to start preparing for retirement.

Being a no-planner doesn't mean you are a no-hoper. Dreamers can have financial dreams of grandeur, but no executable plan to get them there. They have a tendency to put their faith in the universe. If someone helps a no-planner develop a plan, they can buy into it, provided their 'free spirit' is not too clipped in the process.

Combining money personalities and strategic personalities

Like salt and pepper, Batman and Robin, strawberries and cream, some things are made to go together. When it comes to money personalities, the same thing applies, although not in the combinations you might expect.

A combined shopper/dreamer personality is common, but so too is the shopper who likes to play it safe strategically. The problem for these poor things is that their tendencies are competing, which means they have the urge to spend money (or at least not save) but then feel bad about it. This guilty feeling gets worse as you get older, and don't have a plan for the future.

The saver/safety warden combination is also common. These people can go without, but don't have an effective strategy to take them forward faster. My husband is a saver and a dreamer. I am a shopper and an adventurer. My daughter is showing saver and safety warden tendencies (just like her grandmother). My son is looking like he will take after me.

Typically a shopper will have an adventurer tendency, and this will often become their secret weapon if they can unlock it. Shoppers may be useless at saving, but when it comes to growing wealth they are 'all in'. They can see the connection between saving and how hard their money can work for them. Provided they can see wealth building quickly, they will happily save to unlock more opportunity. But they have to see the results, and the results have to excite them.

Remember, each combination is no better or worse than the others. They all have their own challenges, which usually come to light when you try to combine your personality with a partner's.

Face up to your debts

When you know you're not in control of your finances, it can be easier, for a short while, to avoid the issue. But the ostrich effect — burying your head in the sand — is one of the biggest threats to a relationship and financial progress. Avoiding dealing with money issues easily lends itself to anxiety and a feeling of helplessness around money. It feels bigger than you, so you ignore it and pretend it doesn't matter.

But money is never bigger than you. With the exception of compulsive debtors, there is no financial problem so big that you have to relinquish control. Don't be the poster child for 'someone else will save me' — the belief that you will be rescued by someone or something, that if you just keep going somehow it will be OK. It won't.

If you have a stack of unopened bills in front of you, it's OK to be scared. But open them anyway. Remember, being scared isn't the issue; continuing to do nothing is. Open them now and write out a list of what you owe.

3. Budgeting — creating a cash surplus

Tell your money where to go instead of wondering where it went. —C. E. Hoover

Irrespective of income level or age, too many of us can relate to the definition of the new poor: when there is too much month left at the end of your money.

The cornerstone of financial success is having a cash surplus, yet it is the most neglected of all financial principles. It's not particularly engaging or sexy, but it's the foundation stone to wealth creation. *You must have money left over* if you want to get ahead.

This leads us to the first question: do you? You won't need to complete a budget or analyse your bank statements to answer this. You don't need to be earning a low income to have no money left. In fact, the higher your income, the more likely you are to be living pay day to pay day. Living *well* pay day to pay day, but pay day to pay day nonetheless.

Having money left over at the end of each week, month or year is critical to achieving any form of financial progress, and this is where most people trip up. However, once you have mastered the ability to create a cash surplus, you can then move on to creating a productive investment with this cash, which gets your money working harder. This is the precursor to wealth, or growing your value.

In New Zealand — whether because of our 'she'll be right' attitude, or our lack of financial know-how — it seems we are particularly good at spending money and financial drifting. We pretty much spend everything we earn, however much that is. This doesn't seem to bother us until we get to our fifties, when we first become aware of our limited income potential. Up until this point, increasing income or increasing property values have distracted us from our overspending. We are lulled into a false sense of comfort, which seems to give us permission to care less and less about the speed at which money is leaving our bank accounts.

Among people who don't yet own property, many believe they can never own a property, losing hope before they start a financial plan, and never bothering to try. And let's not forget, there's always credit: loans or buy-now-pay-later schemes that make it easier to focus on instant gratification, and even facilitate your overspending or catch you after you have stepped off your financial ledge.

While having a cash surplus doesn't sound particularly sexy, the lack of a surplus will catch up with you — and maybe not in the way you expect. Sure, the obvious end point is that you run out of money, creditors come knocking, debts are called, assets are sold and, at its extreme, you may go bankrupt. In reality, the lack of a cash surplus initially leads to frustration, stress, anxiety, lack of sleep and relationship pressure. But at a more basic level, it just means you're not able to benefit from any opportunity and you won't be able to retire comfortably. This usually means you then have to work longer, downsize your home sooner and accept that you won't be able to help out your kids or family as much as you may have hoped. Sure, you'll still be OK — but there are real consequences that will respond to whatever action or inaction you decide to take. The lack of a cash surplus is directly linked to your personal wellbeing.

Creating a cash surplus can be hard, but planning and controlling how much you consume are key components to wealth building, so you must master this skill. If saving doesn't come naturally to you, get help. Your advantage is that you know this about yourself. Finding time to exercise might not come naturally to some people, but just because it doesn't come naturally doesn't mean you shouldn't do it — you just need extra help, or a different environment to support you to do certain things. For me, I know that I am time-poor and get bored easily; this means that I can easily fall off a wagon of good intentions. I need structure and accountability.

Last year I trained for my first marathon. I downloaded and attempted to follow a basic running plan. This plan took me from couch potato to being able to run 10 kilometres, but that is a long way from the 42 kilometres I wanted to run. This is when I decided to engage a running coach who could provide the right support to keep me on track and the right strategies to ensure I was focusing on things that would make the most difference on race day. Whether you are thinking fitness, nutrition or finance, enlisting an expert gets you to your goal faster and allows you to dare to dream bigger dreams.

It takes time to plan a budget. A budget is only one component of a financial plan, but if you don't take the time to do the budget first, you can't make that plan. Being time-poor is no excuse; if you don't have time to do it, pay someone else to prepare one for you.

Operating a household without a budget is like running a business without a plan, without goals, without direction. If you're spending more than you earn and you can't manage to change this, you need to enlist expert help to kick-start your progress.

What is a budget?

A budget is an estimation of incomings and outgoings over a period of time. It allows you to think about money in an analytical way and, most importantly, is an effective tool to help you get your finances under control.

The purpose of a budget is not to tell you where your money has gone, but where your money *should* go. It is forward facing, not backward facing. If done right it can help you to:

- feel in control and take responsibility for your life
- make informed projections about your financial situation
- set big progress milestones each year
- understand the volatility of your progress and adjust your efforts to respond to real-time opportunities or setbacks
- enjoy a better quality of life
- anticipate curve balls ahead of time
- get in control and allow you to plan for financial changes
- sleep better
- achieve peace of mind
- make your money work for you
- improve your personal relationships.

Despite these many and varied benefits, a lot of us have never set a budget. For the few who have taken the initiative to create a budget, most will attest to the fact that sticking to it is no easy task, with the best-laid plans often ruined by impulsive spending, impetuous decisions or a lack of obvious progress.

This chapter talks about how to set a budget that works, while remembering that the best budgets will create a feeling of consciousness around your spending without leaving you feeling deprived.

> **Tip:** If you want to get ahead, get organised, as financial opportunity tends to run in organisation's shadow. Diligence is the mother of good luck.

Jotting down expenses and making some sweeping assumptions about your financial capability does not create a budget. It might create a table with numbers on it, but this does not in itself make a budget.

A budget must be considered and set — but this is just step one. Assuming you successfully set a budget, you will quickly realise that committing a plan to paper and actually achieving it are two very different things. While setting the budget is important, it is in fact the easy part. Sticking to the budget takes skill, better habits, discipline and support. This is step two.

> The goal of a budget is to achieve a cash surplus. It is the size of the surplus (not the size of the income) that matters.

How to set a budget

Setting a budget requires taking certain steps in a particular order. Each step is as important as the others. When I'm setting budgets for clients, I start with their best guess of where their money goes. I then benchmark this spending against other clients earning similar levels of income. This highlights where they are overspending or undercooking some costs. Next, I factor in their non-negotiable costs (what they enjoy spending their money on) and I see what's left over. I calculate whether this is 20 per cent of their income; if it isn't, I then refine the spending further as required. I'm trying to create the least amount of friction for the client by focusing on squeezing out any inefficiencies on costs they don't care about before I tackle the more sensitive costs (their discretionary spending and non-negotiable costs). Wherever possible, I try to minimise any changes to these more sensitive costs.

Step 1: Understand where you have spent money in the past

If you're going to develop a budget, first find out where your money is going so you can learn to catch it before it gets spent. The first question I ask is: how much money was saved in the past 12 months? If the answer is none, then I know you are spending all your income, whether you have categorised your spending correctly or not. An indicative assessment is easy — if your savings are depleting or you are using debt to live, you are likely to be living beyond your means by spending more than you earn. But the size and scale of the overspend are key. Do not rely on your instincts to determine this, as you will be likely spending more than you realise across a number of different costs. Little but frequent (and often forgotten) costs can create the most lasting damage.

You need to *actually look at where your money has gone*. This is called an analysis of spending, and a template can be found in Appendix III. However, a summary of your spending to date is not a budget. The purpose of a budget isn't to determine where your money has gone, but where it *should* go. Knowing where your money has been going will help you to understand where it is likely to continue to go if you do not take considered steps to change it.

> **Tip:** Think carefully about the categories you use to classify your expenses. Lots of people over-simplify their budget. Instead, list your expenses in as much detail as possible to give you a more accurate summary. For example, 'vehicle costs' does not just cover your WOF and petrol. It includes maintenance, insurance, road user charges, AA levies, services, tyre replacements, parking costs and speeding and parking tickets.
>
> The timing of costs is also important, as this helps us understand the rate and volatility of progress we expect to see over the course of the year. The devil is in the detail.

Print out your bank statements for the past 12 months. If this is too onerous, then print out your statements for the past three months, provided they are from a typical financial quarter. Extrapolate your quarterly spending into an annual amount. *This amount is what your life is costing you.*

List all your income earned, by income type (salary, bonuses, regular overtime, cash jobs and so on). Add up all income you've received, then subtract your expenses from your total income to see if you are going backwards or have a cash surplus.

If this exercise shows that you don't have enough money coming in to cover all your costs, it will show as a negative number (known as a deficit) and your bank balance will likely be reducing or your debt (mortgage or credit cards) increasing. A deficit means that you are going backwards. Some of this shortfall may be made up through creating efficiencies within your budget, capturing the money that is currently getting frittered away (see Chapter 4), reprioritising goals, structuring debt better and getting serious about your financial future.

The second prong to this exercise is that it allows you to *determine what you can actually afford to spend* and how much ground you need to make up when you set the budget.

Your initial budget target is to generate a cash surplus of 20 per cent of what you earn, which can be used to reduce debt or accumulate wealth through investment. (If this isn't possible, start with a 10 per cent savings target.) This means that you have 80 per cent of your income to allocate to your living costs.

> **Tip:** Write down your expenses by what they are rather than where you purchased them, so you'll be able to figure out later how much you spend in particular categories, e.g., groceries, takeaways, coffees, clothes, etc.

I once had a client who proudly presented her previous seven years of spending on a spreadsheet. She told me she knew exactly where her money went and she felt completely in control of her spending as a result. I asked her how much she had saved each year, over the past seven years. Outside of her KiwiSaver contributions and mortgage payments, nothing. All this information showed me is that she is good at spending her money. It didn't tell me what she is capable of, and it certainly hadn't changed how she manages her money.

Step 2: Understand your expenses

Most budgets don't work because insufficient emphasis is placed upon the different types of expenses and their timing, instead assuming that all costs are linear (that is, always the same amount and incurred evenly throughout the year), within your control and of equal importance to you. But this is not true. While you might be able to annualise costs then divide up how much you need each month, in reality, it's crucial to understand the timing and sensitivity of those costs. Failing to understand the volatility of their spending is one of the leading causes of clients no longer sticking to their spending and saving plan. Despite consistent effort, the progress will be different each month, usually as a result of timing pressures. Knowing what progress to expect is key for keeping your head in the game.

Expense types include:

- Operational costs — these are the costs you are likely to incur each year. They can include regular, occasional, discretionary and non-negotiable costs.
- Regular — both fixed costs (bills) and variable costs (discretionary spending).
- Occasional — perhaps annually or bi-annually.
- Discretionary — money you spend outside your basic commitments (holidays, gifts, hobbies, etc.).
- Non-negotiable — important costs, sometimes frivolous, but bringing a sense of joy. They are usually a subset of discretionary costs.
- Curve ball — unplanned but manageable. Could be good or bad.
- Mack Truck — usually bad, serious and causing a reset around the finances.

The type of expense dictates whether you can reduce it or not. Don't bother trying to change things outside of your control; focus only on costs you can manage.

> **Tip:** When you are looking to give yourself a money makeover, focus only on the areas that you can actually change.
>
> If you have a mortgage, 80–85 per cent of your operational costs are normally attributed to your standard living commitments, with 15–20 per cent left over for discretionary spending. Usually half of your fixed costs relate to mortgage payments.

You need to plan for both fixed and variable expenses.

Fixed expenses are items like rent, mortgage and health insurance. The costs are fixed and do not differ depending on how much you consume.

Variable expenses are things like utilities (e.g., power, water) and petrol. Some costs, like groceries, can fall into either category, depending on how much self-control you have. Remember, all necessary costs such as groceries, clothing and power can quickly become unnecessarily expensive if you have champagne tastes or fail to track your spend. People often get confused about spending on necessities, but the inevitability of a purchase does not justify spending more than you need to. For example, of course you need to buy food, but that doesn't mean that anything and everything you spend on food is justified. The table below shows the range in weekly food costs for a basic, nutritious diet, then a moderate diet, and finally a liberal diet including more convenience and imported foods, out-of-season fruits and vegetables, higher-priced cuts of meat and some speciality foods.

New Zealand*	Basic $ (mean)	Moderate $ (mean)	Liberal $ (mean)
Man	88	115	149
Woman	75	98	127
Adolescent boy	93	121	157
Adolescent girl	77	100	130
Child 10 yr	65	85	110
Child 5 yr	56	73	94
Child 1 yr	37	48	62
Family (two adults, two children 10 and 4 years)	273	355	462

* Calculated from average costs from 16 supermarkets across New Zealand, including Auckland, Wellington, Dunedin and Christchurch.

Source: Department of Human Nutrition, University of Otago, 2023

You need to plan for *occasional expenses*, whether they are fixed or variable. Budget for expenses that happen only a few times a year, such as gifts, birthday parties, doctor's visits or car maintenance. If you have enough room in your budget, you can pay for these as they occur. If you're on a tighter budget, set aside additional savings ahead of time. There's no excuse for going into debt because you 'forgot' that Christmas happens every year. Too often people blame the less regular costs for their financial impotence. Some people try to spread these costs over the year rather than make a single payment, which has some merits, but spreading payments doesn't fix the problem if there are insufficient funds in the first place.

Non-negotiable costs are things that may be frivolous but make you happy, or make your life better. These costs are more sensitive to you, so put them in the budget first. You are more likely to stick to the plan if these costs are factored in. Remember, if the cost is important to you, then it needs to be in the plan.

The other two types of costs, curve balls and Mack Trucks — are a bit harder to manage. *Curve balls* are one-off major costs such as having your car blow up, or needing expensive dental work. Your budget needs to be able to absorb curve balls, so you need to work hard on it to build up a buffer of some savings. It might be tough at the start, but once you've built a buffer things will get easier.

Financial Mack Trucks are impossible to plan for: things like relationship breakdowns, serious illness or redundancy, which flatten you financially. These things might push you back to the Starting Out phase. Your 'financial resilience' plays a key part in protecting the progress you have made to date. Mack Truck events often require the plan to be completely reset for the new situation.

The seriousness of your situation will determine to what extent you can afford to be generous with yourself. For some, $50 per week to spend on coffees may be all they need to feel OK about sticking to a budget. For others, spending only $5000 on clothes is considered a grim reality, while for others, having $300 to spend on Christmas is considered a luxury.

Assuming you have a cash surplus, you are entitled to some non-negotiables. If you do not have a cash surplus, then all costs are on the table and could be slashed to achieve a cash surplus.

Cash position	Sinking	Floating	Flying
Number of non-negotiables	0	2–3	3–5
Strategic focus	Stabilise/detox	Optimise	Maximise

Most people have at least two to three things that are so important that they can identify them as deal-breakers. Work out what these are for you and look for ways to reduce spending on everything else to create a cash surplus. To help you identify areas of spending that you may be able to cut, I have found the most common types of casual wants can be roughly categorised by gender.

- Women tend to like good food, grooming, holidays and buying presents for friends and family.
- Men tend to like buying 'toys', family holidays and alcohol, and spending on sports/hobbies.

Have a think about all the money you spend and distinguish between desires and needs. Remember when you received your first pay cheque — it went a long way. You were earning less and spending less, but were just as happy (I presume). Some frivolity is needed, but think carefully. If all your desired spending can't be incorporated into the 80 per cent of your income allocated for spending, recognise that you must let those desires go unsatisfied and move on.

Keep adjusting your budget until you are pretty happy with it. Consider what you really want — nice clothes, a bit of finery, more coffees? Or do you want more substantial assets, the opportunity to work less, to be mortgage-free or pay for your children's education? Do you want to have a retirement you can enjoy? The 80 per cent you spend covers the basics, the 20 per cent you save brings the extras.

Pay attention to the rhythm of your spending. Do you spend more during the week or on the weekends? What are the behaviours you want to maintain? Think about any costs attached to the way you want to live your life.

Step 3: Set the budget

See Appendix III for a budget template. Our budget spreadsheet is easily adjustable to accommodate different budgeting needs and styles. An example is on the following page.

Remember, the purpose of a budget isn't to determine where your money has been going, but where your money *should* go, and to help you to calculate how long it will take you to create a cash surplus.

With my clients I work to an annual target, broken down into quarterly check-ins with weekly targets. With all successful budgets, *consistency of effort is the single most important component*. It's not about starting off hard and fast and ending up with a budget blowout, but about conscious spending and saving. Make small initiatives often. You need goalposts of where you need to be, and by when, to make sure your budget will work. You then track, measure and tune.

Start with your regular income and fixed expenses. Then overlay your variable costs, and less regular costs. If your income varies over time, maybe due to bonuses and commissions you receive, base your budget on your predictable income, what you expect to earn under the most conservative of assumptions. Have a conservative discretionary spend to match this. This means dialling back your discretionary spending to match the income that you expect to receive. If your income increases, then you increase your discretionary spend accordingly.

The easiest way to illustrate this is with the family holiday cost. If you earn a bonus, then of course take a bigger holiday. But if you don't, it's inappropriate to have committed to the higher cost. It's impractical to ignore a likely bonus but still stretch your discretionary costs to their limit as if the bonus had been received.

Monthly budget

Income

Work (after tax)	7,000
Total	**7,000**

Fixed Expenses

Rent	3,000
Groceries	800
Petrol	250
Health insurance	200
Electricity & gas	350
Internet & phone	100
Pet costs	100
Total	**4,800**

Variable Expenses*

Car maintenance/repairs	120
Doctor visit	35
Gifts	100
Entertainment (concerts, movies)	100
Clothing and shoes	200
Makeup	50
Total	**605**

Miscellaneous

Books	25
New sheets	40
Prescription	10
Massage	50
Total	**125**

Total Income	7,000
Total Expenses	5,530
Remaining / Surplus	1,470
Annual surplus	**17,640**

Target savings = 20% of income = $1,400

Budgeted surplus: $1,470

*The amount you spend on variable costs will vary from month to month. Typically you annualise the cost, and then break this cost into monthly portions.

Step 4: Tracking your spending

To stick to a budget, you need to record your actual spending against the budget. So, before you kick-start your new regimen, you need to choose the tracking system that will work best for you. You could use:

- a notebook and pen
- a spreadsheet
- an app (such as Moneyfit.me, YNAB, Xero, CashNav).

I prefer to use a financial tracking application and use our in-house tracking app, Moneyfit.me. You can use this app without being a client of enable.me. Remember, your system of budgeting shouldn't require heroic effort to stick to it, but will require you to track your spending against a target amount.

Tracking your spending tells you where the money has been spent after you spend it — but it doesn't easily alert you to the fact you are about to overspend before you do. This is where your bank-account structure and how your money flows between accounts can provide a layer of control and protection. If a bank account has been set up to cover a particular cost, like food (I discuss multiple bank accounts in Chapter 6), once the money has been spent, it will show as a nil balance, whether you have tracked and coded your spending or not. If you went to spend money from this account, your card would be declined, making it impossible to overspend. Your bank account forms part of the structure to protect you from inadvertently overspending.

Review your weekly tracking and determine the areas in which you are overspending, or where you could spend less. Continue with weekly check-ins for each of the 12 weeks. Weekly check-ins give you the chance to reflect on what has been achieved and to mentally prepare for what's coming up in the week and month ahead. I set my clients a monthly (and quarterly) savings target, spending target and mortgage-reduction target. I also give them a stretch goal to hit within the quarter. After those first three months, review your position to determine if you have achieved what you'd planned within that timeframe.

Review your budget and tweak it for the next quarter. If you are under-earning, then the solution lies with you (see page 88). Likewise if you are still overspending.

If you have set your budget correctly and, despite trying hard, you are not managing to make the progress you expect, there are four likely causes.

1. You have overstated your regular income, or understated your regular costs.
2. Your progress could be more volatile, with fluctuations in income and expenses each month, than the budget has recognised.
3. You are not financially aligned with your partner, so one of you has disengaged.
4. You have been hit by a curve ball — something unplanned that has knocked you over or at the very least pushed you into 'survival mode', with financial progress taking a back seat.

The most common cause of struggling to keep to a budget has to do with the *timing* of income and expenses. Some income, despite being fairly certain, should not be counted on in the budget until it is earned. An example of this is bonus income. Even if you are virtually guaranteed this income, unless it is received regularly it cannot be counted on for budgeting purposes. It needs to be removed from the budget along with any discretionary costs that would normally be paid for from this income, such as holidays and presents. Rework the budget, reducing costs as needed to make sure you stay within the lower income amount.

Pay attention to the timing of annual or less regular costs for the coming quarter, then overlay any favourable income adjustments for the quarter. This might include a bonus that is due to be paid, a commission or dividend.

If your lack of progress stems from misalignment of financial behaviour and goals with your partner, then you are not alone, but you will need to take some serious measures to fix this situation (see Chapter 8).

Frugal fatigue

A word of warning: if you set a budget that is too harsh, you will probably lose your motivation to follow it and get budget burnout or 'frugal fatigue'.

My experience is that people are prepared to make concessions if their cutbacks lead to immediate progress and a measurable result. If they don't see the result quickly, they will give up. Understandably so. I wouldn't keep trying at something if it isn't giving me the results I expect. This is the main reason why clients work with me as their financial personal trainer. They want to get results, they are happy to be told what to do, but ultimately they want to know that they will achieve their financial goals. Most say they are prepared to do 'what it takes', but the psychology of behavioural change suggests the easier a change is to make and sustain, the more likely you are to lock it in. So we always aim for the least amount of change required for the outcome we are seeking.

One potential pitfall of frugal fatigue is that eventually you simply get tired of being so deliberate with your money. As a result, you might start splurging unnecessarily, with the risk being that, once you start to overspend, you might as well spend up large — much like when you are dieting and open a packet of chips promising you will only eat a few, only to find your willpower disappears along with the rest of the packet. You decide you've already fallen off the diet wagon, so you might as well fall off in style.

It's important to recognise frugal fatigue if it begins to affect you. If you feel totally bored with budgeting you aren't going to stick to it for long as it will feel like a detox, which is going to put you more at risk of a spending bender. Don't give in to the temptation.

Remember what you are working towards, and if it seems too far away, have a review with your financial personal trainer to see if you can get there faster. If you aren't working with a money coach, I encourage you to set your own savings, spending and mortgage-repayment targets each month and to take the time to measure progress each month and quarter to make sure you remain on track. If you are struggling to stay on-plan, then engage more support.

> **Tip:** A good measure of progress is feeling in control and seeing actual financial results. Progress takes the form of your debts reducing faster or your savings increasing more speedily.

4. The fritter factor

I find that people tend to fritter away between 10 and 20 per cent of their income. By 'fritter', I mean inefficient, unthinking spending. Or perhaps they do realise, but are unaware of the extent to which they are spending, and that this spending is not making them any happier.

To understand what frittered funds are, you need to understand the law of diminishing returns. This law is one of the most famous in all of economics and production theory. The basic definition is that, in a productive process, if you keep adding one more unit of something while holding all other components constant, at some point the unit added will produce less. For example, you may say that watering a plant will produce a better flower, and the more you water it the better the flower — to a point. You can continue to water the plant, but eventually it will reach a point of optimum water consumption; you could keep watering past this point, but you won't get a better flower. Indeed, if you overwater, you're likely to undo all the good work you did watering it in the first place.

Another example would be an athlete training. There is an optimal level of training and rest for every athlete to enable them to reach their peak performance. Training beyond that point will not produce better results, and can actually have a detrimental effect if they are not refreshed on race day due to excessive training.

The same can be said for money and happiness. Money can buy you a warm home, put food on the table, pay for holidays and allow you to be generous with yourself and your friends. It allows you to do things that make you happy. But if you keep spending on a particular thing you will hit a threshold, a point of optimum spend, where your happiness or satisfaction will start to drop off.

For example, I love to buy a coffee from the local café. I love visiting the café and chatting with the barista. I love how they remember my order. The coffee smells great and I thrive on the caffeine hit every morning. Whether the coffee is a necessity or not is irrelevant; it simply makes me happy. It's my little non-negotiable. To some people it would be something they could take or leave, but for me it's staying.

But, if I were to buy *two* coffees a day, the experience of the second cup would not be as special as the first. I would still enjoy it, but less so than the first cup. If I were to buy a third, my enjoyment would reduce even further. I would have well and truly hit my saturation point. And some people might be just as happy to make a coffee at work and save themselves the money.

There's no judgement here over what you spend your money on, but there needs to be a self-imposed gauge as to whether you need to spend to the same level on certain items to be just as happy. Unfortunately the only way to test your threshold of happiness is to spend less and see if you feel it. If you can spend less on a cost and not feel that it affects you differently, then quite clearly the higher amount is now a frittered cost.

Around 15 per cent of the money you spend is not making you incrementally happier. This money is what I describe as 'fritter'. That is, you could not spend it and still be just as happy.

The trick to identifying your fritter areas is to know yourself well, and to go through a period of testing. What might be fritter for you might be a non-negotiable for a friend or spouse. Interestingly, what might have been a non-negotiable cost for you previously may become a fritter with time. More likely a reduction in spending on this cost could release a bit of fritter, rather than removing the cost outright.

> Fritter is like a virus with few symptoms. It creeps into your spending without consciousness and, before you know it, you are spending more than you realise on things that do not necessarily improve your lifestyle.

The following graph illustrates how fritter works. Money makes you happy to a point, with the more money you spend supposedly making you happier and your life better. But you will reach a point where you could spend more and more on a particular cost that would typically create enjoyment, but it does not make you any more satisfied. This is the happiness saturation point, or the point at which spending on a non-negotiable and possibly frivolous cost becomes fritter. If you continue to spend freely on this particular cost it may produce less enjoyment, even to the point where it produces dissatisfaction.

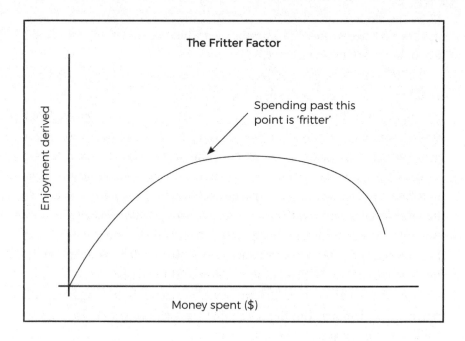

The Fritter Factor

Enjoyment derived

Spending past this point is 'fritter'

Money spent ($)

In assessing the extent of your frittering, you must understand what your 'wants' actually cost. Do you want these things because you've always had them, have always wanted them, or because they truly make you happy? If they make you happy, and you are determined that a cost is necessary even if it is frivolous in nature, then you need to ask yourself if you could satisfy the need more cheaply. The answer may be no, but you still have to ask, and in many instances you might surprise yourself. For example, the most common non-negotiable cost is a family holiday. Knowing this, we'd pop this into the budget. You might look to spend $8,000 a year, because that's how much you spent on your last two holidays. The allocated amount is verified, but the question to ask is not whether you should holiday, because we have assumed you will, but whether you could spend a fraction less and still feel just as refreshed, and possibly a bit smug for the underspend? As a rough rule of thumb, aim to cut back your non-negotiable spending by 10 per cent.

Just because you have always spent money on something doesn't mean that it makes you happy having it. Some people spend simply because they haven't had a reason *not* to spend.

Remember, the best budgets create a feeling of consciousness around your spending but do not leave you feeling deprived. Every budget has an optimum balance between progress and sustainability. Finding this balance is the main challenge for setting and sticking to a budget.

Expenses are necessary, even if some of them are frivolous; and, within the frivolity, there will be good and bad expenses. Just as with food there are good and bad calories, it's the same with your budget. Good expenses are the expenses that provide you with maximum enjoyment at the lowest cost, while bad expenses might give you buyer's remorse or at the least not even improve your day.

Whether we know it or not, we are living in an age of luxury and convenience. One area where costs often sneak up and bludgeon your monthly budget is through your food spend. We tend to spend a little more than we think, a little more often than we realise. We can usually cut back food spending by 30 per cent if linked to a plan with a big financial goal. Similar creep occurs with the services you receive. Getting the lawn cut, the house cleaned or having all the online entertainment subscriptions may be a luxury you simply cannot afford. Spending money on these costs on a regular basis is one of the quickest ways to reduce your disposable income.

Budgeting will take sacrifice, and means you need to make better choices. Sometimes these choices hurt. Sometimes it means you don't buy the biggest house on the best street. Sometimes it means you have to settle for a second-hand car instead of a new one. Sometimes you have to link your holiday budget to your annual bonus, and if the bonus isn't paid then you aren't going on holiday.

Budgeting hurts sometimes. Stay on guard though, because when it hurts is when you are about to unlock better outcomes. Pay attention to your rate of progress. You should be able to see and feel yourself pulling away from your current position. If you don't, then get an independent opinion — but don't keep putting in effort if you're not getting the result you expect. Instead, pause and enlist help.

Remember, banks and businesses offer credit cards and interest-free loans to help you justify spending on something you cannot afford. They make the pain of paying so low that it's hard to not be tempted. So stay alert.

Credit cards offer you up to 60 days of free credit, but in most cases you will pay for this little perk well after the 60 days have ended. You need to understand the history and psychology of credit cards to ensure you no longer fall prey to these little weapons of mass destruction.

5. Credit cards — don't trust them

Although the concept of credit has been around for centuries, the idea of a card that could be used to buy products in more than one place was novel when it first appeared in 1950, courtesy of Diners Club. Since their inception, credit cards have become a phenomenon, a way of pushing a spending culture to hedonistic heights. American Express jumped on the credit-card bandwagon in 1956, using the phrase 'Don't leave home without it' — an instruction too many have taken to heart!

Some take comfort from the fact that their credit card is paid off in full each month. But just because it's paid in full doesn't mean your credit card isn't harming you. Don't confuse being able to pay your credit card off each month as a measure of your financial progress. All it shows is that you're living within your means — which, while positive, is not an indicator of success. Your credit card might be allowing you to spend more without realising, creating wastage and enabling frittering.

The reality is that almost 33 per cent of people with credit cards don't pay them off in full each month, and that the average credit-card limit per household is around $30,000. Broadly speaking, if you have to use a credit card to pay your bills because you don't have the cash sitting in the bank, you're going backwards (see Chapter 6). Buy-now-pay-later schemes are the first cousin to the credit card, younger in age but just as harmful. In fact, if you get too familiar with a pay-later scheme or credit card, it is the fastest way to end up poor.

Understanding how credit cards work

Credit cards are a financial product issued by a bank or financial institution which allow you to make purchases or cash advances. They are essentially a line of credit that you can spend, up to a preset limit.

The bank charges an annual fee for you to use a credit card. When you use the card, the bank pays the merchant within a day of processing and you are given up to six weeks to come up with the money to pay the bank for the purchase.

Some banks promote that credit cards save you money (which in my opinion is a bit of a stretch). In truth, credit cards are more likely to introduce spending inefficiencies that weaken your financial foundation and make it difficult to capitalise on opportunity. If you pay off the credit card within the allocated grace period, the purchase hasn't cost you anything extra. If you don't pay it off, then you are charged interest on your purchase. And this is where it gets both interesting and scary.

A charge card has to be paid in full each month. A credit card doesn't. A credit card allows you to carry a balance indefinitely, as long as you make the minimum monthly payments.

The money you owe is subject to an annual percentage rate or finance charge. While it can vary between cards, it is normally in the range of 12–28 per cent with the average interest rate around 20 per cent. Cash advances attract a higher finance charge (sometimes up to 30 per cent) and don't have a grace period (that is, you start being charged interest on the money right away). Interest is compounded daily, which means you pay more interest than you think.

In conjunction with the annual fee and finance charge, you can also be charged late-payment fees and a higher interest rate if your transactions exceed your credit limit. If you avoid these fees and are able to pay the credit card in full each month, then this means that you have earned enough money to pay your bills — which isn't an achievement, as such. (Read Chapter 16 to better understand the damage a credit card can inflict when you're trying to repay your mortgage.) Also, due to the delayed processing times and application of funds to your account, it can be hard to determine what you have actually spent at any one time.

If you cannot afford to pay off the card in full each month, the minimum payment that the bank requires its customers to make is set at 2–5 per cent of the original purchase amount. That means that the lion's share of all minimum payments simply covers the interest charge (and sometimes not even that), and only a fraction of the payment actually reduces the balance. Even more disturbing, each month, if you don't make any more purchases, the minimum payment reduces further — it's like the bank doesn't *want* you to pay off the credit card. (I wonder why that is?) The result is that by just paying the minimum payment every month, you could take up to 40 years (*yes, 40 years!*) to pay off the original purchase, with the interest you pay being a lot more than the original purchase price. Not surprisingly, banks find their credit-card divisions are among the most profitable parts of their business.

Understanding the psychology of credit cards

Apparently, seeing a credit-card logo such as Mastercard or Visa on a website increases the chance of an impulse buy.

In a study comparing spending patterns when using cash versus credit cards, people valued credit-card purchases at 50 cents in the dollar when compared to paying for the same item with cash. Or, put another way, a purchase feels half as expensive, or people are willing to spend twice as much for the same item when paying with a credit card. Another study suggested that using a credit card instead of cash could increase your spending by 30 per cent.

The 'pain of paying' is a term coined to describe the negative emotions we experience when we part with our money. It seems that less tactile and transparent forms of money like credit cards, digital payments, Apple Pay and Google Wallet tend to be treated like 'play money' with the 'pain of paying' removed. They disassociate the pain of the payment from the purchase. Low pain, more spending. The harder or more painful it is to spend, the less you will buy.

Credit cards allow you to avoid the reality of your spending, and in doing so inadvertently encourage you to keep spending. When the pain of paying is lowered, you will need to reintroduce friction to the payment process. If you want to slow your spending down, introduce some friction, such as using cash for purchases, getting a notification when you spend money, and tracking your spending.

Even though we end up spending more when we use a credit card, some people rationalise this because they're earning points. I'm all for getting points, but logic needs to prevail. If you have no money left because you have overspent, you need points to get stuff. But if you hadn't spent as much, you would have money left to buy the item the points are giving you, in half the time. Even if you pay the card in full each month, the fact you will most likely have overspent offsets any savings or reward points.

There's no doubt that you spend more with a credit card than with cash. The gap between the two payment methods is increasing, with both volumes and the values of credit-card payments increasing.

Paying with cash elicits greater psychological pain than other modes of payment (and the larger the note you have to break, the harder it is to break it). Studies suggest that this is to do with the 'decoupling' of the actual purchase from the pain of paying for it. In other words, paying cash to someone for a product links the loss of money with the purchase — you have given something up for something else. By paying with a credit card, consumers don't link the purchase's actual cost with the purchase itself.

The challenge today is not all businesses accept cash payments, and some actively discourage them. This does reduce the pain of paying and means that your money will need to be more proactively managed and progress tracked if this defence mechanism is no longer allowed.

> **Tip:** If you are unable to pay the minimum payment on your credit card then you are almost sunk, and it is time to administer some tough love. Deregister it from your device, and if you are at the credit-card limit, cut up the card. Try to refinance the card with another bank to secure a lower interest rate to help you pay it off faster, then get to work paying off the balance.

If you are able to use a credit card correctly, paying it off in full each month, and only buying items within your planned spending budget, then it can be a source of flexibility which you can continue to enjoy (subject to some parameters). Read the following tips to ensure you are not paying more for the privilege of a credit card than you need to.

- Always ask for annual fees to be waived. These can range from $20 per annum to $325 per annum. You might not always get lucky, but if you are refinancing your mortgage to a new bank (who is issuing the credit card) or working through a mortgage broker, or have physically visited a branch, you may have more success.
- If you have more than one credit card, combine the limits on one card and close the others to avoid multiple fees for the same credit limit.
- Check monthly statements to ensure all credit card charges are your own.
- If you incur work expenses, ask for a work credit card. If this isn't possible then run a separate credit card for work-related costs only.
- Use a debit card rather than a credit card to ensure you are always spending within your budget. If you prefer a credit card, run this to a zero balance, repaying all costs within 24 hours of charging the card.

- If you are using the credit card for its points, then limit your usage to bill payments, provided you are not charged more to pay by credit card.

> **Tip:** Don't use your credit card for at least three months to get a better idea of what you are capable of when the pain of paying is higher. You will always spend less. Let this three-month hiatus become the gauge of what you can do without credit. If you insist on using a credit card after three months, ensure you continue to spend in line with your credit-card-free levels.

6. Going backwards? What you need to do

If you are in a financial hole, you need to stop digging. This sounds sensible, even simple, but for many it is far from easy.

When you are sinking, you need to take immediate action. There is no room for wastage and no time for delay. Depending on the severity of your financial situation, a hard and fast detox may be just what you need.

It may be a case of calling time on a dud investment or a spouse who remains disengaged from your plan and their spending behaviours. Both are harder to address as emotion can be running high and you don't always identify the right problem to fix. Or you identify the problem correctly, but your strategy for solving it might be ineffective.

Calling time on an investment that isn't performing is hard, but it is significantly easier when you have a one–two punch combination to follow. This means you need to know what your next move is going to be after you realise the loss; simply realising a loss is seldom effective in isolation. Knowing what your strategy is to make up the loss makes it easier to make bold moves. It also allows you to face forward, which is immeasurably better than relitigating and regurgitating the past.

As a rule I prefer to avoid changes that are unsustainable, but in some instances this may still be necessary, even if only for a short time. People lose money in many ways — whether they are disconnected from their spending or they are incurring interest costs is irrelevant. We all fritter. We all lose money. We all agree that to get ahead, we have to stop this.

Remember, society has removed a lot of the natural guardrails that used to be in place to keep us on track and aware of our spending. Digital money makes it easier to pay for things, removing pain and the necessary friction that helped minimise overspending. Easy access to credit (credit cards and buy-now-pay-later schemes) create the wrong money habits and nudge you backwards. To combat the changing way we interact with money, we need to establish new controls and money systems. When working with clients I take a few weeks to get the right structures and way of thinking in place, to help them engage and put them in the right head space to get results.

Warren Buffett has been quoted as saying that 'the first rule of money is never lose money', and 'rule number two is never forget rule number one'. There are many ways that you can save money on living costs, and in most instances you simply need to be more organised. More payment convenience usually means less savings.

Below I deliberately introduce the friction needed to rebalance your spending decisions and tilt your behaviour towards saving and making progress.

How much does it cost in work time?

A great way to demotivate yourself from spending is by calculating how much you need to work in order to purchase an item, or how many hours of work have been allocated to an annualised expense category.

Divide the cost of the item by your hourly rate to calculate how many hours you need to work to afford to buy it.

> **Tip:** Divide your annual salary in half and take off the zeroes to quickly calculate your hourly rate. For example, if your income is $80,000, then your hourly rate is $40 gross (before tax). Take 33 per cent off this number (multiply by 0.67) to get your after-tax income of $27 per hour. If you wanted to buy a $400 tool or top, then 15 hours of your work needs to pay for this ($400 divided by $27).

Use cash

As we saw in the previous chapter, digital money or contactless spending encourages spending. Whether it is Apple Pay, Google Wallet, tap-and-go or swiping a credit card, the pain of paying (the negative emotion we feel when we part with our money) is lower for digital payments than when we use cash. We try to reduce the pain of paying by delaying the pain of parting with our money, which nudges us towards spending more without even realising it. Lifestyle creep is easier than ever before, and this is linked to unconscious spending fuelled by contactless money transactions.

Although credit cards are a convenient source of money, if they're not repaid on time they can easily become a drag on your income, eroding your cashflow and costing you extra in interest (see Chapter 5). Buy-now-pay-later schemes might not incur much interest but they cost you dearly by undermining your behavioural-change goals and weakening your money mindset and the discipline needed to get ahead. This further impacts your ability to achieve your financial milestones.

In addition, credit cards encourage spending — most people are willing to spend more when they use a credit card than when using cash.

Studies have shown that less transparent forms of payment tend to be treated like play money and are therefore more easily used. Cash is viewed as the most transparent form of payment, so use cash where you can. In fact, I require my clients to use cash for their most frequent discretionary costs as well as having their most regular expenses (such as food, drink, fuel) paid from a separate bank account that is tracked closely. People usually overspend on their most regular costs, as they repeatedly spend a little more than they realise, a little more frequently, which quickly adds up.

> **Tip:** Fill your car up every week, not just when it is empty. This helps smooth your regular outgoings and to see and feel more consistent progress each week of the month.

For practical reasons you may wish to keep one credit card and limit its use to occasional purchases when other methods of payment are not appropriate, for example, internet purchases. Run the credit card to a nil balance. This means that as you charge something to the credit card you are transferring money from a bank account to the card to pay it off. This introduces a little friction designed to trigger more consciousness around your spending. All other cards should be cut up and thrown away.

> **Tip:** Use a debit card rather than a credit card for internet purchases. If you need to use a credit card, repay it within 24 hours, so it stays at a nil balance and the cost of the purchase is reflected in your accounts immediately.

Bank account structure

How your money flows between your bank accounts is one of the first lines of defence in sticking to a budget.

For my clients, I take time to structure their bank accounts by the frequency of their spend, and usually set up a three bank-account structure.

- One account is for their most frequent costs (food and fuel). I have a weekly automatic payment going into this account to cover these costs. This account is a standard cheque account that does not have the ability to go into an 'unarranged overdraft'. Where possible, I try to encourage the use of cash as a payment for these costs, because otherwise you tend to spend a little more than you think a little more often than you realise on food and drink. Cash introduces awareness and friction. Whether you use cash or a debit card, this structure will alert you to overspending, because once the money runs out, the money runs out.
- Bills are grouped into a separate account that is topped up monthly. I set up an extra one-off payment of one-third of the expected monthly payments, to give a buffer for some of the costs that fluctuate over the course of the year (power) or that aren't paid monthly (rates). This account can be replaced by a credit card, if all bills are already charged to one.
- The third account is called the main account. This is the account that all income is paid into, and the automatic payments to the bills and everyday accounts are made from. The main account is where your overall progress is measured, and less frequent costs are paid from (e.g., holidays).
- An optional fourth account is used if a client wants a pocket money account to manage outside of the main budget.

Work-cost reimbursement

People often pay for work-related things, such as taxis or lunches, with their EFTPOS or credit card. Although the money will eventually be reimbursed, this can put unnecessary pressure on your personal finances in the meantime. There is also the risk that you will forget to claim the expense, or not do it in a timely manner.

I recommend you have a separate credit card for these types of situations. You only use it if you are incurring costs for others that you know will be reimbursed later. It keeps things clean, and it avoids any costs or delays in reimbursement straining your personal finances. Better yet, ask your work to provide you with a credit card.

Keep business and personal finances separate

This is a biggie. Many self-employed people run their businesses as an extension of their personal finances, or vice versa. Everything tends to be intertwined, which just means things are a mess. Financial statements are usually manipulated to ensure profit is low, so that the tax they need to pay is low, with little regard for how much money the business is actually earning and what level of progress they are making overall. We need to pay separate attention to both business performance and personal spending to get a better sense of where the weaknesses sit and opportunities hide.

If it's common to be short of money in the business, people may willingly top it up from their personal finances, or not pay themselves a salary. Some business costs get paid from personal accounts or by credit card, and some business owners and self-employed people are more comfortable spending because they believe some costs are tax-deductible. Any combination of these points usually ensures they are not taking from the business what they could and should.

Very few small businesses actually forecast earnings, instead reacting only to provisional tax payments. Forecasting is key. Tracking to a business plan is key. Business strategy is imperative if you are going to grow your business the smartest way.

Another key benefit of keeping everything separate is that it will highlight actual business performance and whether the business in its current state is viable. Not all good ideas translate to good businesses, and not all good operators have a viable product or service to sell. When trying to untangle personal costs from the business, start with business income and deduct business costs before you push any personal costs into the business. From whatever amount is left over, take off tax (28 per cent) to find the business working profit (for the purpose of this exercise). Separately consider what your personal living costs are and if these can be ring-fenced and reduced. Your personal living costs will be the cash drawn from the business. Does the business have enough profit to pay for these costs outright? Don't mix your drinks on this. Let the two entities — business and personal — stand independent of each other to help you pinpoint where the problem sits.

Manage big fluctuations in income

The feast-or-famine nature of being in business or being self-employed makes you think that planning is a waste of time because of income fluctuations. Some months it's up, some months it's down — which makes it feel hard to get a sense of what progress you are likely to make. The sentiment is real, but the response isn't quite right. Volatile conditions mean you need to plan more, not less, because you need to respond in real time to your changing situation.

Inconsistent income is a headwind that requires special navigation techniques. You want to avoid the feast-or-famine sentiment at all costs as this volatility leads to financial chaos. I had one client who earned $1 million per annum but whose income was up and down over the course of the year. Some months they received no income, other months a lot. They never knew where they were at, and failed to make any real progress despite such a huge income. Another client who earned less and was paid commission for sales struggled to balance the inconsistency of income with measurable progress.

To manage a fluctuating income, start with understanding your minimum living costs. What does it cost you on a monthly basis to keep afloat and cover your most basic non-negotiable costs? This is the minimum after-tax income you must make. As you build up beyond this minimum threshold, you have to set this extra money aside, and slowly build up three months' worth, so you have the buffer to spend normally even if the income falls below the minimum threshold set. If you smash your income goal, then the extra income can be split between extra discretionary spend and savings. For example, under your preferred operational budget, you might want to spend up to a maximum each year of $3,000 on clothes and $10,000 on a holiday. You don't have to spend to this level, but you would prefer to if you could. Know your preference, then consider your minimum spend. You know you need to spend at least $500 per year on clothes and $1,500 on a holiday. These numbers, along with your basic living costs, help set your minimum income target. If your income exceeds the minimum, then 50 per cent of every extra dollar made goes towards your higher discretionary spend until you have met your maximum, and the other 50 per cent goes towards savings.

How much business profit needs to be achieved to allow the business to function and pay you your minimum living costs? Set this as the minimum output for the month. Link the result to an input. How many sales do you need to hit or jobs complete to get to this break-even amount. You will need to achieve this each month. Of course some months it won't be possible, but set an expectation around it being achieved within each quarter. If you can't commit to this, then you probably shouldn't be in business.

Next, list your monthly discretionary spending. Once you have hit the business profit needed to cover your minimum living costs, pay yourself this amount (usually in the form of drawings). Profit after this is split 50:50 — with 50 per cent being paid out to the business owner to cover their discretionary (or fun) spending. Basic living costs aren't typically included in this discretionary spending amount. The remaining 50 per cent stays in the business.

What you spend on holidays, clothes and gifts tends to swell as you earn more money, and rightly so. I don't begrudge you the extra spending; in fact this is a great money skill to have (delaying your gratification until you can afford to pay for it), but I still want you to be more deliberate with how you manage this. List both the minimum and the maximum you want to be able to spend on these costs. The first tranche of profit ensures your minimum desires are covered. Further profit goes towards the larger spending amount. We put a number on the maximum we will spend. Once the 50 per cent profit gets to this level, stop drawing profits for spending purposes and redirect the profit into your personal wealth plan. This process is considered and deliberately sets out to reduce big fluctuations in your spending levels.

Pay less tax — legitimately

A lot of people believe it is only the self-employed who can find ways to pay less tax, but this is not the case. If you are an employee, there can still be opportunities to claim a tax refund.

For instance, if you pay school or other donations or pay income-protection insurance, you are likely to be entitled to claim these expenses against your pay-as-you-earn (PAYE) income and receive a tax refund, provided you actually complete and submit a tax return. Further, if you have not worked a complete financial year at your current place of employment you may have overpaid your tax, which would also trigger a tax refund.

> **Tip:** The Inland Revenue Department (IRD) doesn't know whether you've paid a cost that might trigger a refund unless you tell them. If you have paid a donation, you can submit a tax return for a refund of one-third of the amount donated.

If you are self-employed, work with a good accountant to understand what deductions are available to you. Check that your accountant hasn't missed anything. The first thing you should look at is what has been coded to 'drawings'. Print off the breakdown of this account and review it. Identify and highlight any costs that are genuinely related to the business as these should be put back into the business so you get a tax saving on them.

Often an accountant may err on the side of caution and code costs to drawings genuinely thinking they were personal in nature. When I review new clients' financial statements, I usually find at least $5000 of tax savings that have been ignored through lazy bookkeeping. Make sure your accountant is picking up on any little areas of tax savings.

Consolidate debt onto your mortgage

I recommend consolidating outstanding debts onto your mortgage. Although this means you will owe more on your mortgage, you should pay less interest overall — all your credit-card debt and personal loans would now be at mortgage interest rates, which tend to be lower than credit-card rates. Importantly, without other payments dragging on your income, you will be able to apply more of your surplus income to paying off your higher mortgage. However, unless you accelerate your repayments on your new higher mortgage, you run the risk of paying more over the life of the loan. I track this very closely, because freeing up your cashflow through debt consolidation too often leads to lifestyle creep, not a faster repayment of debt.

For example: You have a credit-card balance of $10,000 at 20 per cent. This is compounding daily. So it's going to cost you $2,247 (not $2,000) in interest per year. Let's say you are due to pay it off over two years. (For simplicity's sake, let's say you were going to make a lump-sum payment in two years of $15,000 to clear the credit card, which is the $10,000 debt plus two years' worth of interest, compounded daily.)

If you put this debt on your 25-year mortgage, the interest rate would be lowered to 6 per cent, which would incur $600 in interest every year. But your mortgage is set up to be paid off over 25 years. This means that, unless you channelled that $11,200 (the $10,000 debt plus two years of interest) into repaying the debt within two years, you hold the consolidated loan for longer, and the overall cost would be higher.

While debt consolidation can be a good strategy, *it is only effective as long as you do not accrue further debt*. Data from debt consolidation companies estimates that up to 78 per cent of people who consolidate their credit-card debt will incur more debt, which will again need to be consolidated. And, as we have seen above, the long-term impact of adding extra costs to your mortgage can actually be more expensive if the overall debt is not paid off faster. This is one of the reasons it's imperative that you measure your performance to make sure the debt is reducing. The interest rate and the length of time you have the debt for will be what determines the overall cost of the debt.

If you have insufficient equity at your existing bank to consolidate your other debts onto the mortgage, then consider refinancing with another bank.

Debt consolidation — no mortgage

If you don't have a mortgage, it may be worth consolidating your credit-card balances to one card with a low interest rate. Some banks allow you to transfer the balance of your credit card and pay no interest for the first six months. However, after six months, the interest rate will increase. Some banks allow you to have a low interest rate for the length of time it takes you to repay the transferred balance, but the minimum payments will be set at a higher rate than you are currently paying. This isn't a bad thing, as it means you are forced to pay off the debt faster, but this extra cost could put too much pressure on your cashflow.

> **Tip:** If you are transferring your balance to a low-interest credit card, it is important that you use the respite of lower outgoings to repay the debt balance faster.

If you are unable to consolidate your debts, rank all of your debts according to interest rate, size and monthly payment. Determine which debt-repayment strategy is going to work for you best, to help you build momentum quicker. The three key methods for repaying debt are the Avalanche, Snowball or Ski methods. You can apply any of them in their purest form or take a little of each. Sustainable progress is key.

The Avalanche method prioritises debts with the higher interest rates. This saves the most interest, but if these debts are high it can feel like a Herculean effort and you may lose your motivation.

The Snowball method focuses on the size of the debt. You chip away at the smallest debt first, building momentum as you go. You might not save as much in interest, but you are likely to stick at it for longer.

The Ski method is my hybrid version of the other two. Here I adopt the Snowball approach, chipping off the smaller debts first — but I rank all debts based on the monthly payment amount, focusing on getting runs on the board (paying off the smaller loans), but being strategic in the loans I prioritise to save me the most cashflow each month, so I can channel more cashflow into faster debt repayment of the remaining debts.

If you have short-term debt, this usually means your money behaviours and money management are weak. You also most likely have a poverty mindset. Fixing this requires deliberate action and support. To help support you in this journey, join my Debt-Free Me Masterclass to get in control of your money once and for all. More details, including a discount code, are included at the back of the book.

Structure your debt better

It might be time to change banks. Look at interest rates, lending terms and your ability to access any equity in your property to consolidate debt. Each bank will have different ways of calculating this, and it will result in slightly different offerings from bank to bank, so compare banks. Factoring in break costs, cash clawbacks and possible penalties, should you change the length of your fixed-term loan? Would you be better off refinancing with another bank? Often the answer is yes, if it unlocks your ability to stop sinking or to grow wealth faster, but this is not always the case and you don't want to change banks for the sake of it. Complete a quick cost–benefit analysis before incurring any costs.

Remember that each bank has slightly different lending criteria. What is a negative for one bank might not be onerous to another. If you do refinance your mortgage to another bank, you can still keep your day-to-day banking at your old bank if this helps reduce the faff of moving banks. Even if the new bank requires you to deposit your salary into one of their bank accounts, you can easily transfer this money into your old bank account by setting up an automatic payment to pay this money across the next day. Open banking, which shifts the control of data back to users (and not with the bank), will make it easier to move banks as your banking footprint will be easily accessible and transferable between banks. That is still a little way off though, so for now weigh up the benefit of staying with your bank while restructuring your mortgage, or making the big move to another bank.

Tackle bank fees

Ask for all unarranged overdraft capability to be removed from your bank accounts. This way, should you be about to make a purchase without sufficient funds in your account, you will be declined. This will prompt you to decide if you do in fact need the item you are trying to buy. If you did decide to go ahead with the purchase, you would have to use an alternative payment method (a credit card or money from a different account) and avoid the $15 or $20 unarranged overdraft or 'account out of order' bank fee.

In approximately half of these purchases, most people don't go ahead with the purchase once alerted that the cost would mean they were about to overspend and come off their plan. All they needed was a reminder *before the purchase*. An unarranged overdraft fee tells you that you have overspent *after the fact*, which is useless information. Going into overdraft suggests you are going backwards or at the very least you have lazy money management. (Many of my clients had an average $500 per annum of avoidable fees. The worst I have seen was a client incurring $4000 in avoidable fees. Too much money, not enough care.) Unarranged overdraft and poor bank account conduct fees show a pattern of financial neglect.

If you have multiple credit cards, you will be paying multiple fees. Look to combine the available credit between credit cards and apply for one card, increasing its limit accordingly. Cancel all of the other cards to save in fees.

Reduce your living costs

The best way to reduce your expenses is to go through them one at a time and look for ways to lower the amount you are spending.

Groceries and food

Food wastage tends to be the biggest cost in everyone's grocery budget. Set a budget, write a menu plan, translate this to a shopping list and take a calculator to the supermarket with you.

If you struggle to stick to a tight shopping budget, consider shopping online as it allows you to sort by specials. Online shopping for groceries also eliminates the spur-of-the moment items — usually expensive treats — that get thrown into your trolley as you walk the aisles of the supermarket. With online shopping, you pay a small extra charge for packing and delivery (if required), but this will more than likely be offset by the money you save by not giving in to temptation and purchasing specials. Make sure you order a day or two before you need the food to save on impulse purchases.

Here are some more tips for reducing spending on food.

- Cook and pack your own meals, making enough so you can take leftovers to work the following day.
- Reduce the amount of takeaways you consume.
- Buy produce in season — otherwise you end up paying a higher cost

because the food is flown in from the other side of the world.

- Buy non-perishable items in bulk.
- Start a vegetable garden, as it can often pay for itself within the first season of produce — not to mention the satisfaction of preserving your own produce. Focus on vegetables that are easy to grow and are prolific, such as tomatoes, spinach, cabbage, herbs and so on.
- Buy non-brand products where you can. Compare the ingredients between the labelled product versus the non-branded product and, if the ingredients are the same, opt for the supermarket variety.
- Attend local markets to buy fruit and vegetables.
- Do a weekly meal plan and make a shopping list.
- Buy foods on sale, especially meats.
- Consider buying a coffee pot or machine for home. Spending $1 on a coffee from home saves you $4 or more compared to buying a similar-tasting coffee from a shop.
- Shop online.
- Never shop hungry. Don't shop in the evenings if you can avoid it.
- Families often run out of bread and milk during the week and frequent their local dairy to top up on necessities. Buy what you need each week at the supermarket and freeze part of it.
- Use store points/vouchers towards grocery purchases.
- Food subscription boxes (Hello Fresh, My Food Bag and others) can be helpful in sticking to the budget and having leftovers for lunch the next day. This doesn't work for everyone, but might help you.
- If you do want to buy your lunch from a café, get crafty and pick up leftover food from your favourite café for half the price. Foodprint is an app designed to reduce food waste and enjoy meals at a fraction of the price from your local café or restaurant. The app notifies you of food that hasn't sold which you can buy for a reduced price.
- There are many amazing budgeting groups on Facebook that can help you spend less money each week. Join a few to get some great ideas on how to live more frugally.

Tip: Combine what you spend on groceries, takeaways, cafés, restaurants, work lunches and coffees into one amount. Withdraw this amount in cash each week to pay for these items, and manage your spending based on the remaining funds.

Travel expenses

- Consider public transport as an alternative to driving to work.
- Consider carpooling — your costs can be shared and you get to use the commuter lanes.
- Sell any unused vehicles. Many of my clients seem to have a car or motorbike that isn't being used but is still taking up storage space and requiring annual registration and insurance. Flick it.
- Keep the tyres on your car inflated properly. Once a month, stop by a local petrol station to check the air pressure on your tyres. Make sure they are filled to the recommended level. Your petrol usage will improve by 1 per cent for every PSI of air you are able to add.
- When petrol was rationed during World War II, a popular slogan was 'Is this trip necessary?' Ask yourself this every time you drive.
- Clean oil and a well-maintained engine can save you money.
- Top up your petrol weekly, even if the tank isn't empty. Smoothing your petrol costs to weekly will help you stick to your monthly budget.

Energy bills

- Unplug all electrical devices when not in use, as most electric devices will still use a small amount of electricity (called a phantom charge) even when they are not turned on. Of the total energy used to run home electronics, 40 per cent is consumed when the appliances are turned off but still plugged in.
- Turn off all unused power switches. Your hot-water cylinder is likely to be hotter than it needs to be, and will also lose a lot of heat to the environment. This means you use a lot more energy than you realise to keep the water hot. Install an insulation blanket on your cylinder and drop the temperature to 60 degrees Celsius.
- Use a programmable thermostat for heaters.
- Stop the drafts by buying a roll of adhesive foam door sealer and close up the cracks.
- Insulate your property.
- Consider investing in ceiling fans, as they reduce the cost of both heating and cooling by circulating the air more efficiently.
- When you leave the room, turn off the light.
- If you have children, give one the role of being the family 'energy saver' or let them take turns. Their job is to make sure the family is

saving as much electricity as possible.

- Wash your clothes in cold water.

Entertainment

- If you are going to the gym less than once a week, cancel your membership.
- Trim back on your Sky package, or consider going TV-free or basic free-to-air for three months. See if your life falls apart.
- Don't always buy books; visit the library or use a Kindle.
- Cancel unused newspaper, magazine and online subscriptions.
- Consider putting online subscriptions on a quarterly roster, cancelling one and signing up to another, in repeat.
- Any unhealthy 'habit' such as excessive drinking or smoking needs to be addressed. If you are ready to kick this habit, use your new financial plan to motivate you. Your wallet will breathe a sigh of relief, not to mention your body as well.

Insurance

- Shop around for commodity-based insurances (home, contents, car, etc.). Use the code at the end of this book to access a discount on your commodity insurances.
- Review your life-insurance policies each year to determine if you can lower the coverage. As you age, your life insurance needs should reduce, because you have fewer years to cover. Also, as you kill your mortgage, your life-insurance needs should further decrease because you have less debt to be repaid in the event of your death.

Communications

- Look at getting a prepaid cell phone if you don't use one all that much.
- If you do use your cell phone a lot, look at the features you are paying for and determine if you can trim these back.
- If you do use a cell phone, do you need a landline at home?
- Bundle your communication services (phone and broadband).
- Know your data usage and choose a plan that best suits this.

Children

- Look to reduce organised children's activities.

- Give your kids jobs to do to fill some of their 'twiddling their thumbs' time.
- Buy second-hand school uniforms and clothes.
- Bake, instead of buying, snacks.

Household costs

- Live small, with just the basics. Think back to what it was like when you were a student or starting out working, when it was OK to just survive rather than having a life full of stuff.
- Eliminate the cleaner, or reduce their frequency from weekly to fortnightly. Better yet, get your kids to do some of the cleaning in exchange for pocket money.
- If you give to your local church but are struggling to maintain the encouraged levels, speak to the leader of your religious group and explain that you would like to contribute time instead of money for a period, while you get your house in order.
- Save water, save money. Invest in a shower-reduction kit. These kits work by reducing the flow of water to the showerhead, meaning you use a little less water, although the change is barely noticeable when showering. Better yet, time your showers.
- Repair leaky toilets and taps.
- Reduce your garden watering to a minimum.
- If you have a pool, keep it covered when it is not in use to reduce evaporation.
- Invest in a thermal blanket for your pool.
- When brushing your teeth, turn off the tap when not using the water.
- Use the microwave more than the oven where possible, as the cost just to preheat your oven is more than it costs to use the microwave.
- Stop using paper napkins and paper towels. Cloth towels are absorbent and can be used repeatedly. Cloth napkins can be made from old tablecloths and clean better than paper ones.
- Limit alcohol consumption.

Clothes and grooming

- If you spend a chunk of your money on clothes, aim to reduce this spending by 50 per cent. Not surprisingly, spending on clothes is one of the largest cost categories for women. I had one client who spent $60,000 a year on clothes; not a worry if you earn more than a million dollars a year, but if you don't then that is an extraordinary amount that suggests some other issues are in play.

Gifts to ask for

It's frustrating that if you want to reduce your daily costs you might initially need to outlay some money in order to save money in the future. To minimise this initial outlay, consider asking for some of the following as gifts so you don't have to spend your own money on them.

- If you are an avid magazine reader, ask for a magazine subscription.
- If you are a bookworm, ask for an e-reader, so your books cost less.
- If you are a foodie, ask for help setting up a vegetable garden.
- If you love clothes, ask for a clothes voucher.
- For caffeine addicts, ask for a good-quality coffee machine, so your daily coffee costs you $1 per cup instead of takeaway prices.

Do your tax return

If you have worked for part of the year, made a donation, paid school fees or have income-protection insurance, you are likely to be due a tax refund of up to 33 per cent of the amount paid.

Take advantage of opportunities

Part of managing money when you're broke is increasing your income. For example, you might be able to:

- sell stuff
- get a better-paying job or ask for a pay rise (see Chapter 7)
- get a second job, side hustle or additional income.

These options aren't available to everyone, but ultimately it's about being resourceful. Look for opportunities to earn more and save more money, then seize those opportunities. Sometimes they might look more like sacrifices in the short term, but be brave and start banking the extra money.

Sell stuff

If you have assets but are income-poor, consider selling things you don't need or use in order to liquidate funds and repay debt or create a buffer. For every new thing you buy, try to sell the old one.

> **Tip:** Sell any asset that is not being used but has a holding cost — for example, an unused car.

Get a better-paying job or ask for a pay rise

See Chapter 7 for more on this.

Get a second job or a side hustle

Getting a second job sounds intense, but it can be an effective way of propping up your income. Babysitting, mystery shopping, gardening, cleaning and dog walking are all examples of 'extra' income that can be earned without specialist training. I have had some clients pack supermarket shelves at night in order to supplement their income. This works for people who have time. If you are time-poor, then the easiest way to supplement your income is by getting a boarder or flatmate to share your accommodation costs. This income tends to be tax-free.

International schools are often looking for homes for their students, and will pay up to $300 per week per student. Even if you had a student guest for only six months of the school year, this is $6000 of tax-free income.

> **Tip:** You need to have time for a second job, whether it is evenings or weekends. But small amounts of extra income add up.

I find that clients are prepared to go through a little bit of pain provided it is going to get them where they want to be, they have a plan for how they are going to get there and they are able to track progress against this plan. Anyone can handle a little discomfort if you know how long it will last. What people can't handle is ongoing pain or inconvenience without any gain.

Come up with a plan. Set small milestones. Seize opportunities. Overall, this will help you to take control. Once you do, you might be surprised at what you can accomplish.

7. Negotiating a pay rise

For most of us, the idea of asking for a pay rise is really challenging. Women are especially reluctant and are the first to accept less than their value, often because the fear that 'pushing your case' (in the exact same way a male might) could be perceived as being bossy or demanding.

However, a universal barrier to getting a pay rise is *not knowing how to ask*. It's easy for me to tell my clients to earn more money, but advising them *how* to do this takes more effort.

Some of my clients, usually female, take the view that you shouldn't have to ask for a pay rise; if your employer values you, they will give you a pay rise without you having to ask. In some instances this may be the case. But, for the vast majority, this is a naïve view. If the system was going to do right by you, then women wouldn't be paid on average 9 per cent less to do the same jobs as men. Managers are often too busy doing their own work — and ensuring *they* get a raise — to give too much thought to you.

Salary negotiations (like most negotiations) can be difficult, are usually handled poorly and can cause uncertainty and disappointment. Knowing how to ask for a pay rise is a learned skill; and, actually, asking for something is a life skill — and one that less than half of us have. As a UK poll found, more than half of those surveyed had *never* asked their boss for more money, with the most common reason being fear of damaging their relationship with their employer or becoming the first to go in the event of a restructure.

For many of us, part of managing money well is increasing our income. Just because you feel uncomfortable, don't be afraid to ask for more. Before you ask, though, it's important to be prepared, by researching the job market and knowing your industry and remuneration bands, otherwise you are likely to end up disappointed.

Wanting, asking and getting are three different components of the pay-rise process. Understanding each component will increase your chances of getting what you deserve.

I recall asking one client when she'd had her last pay rise; it was three years earlier. I asked where her salary sat in terms of the market average. She confirmed she was towards the top of the band but she was demoralised that her manager wouldn't give her a performance review, much less a pay rise, despite her asking repeatedly for a review. Her response was to stop asking and just get on with the job.

This can be a valid short-term plan, but taking this path means your job satisfaction will drop over time, as you'll not be able to help feeling undervalued and unappreciated.

I guess it would be natural to start looking for other employment in this situation, but since my client was at the top of her salary band all the other jobs she looked at paid $10,000 less than what she was currently on. Her financial plan didn't allow her to take a pay cut this big — or, more accurately, if she were to take this cut she would need to know how long it would be before she'd be back on her current salary. No prospective recruiter could answer this satisfactorily, so again she felt stuck in her current job.

When I started working with her to improve her overall finances, I said she needed to speak to her boss about having a pay review. In fact, this became one of the pieces of homework I assigned her.

As expected, she felt this was an uphill battle. So together we wrote an email for her to send to her HR department. We spelled out her case as to why she needed and deserved the pay rise. She sent the email and was then called to a meeting.

At the meeting she was able to communicate her case — reiterating the points of the email, which acted as her agenda. She tried hard not to treat the result of the meeting as a foregone conclusion. She felt sick beforehand, during and after the meeting. But she got the pay rise, and it was backdated two years! All she had needed was the confidence to ask, accompanied with a solid case to justify her request.

In my opinion, actually getting a pay rise is of less consequence than sticking up for yourself or making the effort to stand up and be heard. The worst that could have happened for my client was that she remained on her current salary. But the exercise of asking for a pay rise was a great way of showing that she thought she did a good job and deserved to be paid more for her work or to be shown the areas her manager wanted her to work on in order to receive a pay rise.

In the last few years, there has been a salary freeze in a lot of industries. This has meant that salaries have not kept up with inflation. At a minimum, your pay should be keeping up with inflation. Asking for your pay to be increased each year in line with inflation is not the same as asking for a pay rise, so don't make this a bigger deal than it is. For example, if you are on a $100,000 salary then this should be increasing by around $5000 each year to keep you on the same after-inflation income (based on a 5 per cent inflation rate). A pay rise is when you receive an increase *above the rate of inflation* for your current role.

If an immediate pay rise is out of the question, consider asking to take on the extra work and responsibility linked to a pay rise, or ask for a performance-related bonus.

Ask what you can do to move up to the next rung on the ladder. If you feel undervalued, say so — and ask what you can do to increase both your contribution and your remuneration.

Things to remember

- In most situations, it's easier for your employer to keep you happy than it is to recruit someone else to take your role.
- Know your worth. What is the market paying for your role? Speak to recruiters to get a sense of what the market is offering and look on different job websites. How much would it cost the company to replace you (in both recruitment and training)?
- Make sure you have leverage. Getting a pay rise without leverage is hard to do. The most effective form of leverage is another job offer that pays more than you are currently getting. (Make sure the offer is real, in case your bluff is called.)
- Know the difference between the value of the role and *your value*, and don't confuse them. If you are not getting a pay rise it could be because your employer is putting restrictions on the value of the role. Most roles have a ceiling remuneration. Remember, it's easy to believe you are worth more, especially if you feel like you're giving 150 per cent every day, but you need to be able to demonstrate this objectively by assessing your worth against others in the same

industry. Many employers don't give a raise until the employee is doing 20 per cent more work than they did when initially hired.
- Salaries are often dictated by market forces rather than individual abilities.
- Determine if you could take on more responsibility or duties to warrant higher pay.

Not all employers will be in a position to give a pay rise, so find out what else is available. Some things you might ask about include:
- extra training
- education
- professional development
- increased KiwiSaver contribution
- finishing work 30 minutes earlier
- doing your job in four days, but being paid for five
- a bonus scheme, based on you delivering your objectives and then being paid at a later date.

Be aware that many managers are paid to keep the salaries of their staff at a certain level. So giving you a pay rise may come at the expense of their own pay review.

Building your case — the prep work

A key factor is knowing *when* to ask for a pay rise. This will either be set out in the company manual, and is usually on your job anniversary or at a set time every year. If your company doesn't have a manual — or, worse yet, has one but doesn't follow it — then know that budgets are set a couple of months before the start of the next financial year. These budgets typically include funds allocated for increased staff numbers and pay rises for existing staff.

Remember, just because you want a pay rise and you feel like you deserve one doesn't mean that you should or will get one. Asking for a raise is about building a case, not simply making a request. It is up to you to build a case to persuade your employer or manager that you are worth it.

Your case needs to focus on the areas that are important to your employer and demonstrate that you are making their life better by having you working for them.

Your performance is only one of the key factors influencing a pay increase. The performance of the economy, the company as a whole and your overall department will also have a significant influence, and usually has a more far-reaching effect than your performance in isolation.

Furthermore, the strength of the talent market is crucial. What are people in your position being paid elsewhere? Is there a shortage of supply, and what would the company need to pay to replace you (in terms of recruitment and training)?

Review your work history and prepare a list of your accomplishments. Arm yourself with evidence, which can include when you had your last pay rise, the length of time you have been with the organisation, above-average performance reviews (where relevant) and salary surveys (contact your industry association). Be sure to use accurate performance measures, not subjective opinions, to prepare a list of your accomplishments. Consider how your input and general performance has improved quality and increased customer satisfaction, raised staff morale and, perhaps most importantly (in your employer's eyes especially), contributed to a growth in profitability.

Pay particular attention to projects you have worked on and problems you have solved. Consider how the business's operation and profits have improved since you started working there. How can you demonstrate that you have done more than you were expected to do, as your employer will argue that you are already paid to do your job well? The most effective measure of anyone's contribution is how it affects the profit, the bottom line.

Think about the following things.

- Do you work overtime to get the job done?
- Do you take the initiative? List the ways you can demonstrate this.
- Have you saved the company time or money?
- Have you empowered your team to be stronger?
- Are you managing more people than when you were originally employed?
- Have you completed or helped to complete a tough project and got positive results from it?
- Have you completed tasks outside your job description, or gone above and beyond the call of duty?

Tip: Print off your job description then list any additional duties you have completed outside of the list.

Decide how much of a pay rise you want. It is important in all negotiations to appear both reasonable and realistic (not greedy). The common tactic of starting high with the view of negotiating down doesn't tend to work well in pay negotiations, as it can be viewed as taking the mickey.

Remember, some of the best pay rises are tools to help you jump ahead professionally, both within the business and on your wider career path. Be open to taking on other things in lieu of money that may be more valuable in the future, for example, shares in the company, an option, a wardrobe allowance, a company car, a carpark, an increase in annual leave entitlement or the employer's KiwiSaver contributions, professional development or external training.

Even if your requested pay rise is reasonable, expect to negotiate further with your boss.

> **Tip:** Always have realistic expectations and put yourself in your boss's shoes. How do you think they would view this salary-increase request?

Before you have a chat with your employer, always make an appointment. Set time aside. This is an important topic, and it deserves to be more than a water-cooler conversation. Your boss may not be expecting this conversation, so ask to speak with them in private and say that you would like to make a meeting to review your role.

Many of my clients get stage fright at this point. If you find this too hard, you might say, 'Can we please meet to discuss my role and ongoing development? I would like your feedback and advice.'

Avoid mentioning anything to do with salary, reviews or pay increases. If prodded say it is a personal matter, or that you want to present a proposal.

> **Tip:** Avoid meeting on Monday or Friday. Most likely your boss will be busy getting ready for the week on Monday, and thinking about the weekend on Friday.

Once you have an agreed appointment, and depending on your relationship with your boss, you could email them your pitch ahead of time to give them a chance to digest it. For some people this takes the awkward part out of the meeting. If you know your boss won't read the email or feel that the in-person version is the best way forward, then be brave and do just that.

Having the meeting and making the pitch

Once you've done the prep work, it's time to do the asking. It's not until you ask that you will know where you stand from your employer's perspective.

In any meeting or negotiation, present yourself well. Stay positive. Be confident, but not arrogant (sometimes this line is easily blurred). Remember, while the meeting is unlikely to be in your office, you are the one who has requested it, so in a way you are the host. Run the meeting as follows:

- Start by saying how much you enjoy your job.
- Lead into discussion of your achievements.
- Tell your boss what percentage increase in pay you would like. Never just say 'I want a raise.' Be specific and demonstrate that you have thought things through. Incorporate market standards or job comparisons. It is up to you to demonstrate that you are worth it.
- *Never* mention that your personal situation has changed and therefore you need to be paid more. What happens at home has nothing to do with your reasons for a pay rise, and it is insulting to your employer to lump them with the responsibility of having to pay you more because of your personal circumstances.
- *Never* say you are broke. You get a pay rise because you deserve it. Your employer is not a charity.

Record the reasons justifying a pay rise in a written document that can be given to your manager to make their job easier if they need to get sign-off from someone higher up the chain.

The meeting can result in one of four responses from your boss:

1. 'No.'
2. 'I need to think about it,' or 'I need sign-off from someone higher.'
3. 'Yes.'
4. 'Not yet, but let's revisit this at a specified time in the future (say three months).'

No matter the outcome, thank your boss for taking the time to have the meeting. Follow this up with an email reiterating the findings of the meeting and thanking them again.

How to handle the meeting when the answer is 'no'

Never take it personally. If you let the rejection affect your work then your boss will feel justified in their decision. Remember, in reality there is no such thing as 'no'; it is actually a 'not yet'.

It's important to understand the reasons why you are not getting the raise and consider them carefully. Is it because the company cannot afford it, or is there no room in the budget? Discuss non-cash ways the company may be able to reimburse you for your efforts in lieu of a pay rise.

If the answer is no because your employer doesn't think you deserve it, then you need to understand why they have that view and find out what you need to do to achieve a different outcome or more positive perception. Is it about taking on extra responsibilities? Determine how long you will need to take on the extra responsibility before you receive another pay review.

Determine whether the feedback from your employer is fair and right. Are their review points reasonable and is their expectation of what needs to be done to get the pay rise achievable? Speak to colleagues and get their feedback.

> **Tip:** Unless the business is in financial trouble, you should be expecting a pay rise in line with the CPI (Consumer Price Index), otherwise you are effectively taking a pay cut. Your employer will need to have a very good reason why this cannot be achieved immediately, and this could be a warning about the viability of the business going forward.

If you are instructed to take on more responsibility or duties in order to justify a pay rise, then agree to a time that your pay can be reviewed again to reflect the extra duties undertaken. This should be no later than six months away.

Be wary if you are given extra duties with no offer of a pay or performance review. To arrange a discussion about an issue like this, write a basic email to your boss to thank them for the increase in responsibility, which is something you welcome. Say that, while you acknowledge this opportunity, you would still like to review your objectives, future development and rewards, along with other opportunities you wish to be offered.

What to do if your boss is not the person who signs off on the raise

Unless you are working in a small company, you hold a senior position or your direct boss is the CEO, it is likely that your immediate boss will not have the authority to agree on a salary increase on the spot (if at all). In this case it is important that you gain agreement in principle with the case you are presenting. Having prepared a written report will help your boss to communicate the salient points to the higher powers. Make it as easy as possible for them to go in to bat for you.

The value of you versus the value of the role

It is important to recognise the difference between the value of the role and your own value. *The value of a role does not directly relate to the value of you as a person.* If an employer is unable to give you a pay rise, it may be because the role you fulfil in the company has a salary cap on it. If you find there is a big gap between your expectations of what the role should pay and what you are receiving then it's time to find a role which commands a higher value and corresponding salary.

The best time to negotiate a pay increase is when you are starting a new job. You will have the greatest advantage after you have received the job offer and before you accept the role.

What to do when your role has a pay ceiling

If the position you have trained for does not pay enough, and the market agrees with this — that is, no matter where you work there is a salary ceiling on that position — it's time for you to think about your options to earn more money. Some options are:

- take on a boarder
- take on a flatmate
- retrain
- work overtime
- start a side hustle
- get another part-time job.

You need to take control of your career trajectory. It is no longer sufficient to sit in a job and not progress financially or professionally.

8. Money, relationships and being happy

The role money plays in relationships can make getting ahead a challenge. Not surprisingly, studies have found that starting a relationship with consumer debt has a negative impact on the quality of a relationship. Mismatched money personalities and unaligned financial goals and values can also play havoc with any relationship, causing arguments, frustration and lack of sleep.

While sleep deprivation can magnify any vexation, arguments around money still tend to be longer and more intense than other types of marital disagreements. Perhaps most disturbingly, research has found that couples who argue about money early in their relationship — regardless of their income or net worth — are at greater risk of divorce.

Financial honesty is hard to come by in couples. A 2011 US study that interviewed 949 adults between the ages of 25 and 55 in committed relationships (married, engaged or de facto) found that 40 per cent prioritised financial honesty higher than honesty about fidelity. This was up from 24 per cent when the same survey had been completed six years earlier. Despite the growing significance of financial fidelity, almost 30 per cent of those surveyed admitted they had withheld information on their own spending or salary from their spouse.

The survey also reiterated the disconnect between beliefs and actions around money. It found that over 90 per cent of those surveyed agreed on the importance of discussing and understanding each other's financial history before the relationship became serious, yet over 25 per cent tended to avoid the topic completely!

Less than half of us discuss our finances openly with our prospective spouse before committing to the relationship. So it's no surprise that, of all the causes of relationship breakdown, the leading one tends to be financial issues. While it's not particularly sexy to discuss money when starting a relationship, if you want to avoid nasty financial surprises and possible financial losses, be prepared to ask the hard questions up front. At the very least, notice if your new partner shies away from conversations about finances early on in the relationship.

Find out if they are a natural shopper or saver, and if they tend to make purchases with cash or credit. Find out if your potential partner has a history of debt, bankruptcy or outstanding financial obligations. Do they save money? What are their financial goals?

A number of my clients cite relationship disagreements as one of the obstacles they face to getting ahead. This in itself need not be a barrier to financial success, provided both partners are committed to the same financial goals and are prepared to do something about it. The fact that they are speaking with me and prepared to have some honest and confronting conversations about money, including the role money plays in their relationship, suggests they are ready to do something — otherwise why put themselves through the pain?

While the statistics are compelling, money does not have to wreck your relationship. The journeys differ, but I know of many financially challenged relationships where the partners have successfully worked through their issues.

The reason money causes so many relationship fatalities is due to the emotion around it. It's similar to the emotion around being overweight; it's a super-sensitive topic that can cause offence and anger if it's not navigated carefully and thoughtfully.

Personally, I think it's better to receive a tough message from someone outside of your intimate relationship if it relates to your own behaviour, so that you don't blame your partner. I think of my personal trainer. I keep a food diary; she reviews it. If I need to improve, she tells me. I take it on board. In fact, I *pay* her tell me what to do, even if I *know* what it is I am supposed to do. I pay her to make me do it and to tell me things I don't want to hear. I pay her because this transaction makes me show up more consistently than when left to my own devices. However, if my husband said the same things, delivered in the same way, I would be likely to be offended and dismissive. In this example, I don't want to be accountable to my partner about my weight and fitness goals. This is not a dynamic I want within my relationship.

Money is the same. People are prepared to do the right thing and are happy to be accountable to something or someone, but it's usually best if that someone is an expert and independent, someone who can motivate you and keep you on point. Being corrected by your partner, no matter how constructively, is not usually an effective way of growing a relationship.

What makes a shopper?

Your attitude to money is formed by your background, experiences and psychological makeup. Your partner will have their own experiences and spending psychology. How do you engage financially? You need to first understand your own money personality and then your partner's.

This is especially true if you are a shopper. When I ask what has triggered my clients to be shoppers, the answers vary. Some grew up in a financially dysfunctional family and they are simply mimicking their parents. Others had parents who budgeted well, but they never spoke about money openly and so the skill of managing it was never passed down. Some have been over-indulged by their parents and partners, so they continue overspending. Some have had good financial role models and for a while managed to save but, over time, perhaps with excess commitments or time constraints, they replaced good habits with bad. Partners can also lead you astray. Many a good budgeter has been persuaded to loosen their purse strings by a more casual partner. Some just need a compelling reason *not* to spend.

The less obvious reasons for being a shopper can include low self-esteem, avoidance, a need for instant gratification, or even self-medicating for depression. Some people become shoppers because a component of their life is out of balance.

There is another tranche of shoppers more serious than the rest: the compulsive shopper or compulsive debtor. Although society tends to use the phrase loosely, a compulsive shopper has a serious disorder. Shopping is their addiction.

If you are a compulsive shopper, you have a chronic tendency to purchase products far in excess of your needs or resources. Spending money on a particular good or service after making a decision not to, or not wanting to but doing it anyway, are other examples of compulsive spending.

One of the characteristics of a compulsive debtor is 'terminal vagueness', or a systematic avoidance of tracking spending and a reluctance to speak with creditors. This more often than not leads to an exaggeration of account balances and an understatement of debt levels.

Co-dependent debtors incur debt to pay for another person's compulsive spending. Not wanting to see their loved one in financial ruin, they step in and clear the slate. This action, although laced with love, enables the same addictive behaviour to continue.

I have only worked with two clients who have had this degree of compulsion. Extreme measures were taken to save them from themselves. One was single, the other married. The marriage didn't last, as the pressure of living with a compulsive debtor is much the same as living with someone with any other disorder, like alcoholism: it is all-consuming, with each day lived without succumbing to their addiction a day fought bravely, but a constant battle nonetheless.

While some researchers have likened compulsive buying to an addiction, the key difference between compulsive buying and other addictions is that it is largely condoned by society. Consumption fuels our economy. Our leaders do not encourage us to go out and take drugs and drink to deal with the stress of modern life, but we are often told to go out and shop.

Instant gratification is a killer. We want what we want, we have to have it now and the media tells us we *deserve* it now. We are becoming a society of short-term hedonists, spending money we don't have on things we don't need. Many of these extra or ad hoc purchases may give us a quick fix, but this is often followed by a much longer-lasting sense of dread or guilt after the purchase has been made. Such decisions can in fact lead to reduced happiness. Research has also shown that more materialistic people are less happy and have poorer psychological health and emotional wellbeing.

> **Tip:** If a loved one is in trouble financially, encourage them to get help.

9. The property ladder

If you are serious about getting ahead in New Zealand, you need to be on the property ladder. However, owning a property and being on the property ladder are not one and same thing, and this seems to confuse people.

To be on the property ladder, you do need to own a property, but you don't have to live in it. A tenanted property still gets you on the property ladder. The key criteria for either a home or an investment property are a) you own it, and b) it is going up in value (*at a rate higher than inflation*). This means that some properties in small towns, or low socio-economic or rural areas, might not constitute a property investment in the strictest sense of the word. In fact, you would only buy in these areas if a) you needed to be based in that specific area for personal reasons, and b) you couldn't rent the same place for less.

For most of us, the first property we will buy will be our home. If it's in Auckland, it will probably be in an area that is going up in value, so by default you will have taken a step onto the property ladder, even if you are still at the bottom rung.

For you, it might be that living in your own home isn't necessarily the be-all and end-all. In fact, you are just as happy to rent somewhere nice and own a rental property. This tends to make more financial sense, although the typical Kiwi struggles with this logic.

A few years ago, you could buy your own home with a 5 per cent deposit, while to buy a rental property you needed a 20 per cent deposit. This meant it was usually easier to buy your own home first, because you didn't have to save as much to satisfy the bank and you could get on the ladder more quickly. Then the Reserve Bank changed the lending rules, in a bid to slow the property market, and then changed them again. Bank lending is usually capped at 80 per cent for all properties, with the exception of first-home buyers (to whom banks can lend more), or existing investment properties where they can lend less (normally up to 65 per cent of the property's value). A key difference between buying a home and buying an investment property comes down to the level of KiwiSaver you can access, if any.

If you have been a member of KiwiSaver for at least three years, you may be able to withdraw all or part of your savings to put towards buying your first property. The criteria for this withdrawal are that you leave the $1,000 kick-start (from when you first joined KiwiSaver) and you will live in the property for at least six months.

However, even with the lower deposit requirements for a first home and the ability to access the KiwiSaver balance, for many of my younger clients it makes more sense for them to purchase an investment property rather than a home. This gives them the flexibility of living where they want (either in New Zealand or travelling on their OE), still getting a foot on the property ladder, with their KiwiSaver funds still intact for the future. I encourage all first-time buyers to consider whether it makes sense for them to buy an investment property over a home and to compare the financial and practical outcomes of both options to get a sense of which will serve them best in the long run.

The exception to this rule is if being able to access your KiwiSaver becomes the difference between you being able to buy the property or not. If you do access your KiwiSaver, you will have to live in the property for six months, and then consider converting that property into an investment property. Yes, this will mean higher moving costs and that you may lose the property you were renting (if you were previously renting), but in most instances the ongoing gains of owning an investment property versus a home will far outweigh any of the one-off moving costs. In most cases, continuing to rent, board or live at home and buying a property to rent out (even if it is six months later) is usually the better financial option, provided you buy the right type of property. You will incur the same property costs (e.g., rates, insurance and maintenance) whether it is a home or a rental property, but the six key differences between a rental property and a home are:

- The cost of rent versus paying off a mortgage is much lower, and can often exceeding $20,000 in savings. These savings can help you pay down your property mortgage faster, while you live where you want.
- The costs of an investment property are usually tax-deductible.
- You are less likely to pay more for the property than it's worth, because you are not making an emotional purchase.
- You are less likely to over-capitalise on the investment over time, for the same reason.
- The fancier the neighbourhood you want to live in, the more likely it

will be cheaper to pay rent than to own your own home.

- There are tax implications when owning an investment property (tax-deductibility and bright-line — see Chapter 19), which should be considered.

Should you own your own home or rent?

It's often said that paying rent is the same as paying someone else's mortgage (i.e., the landlord's), and that you are better off owning the property and paying your own mortgage instead. Like most financial ideas there is some truth in this, but taken in its simplest interpretation it is downright misleading.

The nicer the suburb you live in, you can usually assume that it would be cheaper to rent the property you live in than to own it and pay the mortgage. This is because *property yields* (the rent charged proportionate to the value of the property) tend to reduce as the property's value increases. If you live in a super-expensive part of town, you will pay more rent than in a cheaper part of town, but the rent you pay as a percentage of the property value tends to reduce.

Rent as a proportion of property price is called the *rental yield* (to work out the rental yield of a property, divide the annual rent by the property value). As a rule, expensive properties have a low rental yield and cheaper properties tend to have a high rental yield. This is the difference between a *cashflow property*, for which you can charge good rent even though the property value is low (see page 107), and a *capital gain property*, which tends to be negatively geared (meaning it produces insufficient income to cover the costs related to it, whether mortgage or running costs, and requires a 'top-up' from the owner in order to cover the outgoings). For the same reason, buying a super-expensive property as an investment doesn't always make financial sense; being the person renting this property does.

I am not saying that you shouldn't own a property. Quite the opposite. For the most part, owning a property (provided it is a good one) makes financial sense. The latest round of government valuations is testament to this, as very few of us could have saved the capital gain that our properties have earned.

Recognising this, why shouldn't you own your own home? The answer is not that you *shouldn't* own your own home, but that you need to recognise that there are *cheaper ways for you to live in a property than being the owner of the property*. If done correctly, you can be financially better off.

Let me elaborate. The higher a property's value, the lower the rental yield tends to be. What a property can rent for and what it can sell for are two very different things. For example, you can rent a three-bedroom house in Ellerslie, Auckland, for $800 per week. This property is valued at $950,000. A three-bedroom property in Mission Bay is worth $1.6 million and rents for $950 per week. So, yes, the rent is higher on the Mission Bay property, but only by $150 per week, or 19 per cent, yet the property value is 68 per cent higher. In this example, the rent has not kept pace with the increase in property value.

Property	Capital value ($)	Weekly rent ($)	Rental yield
Ellerslie	950,000	800	4.4%
Mission Bay	1,600,000	950	3.1%

The Mission Bay landlord is prepared to pay an extra $39,000 per annum in interest costs (using a 6 per cent interest rate) to own the more expensive property, and for this extra cost they are going to receive $7800 more rent. The increase in rent doesn't come close to covering the higher interest costs (and other costs) the Mission Bay landlord will face in acquiring a property and mortgage that is $650,000 more expensive than their Ellerslie counterpart.

As a side note, there can still be legitimate reasons why someone might buy an investment property in Mission Bay or a similar suburb, where the rents don't keep pace with the property values but where the owner's cash position is so strong they can justify the top-ups. Also, the above example does not take into account the capital gains made when the properties are sold. As a rough rule, the higher the value of the property at the start, the higher the gain to be made.

In this example, the cashflow financial gain sits squarely with the tenant. Because properties have increased in value in recent years, not only do home buyers need a larger deposit, but they also need to borrow more money from the bank, which also means more interest being paid back to the lender. As the tenant living in the Mission Bay property, you are paying $150 per week more than the tenant in Ellerslie, *but your landlord is having to pay $750 per week more to the bank in interest alone.* The saying that your rent is paying off the landlord's mortgage doesn't come *close* to being true in this example. Your rent payment is simply a gesture to the higher interest your landlord is paying to the bank; the landlord is not even chipping away at the mortgage with the rent you are paying.

The underlying assumption with the rent-versus-buy argument is that you could rent for less than your mortgage outgoings. While this is usually the case, there are examples where it might not be. Certainly if you could own your home, and your mortgage payments and property costs combined (rates, insurance, repairs, etc.) were less than the rent you would have to pay as a tenant of the same property, then it might make financial sense to own a property, live in it and pay the mortgage.

This type of property is called a *cashflow property* — where the potential rental income outweighs the mortgage and holding costs of the property. Some city apartments or properties in lower socio-economic areas might be an example of this type of investment. Cashflow properties don't tend to experience high capital gains.

For the most part it is the capital gains that create the wealth for property investors, so without a likely capital gain you might need to question whether purchasing this type of property is a sensible idea in the first place (again, there can be exceptions to this).

The benefits of being a tenant rather than a home owner extend beyond the rent paid. A tenant doesn't need to waste their weekend and wallet on repairs and maintenance; a phone call to the landlord will take care of it. There are no council rates or insurance costs to pay, or the threat of higher interest rates to immediately affect you. These extra property costs alone can easily amount to $10,000 per annum, sometimes more. Sure, these costs are tax-deductible for the landlord, but that simply means that they will get *a portion* of the cost back in tax relief — about 33 per cent (the assumed marginal tax rate). In this example, the net cost to the landlord for the property costs would be $6,700 per annum ($10,000 less tax deductions). The tax benefits make the cost lower, *but there is still a real cost that needs to be paid from available cash funds.*

As an investment-property owner it's imperative that you factor in all of the costs related to property ownership. This includes the more obvious fixed costs, such as rates, insurance, regular maintenance and accounting, but also the less regular maintenance costs like new roofs and painting.

As I noted initially, I am not against owning a property, but I am against paying through the nose for a property that you could rent for less. I have many clients who can't afford to buy in the area they want to live in for their kids' schooling. My suggestion to them is to rent in that area, taking advantage of the lower rent yields or the fact that rent hasn't increased nearly as fast as property values.

This recommendation in isolation might improve their cashflow in the sense that their annual rent cost is likely to be lower than their annual interest cost to own a property in the same area, but improved cashflow doesn't necessarily translate to financial progress. For these clients I also encourage them to own an investment property in a different area, with lower-value properties (and a corresponding lower purchase price and interest cost). Maybe they could even consider buying two. If they buy well, the rental income will go a long way to covering the mortgage.

Yes, there will be additional costs on top of that and it is still probable the property will require a cash top-up by the landlord. But the top-up, even when added to the rent they are paying elsewhere, would still be lower overall than the cost of buying a property in the more expensive area and not having any further investment portfolio.

Renting your home might not satisfy your hankering for DIY home improvements, but it can make good financial sense. You can still own a property, but make sure it is in a good investment area, where the yields are favourable, to allow you to improve your cashflow, neutralise the impact of skyrocketing property prices and still provide you with capital-gain prospects, but at a lower cost.

Sometimes moving out of your home to rent feels like a huge sacrifice. Because it is. But if this sacrifice can unlock significantly more gain, then you need to consider it. Moving out of your home, or even selling it, might be in your best interests, provided you can still live in a property you love, and the equity/capital released from the sale of the old family home can be reused as deposits for two, three or sometimes four investment properties. This allows you to get capital gain on two, three or four properties, rather than one (the family home). Eventually some or all of the properties could be sold to get you back into your preferred home (that you would own and live in), hopefully without a mortgage because you have realised enough value to buy your dream home with cash.

How to buy a property

Buying a property, whether it is to be your home or an investment property, is stressful, and not all properties are created equal. It is too easy to end up with a lemon, so make sure you understand the basic buying process. If you are buying an investment property, understand your property criteria. When I work with clients I spend a lot of time setting their criteria for them (see Chapter 19), and shortlisting properties that fit these criteria.

This is because they aren't buying any old property. Instead, I am trying to balance the probability of a capital gain within the agreed timeframe, and maximising the amount of the gain while minimising the hold cost.

The following 18 steps focus on buying your first home. Some of the steps are different if you buy an investment property, which will be noted below each step wherever relevant.

1.

Before you even start looking for a house, you need to think about how much you would like to spend on a property and how much you can borrow. To find out how much the bank will lend you will need to make a formal application to the bank asking for finance. The bank will assess your personal circumstances and make you an offer of finance. The offer they provide is often called a pre-approval or a conditional commitment to advance you funds to buy a specific type of property. Your job is to satisfy all the conditions so you can be comfortable the bank will provide you with the necessary funds to acquire your property.

As a minimum, the bank will want to be comfortable that your income is what you say it is, your deposit exists and that you have good bank-account conduct. They will check your credit rating and review your bank statements, checking for undisclosed debts and the number of unarranged overdrafts. Typically they will request:

- three to six months' worth of bank statements (cheque and savings)
- payslips
- credit-card statements
- evidence of your deposit.

> **Tip:** Use a mortgage broker to manage this process. They have access to all banks and the different mortgage products and loan terms available.

Many people have lousy bank-account conduct. Without realising it, they are in and out of overdraft, incurring unarranged overdraft fees and various bank penalties. One client I worked with incurred $3,000 in unarranged overdraft fees or penalties over the course of a year. She earned good money, but these fees highlighted her lack of care and time when it came to managing her personal finances. Despite satisfying all other bank criteria, her account conduct was so poor that she had to show three months of 'good behaviour' before the bank would provide her with a pre-approval to buy. For all my clients, I spend a month tidying up their bank-account conduct, and then I get them to stick to a fairly strict spending plan for 12 weeks, with the objective of maximising their cash surplus and savings rate, which in turn allows us to secure the most potential lending.

2.

There is usually an assumption from the bank that the property will be a stand-alone property made of appropriate construction materials (not plaster) and be worth what you are prepared to pay for it. The pre-approval will always be subject to a specific property and the way you have acquired the property (e.g., auction or tender), whether it says this specifically on the pre-approval or not. This catches many people out, who innocently look at properties thinking that, because the bank has given them a pre-approval, they are in the market to buy any type of property up to the level agreed on the pre-approval.

However, the pre-approval is generic in nature and applies to standard dwellings bought at arm's length. This means that if the property is non-standard in the bank's opinion (e.g., leasehold, plaster, apartment, rural, still getting built or commercial) the pre-approval may not be valid. To avoid disappointment (and stress), always make sure you advise the bank of the specific types of property you are looking at so they can confirm it meets their standard criteria, to give you confidence that you have the bank's backing.

A generic pre-approval will also assume that the property you purchase is built, that you will pay a fair price for the property and that the price paid indicates its value — that is, that you haven't paid too much for it. If you are not buying through the normal selling process then the bank will likely require a registered valuation to determine the property's true value, and the pre-approval will apply against the lower of the purchase price or the registered valuation. For example, you see a house you like that is being sold at auction. You are prepared to pay $700,000 for it, but the registered valuation for the property is $650,000. You have a 20 per cent deposit ($140,000) and a general pre-approval from the bank for $560,000, so you think you are fine. In this instance, however, the bank will loan you 80 per cent of the $650,000, being the lower of the purchase price and registered valuation, which is $520,000. You then have a $40,000 shortfall that you need to come up with before settlement. If you are buying at auction, this is your problem to solve. If you are buying outside of auction you may be able to re-negotiate the price, if you haven't yet gone unconditional on the contract.

Banks will also usually require a registered valuation for all properties purchased via tender, auction or private sale. If the valuation is lower than what you are prepared to pay, be mindful that the bank will not lend above the valuation, so you could be out of pocket or not be in a position to buy the property at all.

The pre-approval amount indicates what the bank believes you are capable of repaying based on their limited understanding of your finances. In too many instances the level of borrowing the bank is prepared to advance and what you can actually afford to repay are two very different beasts. While this is happening less and less, I have seen clients be offered a loan seven times their combined household income. (For example, their household income was $100,000, but the bank offered them a $700,000 loan.) Because the bank was prepared to give it to them, they were prepared to take it, naïvely thinking that if the bank thought they would be able to repay it then they could.

If you need to save for longer before buying, be OK with this. For every $1000 you save, the bank will lend you an additional $4000 (based on them back lending you 80 per cent of the property's value).

If you are buying a property off plan (whether as a home or investment property), the bank will need to understand if you are buying a 'turn-key' property, or a 'land-and-build'. For a turn-key property, a standard approval will apply, provided you settle the property within the timeframe of the pre-approval. For a land-and-build contract, the bank will usually reduce the pre-approval by 10 per cent to allow for the interest costs you will cover during the build phase. Speak to your mortgage broker about this if it is relevant to you.

3.

Calculate what you can afford to repay based on a higher interest rate than what is being offered. When I am calculating my clients' tolerance to debt levels, I currently apply a mortgage rate of 7–8 per cent, or a rate 2 per cent above their current fixed rate, depending on how long I believe it will take them to repay their proposed mortgage. When determining what you can pay for a home, also be sure to factor in the legal fees, insurances and due-diligence costs. The bank will often pay you a cash incentive when you draw down your mortgage, which can reimburse you for your legal fees and other costs — although this happens at the end of the process so you may have to fund these costs at the start.

4.

Find out if you qualify for any kick-start initiatives from the government or lenders. Visit kaingaora.govt.nz/en_NZ/home-ownership/first-home-grant/. For example, at the time of writing, if you are buying your first home, your combined income is less than $150,000 (for one borrower you can have earned $95,000 or less before tax in the last 12 months) and your first home costs less than $875,000 in Auckland, or less than a figure ranging from $650,000 to $925,000 depending on the location in New Zealand, you may qualify for a $10,000 grant, access to KiwiBuild properties or lower deposit requirements.

5.

Make a list of what you want in your property. Specifically identify your non-negotiables. Is it proximity to work and amenities, the number of bedrooms, an internal garage, or the amount of work that needs to be done on it? Understand your deal-breakers and don't bother visiting properties that don't fit your list. Other things to consider are:

- school zoning
- ease of access
- proximity to public transport
- ongoing maintenance requirements
- whether the property is stand-alone or attached to another one
- level of privacy
- child- and/or pet-friendliness — is the section fenced?
- is the legal title cross-lease or fee simple?

If you are purchasing an investment property, you also need to understand your property criteria. These could include the points above, as well as rental yield, historical capital growth rate, and floor size versus section size.

6.

If you are buying your first home, get a lawyer *before* you make an offer to buy. A good lawyer will help you with the process and provide you with specific clauses to protect you through the sale process. As a bare minimum they should review the sale and purchase agreement before you sign it.

If you are buying an investment property, we usually follow a slightly different process because good property stock that fits your criteria is hard to find, and moves quickly. In response to this my clients often sign a conditional contract to take the property off the market while they work through the due-diligence process. They should only sign this contract if a comprehensive due-diligence clause is inserted into the agreement that allows them the right to cancel the agreement for whatever reason they want. This gives them the wriggle room of then getting the lawyer to review the document and request changes to the contract as needed.

7.

Do your due diligence. This can be quite an arduous and expensive process, as the checks and reports you should do for each property you are seriously considering can quickly add up in value. I personally don't bother incurring any costs until I have signed a conditional contract (with a strong due-diligence exit clause), because I don't want to incur costs unless I know the property will be mine should I want it. This is tricky if the property is being sold at an auction. I had a client who went to 10 auctions before they were able to successfully buy a property. Each property they were serious about buying required a builder's report and a review from their solicitor. Because the houses were being auctioned, my client also had to get a registered valuation for each property to determine its value for the bank and therefore confirm how much the bank would be prepared to lend. Each property cost in excess of $1000 in reports alone. But due diligence is just that: the diligent thing to do.

As part of any due diligence you need to make sure you are aware of any issues relating to the title, the building and the property generally. You need to know that any improvements you want to make are allowed to be done, to what extent the building is in need of repair, what land issues you are inheriting and what is a fair value for the property. Risks can be minimised by doing your homework, or engaging professional assistance.

As a minimum you will need a title search (done by you or your solicitor), a Land Information Memorandum or LIM (by you or your solicitor), a building inspection (by a qualified builder) and a registered valuation (by a registered valuer). Too often the simplest of tools to protect you as a buyer are ignored by the impatient, and often ignorant, purchaser. I have seen smart people buy lemons because they were so sick of looking for properties or missing out at auctions that, when they finally found something that they thought would work, they wanted to secure the deal and put in an unconditional offer without doing their due diligence. Making an unconditional offer can be a good strategy, provided you have worked through the conditions beforehand. Making an unconditional offer before doing any due diligence is stupid.

Doing a title search is the most basic of requirements. Make sure the title of your property is not subject to claims (such as Treaty of Waitangi claims) or unusual cross-lease clauses. Your solicitor will be able to able to interpret what the title search says, as well as obtain and interpret the cross-lease agreement, including covenants and rights of way (easements) as needed. Covenants may prevent you from doing some subdivisions or building extensions. Find out what you can and can't do on the property and what issues you may be exposed to. You can do a basic title search at www.terranet.co.nz — but your solicitor should be doing this for you anyway.

8.

Getting a building inspection is a must. Unless you are a qualified builder, it always pays to know about the condition of the house you are buying, as the largest bills relating to your house will be the ongoing maintenance and improvements over time. As a prudent home owner you need to know what you are likely to encounter and when, and how much it is going to cost you, so you are armed with the knowledge and, most importantly, so you can reflect these issues in the price you offer and in the sale and purchase agreement.

A builder's report or survey is an inspection by a qualified builder which attempts to identify property defects, overdue maintenance, inferior building work, gradual deterioration and other issues. It is distinct from a water-tightness report, although basic leaky issues should be addressed.

A building report doesn't guarantee to find everything that could be wrong with the property, because the builder is limited to a visual inspection and will not normally remove wall linings or floorboards. However, they should make an assessment of the building structure, exterior walls, heating, insulation, doors, windows and ceilings. The inspector should highlight work for which a building permit may still be outstanding, although they won't tend to look at the property records held at council (see point 9 about getting a LIM).

It is important that your inspector is independent of anyone involved in the sale of the house. Get recommendations from friends about who to use.

Some clients prefer to use friends or family members who are builders to do the inspection for them. This can be a cheap way to get a quick understanding of what you are facing with the property and whether it should be ruled out or is worth pursuing further. If you do decide to go ahead and the rest of your due diligence is satisfactory, I would still encourage you to get an arm's-length building review from a qualified and independent building inspector. This is someone who can give you some immediate assurance in a written report that you could later rely on in case something goes wrong.

A building inspection can cost between $300 and $1300, depending on the size, location, age, cladding, access and features of the building. They can take between three and four working days to complete, so always allow a minimum of seven working days as part of your due-diligence process to give your inspector sufficient time to do their job well.

If the builder identifies some issues, this needn't stop you from buying the property, but it does arm you with the facts to make a more realistic revised offer or to push some of the issues back to the vendor to fix before you buy the property. Whether you then re-enter negotiations with the seller to reduce the agreed price or whether the seller agrees to remedy the problems themselves, these negotiations will need to be formalised and included in the sale and purchase agreement.

9.

Review the Land Information Memorandum (LIM) for the property. A LIM is an up-to-date document held by the council on your property. It includes the property's history, where it is and the council's involvement with the property over time.

Much like a builder's inspection, a LIM is very helpful in deciding whether the property is worth purchasing. It details whether building permits have been issued, the property's zoning, any restrictions the property has against it, any history of flooding or subsidence and any resource consents issued for proposed developments in the immediate neighbourhood. The LIM will document if the building or site is historic or has any protected trees, and details land features, such as the potential for erosion or the possible presence of hazardous substances. (Note: Installation of septic tanks and gas bottles may be excluded from the LIM as the council is not obliged to keep this information.)

Once you have the LIM, it pays to go through it with your lawyer. Consider how the findings will impact your enjoyment and intended use of the property.

A LIM can take 10 days for the council to create, so if the LIM is not provided to you by the real estate agent, ensure you allow 15 working days' due diligence from the date of signing the sale and purchase agreement to allow sufficient time to source the LIM and review it with your solicitor. A LIM can cost between $150 and $400, depending on the council and how quickly you need it.

> **Tip:** Councils are not legally obliged to hold information relating to the building prior to 1992, when the Building Regulation Act (sometimes referred to as the Building Code) was introduced. For older properties, some council records may be incomplete. Not surprisingly, councils do not accept responsibility for the accuracy or completeness of these records.

10.

Look at the council-held property file. Within these files you will find details on any works undertaken on the property, including building consents and what structures have been permitted. The file will note the drainage plan and the location of stormwater and sewer drains. Always look at the flood plain. Be concerned if it has flooded the area in the past 50 years. Compare what it says in the report with what you see in reality. If the physical structure doesn't match the theoretical council records, then you could be inheriting an unpermitted structure at best, or an illegal structure at worst. The most common unpermitted structures include carports, ensuites, garages converted to sleep-outs and outdoor areas that have been concreted when they shouldn't have been.

The reason you need to care about this is because your insurance company may not pay out on an insurance claim if the structure was unpermitted. Worse, you could be required by the council to fix it within a specified timeframe or incur a fine or prosecution. If you come across a property that has unconsented works, or consent is not completed, then do your numbers based on what it would cost to put it back to its legal state. If the numbers still work, and the purchase price is low enough to incorporate any additional costs you may incur, then the deal could still work — but sometimes it is easier to walk away. Depending on whether the works were carried out before or after 1992 will determine what needs to be done to remedy the issue with the council.

11.

Find out what the property is worth. Any valuation will always be subjective. Banks would argue that the best way to determine value is via a registered valuation. I'm not sure I agree, but a registered valuation will be accepted by the bank for the purpose of advancing your mortgage. If you didn't need a registered valuation for the bank, you could get an indicative idea by looking at homes.co.nz, oneroof.co.nz, or by visiting qv.co.nz and talking to your real estate agent about what properties are selling for versus the QV valuations in that area. If you engage a registered valuer, the bank will likely nominate who you can use from their list of accredited valuers. A property valuation report costs between $600 and $1,500.

12.

Complete a sale and purchase agreement with your solicitor. In this agreement you build in a negotiation element, in terms of the conditions you include. If you have not already received a builder's report, reviewed the LIM, satisfied the bank's finance conditions and had your solicitor review the deal, you need to put in a conditional offer. Ideally you would give yourself between 10 and 15 working days to work through your conditions.

This offer is then presented to the vendor and they will either accept it or come back to you with changes. This is the counter-signing process. While the vendor may be OK with the conditions, if the price is too low they are likely to cross out your offer and counter-sign with a higher amount. You then have the opportunity to repeat the process, counter-signing their adjusted purchase price or suggesting a lower one of your own. This process can continue until both parties are happy with the set purchase price. At this point the contract is signed by both parties.

Then the conditional period begins. You have this time to determine if you are happy with the property. During this time the builder's report is completed, the bank finance is confirmed, the LIM is reviewed and other development considerations (like putting in a granny flat or deck) are checked with the council, to make sure that you are in fact able to do what you want to do. Your solicitor will work through each of these conditions with you. If an issue becomes apparent during this process — for example, the building hasn't had its code of compliance issued for a recent renovation, or there are maintenance issues — this becomes a bargaining tool to get the price down further, or to put the onus on the vendor to fix the problem.

Remember, if you are buying at auction, all offers have to be unconditional, so you must have all your ducks in a row before bidding.

If you are buying a new-build investment property, the conditions on the contract may be a little different. For example, you are unable to inspect the property because it hasn't been built and the LIM might not yet show the title as the subdivision tends to happen towards the end of the development. To protect you during this process, make sure you work with a solicitor who is experienced in new-build contracts so you feel safe in the process.

13.

Once you are happy that all of the conditions are satisfied, your solicitor will communicate with the vendor's solicitor, confirming that the sale is now unconditional. You are now legally obliged to settle on the property when it is ready. This might be within the month, if an existing property, or in 12 months' time if it is under construction. When you go unconditional on a property you need to pay the deposit, which is usually 10 per cent of the purchase price. Make sure this money sits in a solicitor's trust account until settlement.

14.

Take out house insurance for your new property at this point. If something goes wrong with the property between now and settlement, you could still be obliged to settle.

15.

Inspect the property before settling to make sure that all the chattels that you agreed on in the sale and purchase agreement remain. Common chattels include the dishwasher, curtains, rangehood and alarm. Additional chattels you may request to be included could include rugs, pot plants, fridge (especially if plumbed in), washing machine, table and chairs. If you are unable to negotiate the price, you may want to sweeten the deal for yourself by adding extra chattels without increasing the price — the attraction to the vendor being that the chattels are one less thing to move.

If you have purchased a property off the plans, I would encourage you to engage a qualified builder to inspect the property on your behalf. They will review the plans to make sure the finished product is in line with what you signed up for in your contract.

16.

Confirm the structure of your borrowings and the entity in which you will be purchasing the property with your bank. This is discussed in more detail in Chapter 16. I would initially elect a monthly repayment plan, which means the first mortgage payment will come out one month after you have settled and moved into the property. These extra weeks can be a lifeline if you have already stretched yourself financially.

17.

Settle and move in. Settlement is the official process conducted by lawyers to transfer the ownership of the property between two parties.

18.

Kill your mortgage!

What if you don't have a deposit?

If you want to buy a property, you need a deposit. This is a barrier to entry for many first-home buyers, because they never seem to be able to save enough fast enough.

Banks typically require a 20 per cent deposit before they look at advancing 80 per cent of the purchase price, although you should speak to your mortgage broker to understand the different deposit requirements for each bank. (Refer to kaingaora.govt.nz/ for how to qualify for grants and lower deposits.) For many, saving this deposit is too hard and is taking too long, with property prices racing away and savings not keeping up. If you are buying a property off the plans (not yet built), you can qualify for the property with a deposit as low as 5 per cent, and in some cases no deposit at all. You will still need to be able to save the deposit the bank needs to see before settlement, but if the settlement is more than 12 months away this might be more viable than you realise. Yes, there is fine print, but that can be worked through. All you need to know is you have options.

Remember, the world doesn't owe you any favours, and the universe is not necessarily going to make this easy for you. If you are serious about getting on the property ladder, you need to be prepared to suck it up and start moving forward. Wealth comes to those who not only want it but also do something productive about it. When I work with my clients we try to save enough for a deposit within the first 12 months — but we go hard. We don't muck about. We get creative about how we could get onto the property ladder. We chat about joining forces with friends to buy a property, syndication, cross-securing with parents' properties, and buying properties with a really long settlement horizon. We then get creative about how we could save more, faster.

If you want to fast-track your deposit saving, look to adopt some of the 10 tips below:

1. Move in with friends or family to drop your lodging outgoings. If you are paying rent of $400 a week, but you could move in with friends for six months and pay $100 a week, then do so. Make sure you bank the difference. Alternatively, get some flatmates in to reduce your outgoings.

2. Cut back on every cost within your budget. Look to save an additional 20 per cent of your income. Take a raincheck on holidays, expensive hobbies and technology purchases.

3. Tell friends and family that this is your objective and how much you need to save. Find out how long it's going to take you to get there. If you don't think you'll be able to achieve the goal within 12 months, enlist someone to help you. When working with my clients I make it clear that we only want them to go without if it means they can achieve their goals. Too often people think that if they go without they will naturally achieve their goals, but deprivation and financial success have less of a correlation than people realise. If you want to achieve your financial goals you need a plan that is achievable, with measurable progress.

4. Consider house-sitting as a drastic way of reducing your costs. I had one client who did this for 18 months.

5. Sell some of your assets. Then sell some more assets.

6. Work longer and work harder. Look for a second job. When my husband and I were saving for our first home, we were working four jobs between us.

7. Determine how much you will get from KiwiSaver. Investigate your eligibility for the First Home Grant and other benefits available to you.

8. Lower your expectations as to what your first home needs to look like, and where it needs to be.

9. Consider buying your first property with a friend or family member to lower your deposit requirements. This comes with risks, but I have seen it done successfully, many times.

10. Borrow from your parents' equity to satisfy the bank requirements. This can create real financial benefits for all parties, but can also be a nightmare to administer if not done correctly. Chapter 29 discusses this in more detail.

If you are serious about getting onto the property ladder, then your first property may need to be an investment property. You should be able to leverage the capital growth from this property to get you into an area you prefer. First step: get on the property ladder. Second step: start to climb the ladder.

As I said earlier, determine if you can have a deposit saved within 12 months. If not, enlist help. Before I work with my clients, I ask them if they are in fact ready to do what is necessary to get them into a property. If they are ready to take control, then I can help them. If they are not, then I explain to them that engaging my services is a waste of money and time.

If you are ready, then you are prepared to delay your life for 12 months and do what is required to achieve your goals. Only you can determine your level of readiness.

PART TWO

Killing your mortgage

10. Making a start

**Continuous effort — not strength or intelligence — is
the key to unlocking our potential. –Winston Churchill**

No matter what your starting point — whether you are sinking, floating or flying — you need to have a plan and to begin sorting out your finances. You need to get in control and get your money working harder, which will allow you to start planning for a comfortable retirement now.

To do this, you must be honest with yourself, about yourself. You must understand what you own and what you owe. You need to know exactly how much you earn and what you spend your money on, your tendencies and what motivates you.

Sorting out your finances takes time. If you are time-poor, get someone else to do it for you, but make sure you are accountable for the results. There are no short cuts.

In order to plan any journey, including managing your money, you must understand the exact distance that needs to be covered, what terrain you are likely to encounter and what the best vehicle will be to get you to your destination.

Four big questions

When starting out on your financial journey, ask yourself the following four questions.

1. Where am I financially?
2. What potential do I have?
3. Where do I want to be?
4. What is standing in my way?

Money troubles and denial typically go hand in hand. Refusing to recognise or acknowledge the true situation often causes people to create serious financial issues for themselves. For example, when your bank statement comes in do you open it or do you throw it in a pile to look at later? Do you even know how much money is in your bank account? Do you know how much you saved last year? When was the last time you deposited money into your bank account, not including your pay? Do you even know how much you are paid? If you can't answer these questions you are either hands-off with your finances or in denial about your financial situation.

If you are going to start making progress towards your financial goals, you need to be honest. Leaving everything to your partner is not delegation; it is shirking your own responsibility. Successful delegation means you still have a handle on things, you know what is happening and why, and you could step in at any point.

While managing the finances is often left to one partner, if you're not both on the same page your progress will be unremarkable, if there is any progress at all. Furthermore, the person who is 'carrying the can' often feels stressed or frustrated at their partner's lack of buy-in, leading to conflict or dissatisfaction in the relationship.

Articulating your personal relationship with money and the role of money in your relationship can be stressful for some people, and I must admit that some clients have even been reduced to tears the first time they meet with me.

Working together

The first time I meet with a client, we set about diagnosing where they are at financially. Part of this process is to ascertain if they are naturally on track to achieve their financial goals. If they are on track, we then spend time establishing whether they can reach their goals faster by getting their money working harder as well as doing certain things differently. If they aren't on track, however, I want to find out what might be standing in their way, and what they could be doing to get a different outcome. For most people this first meeting is a pretty full-on but ultimately rewarding experience.

It is compulsory for both partners in a relationship to be at this first meeting, as I think it is important for people to go through this process with their partner — I won't work with them otherwise. This is because, in my experience, someone who's not willing to attend this first meeting is usually a key player in the couple's current financial position. Trying to fix the financial landscape without their engagement is like trying to drive a car with a flat tyre — no matter how much energy is put into steering the vehicle, you will continue to be pulled in the wrong direction.

Strangely, at least 10 per cent of new clients are desperate to attend this first meeting by themselves. I have heard all the reasons you could possibly imagine and then some, including 'I'm the problem, not my spouse', 'My partner has no idea of where things are at — they don't manage the money' and 'My partner doesn't listen to me anyway'. *If you are in a relationship, both you and your partner have contributed to your financial situation.* Therefore you both need to develop new life skills to correct this situation.

If your partner has no idea where things are at, it's time they stood up and started paying attention. Everyone has a moral and social responsibility to know how they are doing financially. Burying your head in the sand is not good enough.

Having both partners at the first meeting gives them each a new understanding of the other and what makes them tick financially. People often incorrectly assume that the spender in the relationship is responsible for their financial demise or lack of progress, but this is only one determining factor. Often the person who is tight on a day-to-day basis decides that when they do want to buy something they will spend 'whatever is needed' to get what they want. Usually it is the spending on big items that creates a problem — not the occasional little treats.

I once had a man visit for a first meeting without his wife because they had a sick child. This was the first time he had truly confronted the state of his finances and he was embarrassed. He earned more than $400,000 per annum and was in a very high-profile job. I emailed a summary of the meeting to the household's joint email address and he called back within five minutes. He asked me to omit certain details of their financial situation from my original email because he didn't want his wife to know the cold, hard truth of their situation.

My reply was: 'You have successfully managed to get your household finances into a mess without your wife being any the wiser. You've had your turn and it didn't work. If you want to fix this situation, you need to do what I say, and that means everything has to be out on the table, because we all need to be on our game to fix your situation.'

In all honesty, I was just as frustrated with his wife, who had happily buried her head in the sand and taken a hands-off approach to their finances, but that was beside the point. Both spouses need to be on the same page, otherwise they are going to have issues.

I did not resend an amended version of my original email. I did, however, send a follow-up email that said no matter how dire their situation seemed it could be fixed, provided they were prepared to do whatever was necessary. If they were, they could be sure of a positive outcome. (You'll be pleased to know that they both came to the next meeting and together we worked through their issues and put a plan together on how we were going to fix things.)

Although I can understand why people might hesitate to share all the information with their spouse, especially when it makes them look bad, it is a pretty short-sighted approach. Everything comes out in the wash in the end, with sunlight often being the best disinfectant.

Omitting financial details is not uncommon for many couples. Somewhere between 5 and 10 per cent of my clients find out information about their joint finances at their first meeting with me that they didn't previously know — possibly because they didn't care to ask. This is consistent with data from the US that has showed that 9 per cent of spouses are prepared to keep silent about aspects of their financial situation because knowing about the issue would worry their partner. (You don't say!) Using a circular logic, 7 per cent of respondents said they'd kept something secret because telling their partner would damage their relationship. One has to ask: if in knowing the truth the relationship might be damaged, doesn't that imply it already is?

Working out your financial position

Whether you know all the details of your current financial position or not is irrelevant before starting this exercise. The objective is to know your position *after* you have completed the exercise. Fill in the worksheets in Appendix III to get a snapshot of your current financial position.

Here is the series of questions I ask new clients to get a snapshot of their financial position.

1. What assets do you own? What assets could you sell if you needed to?
2. What do you owe? What are your liabilities, including your student loan?
3. Do you have any credit-card debt, loans or buy-now-pay-later commitments?
4. Do you pay off your credit card in full every month?
5. Are you contributing to KiwiSaver? If so, at what rate?
6. Do you have savings? If so, how much? How much did you save in the last 12 months? If you didn't save anything, why not?

7. What does your situation feel like? Do you feel in control of your money? Do you feel that you are getting ahead?
8. If you lost your job tomorrow, how long could you survive on your rainy-day fund?
9. Do you have children? If so, how many and how old are they? If not, do you want children?
10. Do you owe tax?
11. Do you own investment properties? If so, are the properties negatively geared or does the rent received cover the mortgage and rates?
12. Is your employment secure? Have you reached your income potential? Are you likely to receive any pay rises or bonuses? How much do you get paid in the hand (going into your bank account) every week, fortnight or month?
13. Are you self-employed? Do you draw a regular wage? Can you put costs through the business? Do your financial statements show income paid to you? Are you paid cash or with contras? Who manages the money? Do you have to juggle things each week?
14. Do you own your own property in a trust? If not, why not?
15. Who manages the money in your relationship (if you are in a relationship)? Why?
16. Are you both engaged with your finances?
17. How many bank accounts do you have and how does money flow between them?
18. Do you find it easier to spend or save?
19. What are your non-negotiable costs? For example, do you have to go on a family holiday each year? Do you want your kids to have swimming lessons? Do you need to buy a flat white every day?
20. Do you think you fritter away your money?
21. What are your financial goals?
22. If you looked 10 years into the future, what do you want to see for yourself?

The answers to these questions help to paint a picture of your current financial situation and what obstacles or attitudes are holding you back. Basically, I need new clients to tell me their stories so I can incorporate everything I notice into a workable financial plan for them.

Once we've established where my clients are at, they need to understand how they got to that point. Is it because they have frittered away money, paid more tax than necessary, overused their credit card(s), made poor financial decisions in the past, structured their mortgage incorrectly, or simply that they need a good plan to stick to? If they've lacked motivation in the past, what will motivate them now? (See Chapter 2 for more on money personalities, common obstacles and money traps.)

Don't judge your spouse's non-negotiables or suggest where you think they fritter money. It will end in tears.

Understanding the nuances of each unique situation is critical when designing the right strategy and developing a realistic plan to help individuals and partners to achieve the perfect balance of financial progress and enjoyment. All these questions need to be answered honestly before I even begin to look at the numbers. Before I consider people's actual spending I need to know how it feels for them on a day-to-day basis.

11.   Putting the plan into action

I spend the first four weeks of my relationship with any new client designing, testing the numbers, setting up better systems and refining their 12-month financial plan. The plan has to be fluid enough to absorb the effects of life's curve balls and unexpected expenses, but also make it possible to get ahead when windfalls happen. Most of all, the plan has to be achievable if it is going to build momentum.

Most people don't know what they're capable of. Looking at bank statements does not define what you *could* do — it simply tells you what you *have done*. I am reluctant to dictate your potential from your bank statements — which is reassuring for many of my clients, who are embarrassed by the state of their spending. I start with the assumption that we are all capable of better outcomes, and then I work backwards to determine how the inputs of the situation need to change, so the outputs can be different. I further assume that the client sitting in front of me has a willingness to sacrifice if required, but only for a time and only if the trade-off gets them what they want.

In developing a plan with my clients, we start with a best guess of what they think they can achieve. I look at what they are currently achieving, benchmarking their spending against other clients who earn similar levels of income, and overlaying their non-negotiable costs to get a better idea of what's possible. We need to get all their ducks lined up so that positive results are evident as soon as the plan is put in place. Basically, in the first four weeks of working together, my clients and I tidy up or restructure everything that has previously been an obstacle so that the odds of success are well and truly tipped in their favour.

In addressing obstacles, the best approach is to work out a budget or spending plan to capture the money that has previously been frittered away, restructure bank accounts so that money cannot be inadvertently spent so easily, cancel credit cards, and restructure mortgages or business affairs to minimise interest and tax payments going forward. Every decision from this point on is going to have an impact that can be seen and felt.

After the first four weeks, often after I have restructured a client's mortgage and bank accounts, they are in a position to start testing their budget. They then have to draw a line in the sand and stick to it.

After the first four weeks of preparation, every client is chomping at the bit to get started, but they are also often a little scared of what lies ahead. But we're now at the business end of the equation, where results need to be achieved. We need to establish if the plan is doable.

Within every plan it is important you have enough money to do the things that are important to you, otherwise the plan won't work. Once my client is comfortable that the budget is achievable, I explain how things need to work on a day-to-day basis. This is quite detailed, including how much money the client has to spend on a weekly basis to cover weekly costs, such as groceries, takeaways, coffees and petrol. This money is put into a separate account using a weekly automatic payment. They can manage this money as they see fit. I encourage people to use cash, but it is up to my clients to take responsibility to ensure that this money covers their weekly costs. If the money runs out, it runs out, and they need to wait until the next week before it is topped up again. Bills such as electricity, phone and internet, rates, online subscriptions, and cable or streaming TV are paid from a separate account to avoid confusing fixed costs with more discretionary weekly expenses.

For the next 12 weeks we track actual spending on the budget, to establish whether the plan is, in fact, sustainable. Twelve weeks is short enough for anyone to commit to, but also a sufficient length of time in which to see a result. Each week they measure their savings and spending progress and complete a 15-minute exercise. The goal is for the client to reach the end of the 12-week period having an awareness of every dollar they've spent, but not to the point where they feel deprived. If they can achieve this, the budget is working and we can all have confidence that it should continue to work. This confidence leads to belief. Belief leads to motivation and a shift in mindset.

It is important that progress is tracked to the dollar. If you should have saved $2,000 in the first 12 weeks, then this saving needs to be visible.

It is also important to know if you will save evenly each month ($700 p/m) or if your progress will be more volatile, as this will change your focus and mindset.

Targets for the next quarter are then set, giving consideration to any unforeseen or unusual expenses or changes. Then we repeat the process of tracking and measuring actual results to forecast capability after another 12-week period.

If clients are on track after the first 12 weeks but their situation feels too 'tight', tweaks are made to the budget to ease the brakes on spending, because if things are feeling tight there is a likelihood that clients will stray from their plan.

For most people, after the first 12 weeks the results speak for themselves. Sure, the plan may need some refinement, but if they can see the result of their efforts, money is no longer a misunderstood phenomenon; instead, it's something that is understood and under control. Money makes friends with those who stick to the rules, and laughs at those who do not. If you stick to the rules, you will get the result, guaranteed.

My job from here on is to keep my clients on track, refine the plan, keep emotion removed from the process and, at times, force the results until the client's confidence grows enough to build momentum. I am accountable for the results as much as my client is because I believe that, once the emotion is removed and the plan is adhered to, the results are sure to follow. I'm particularly eager to get to work on creating wealth, but I need to first get my clients' financial foundations strong, and their resilience improved.

Financial foundations include:
- creating better money habits
- changing money beliefs and strengthening mindset
- setting financial goals
- working to a savings plan, with better structures, targets, measurement and accountability
- building financial resilience.

To keep motivated, you need to ensure you are achieving your targets. Set goals, know what you are capable of, and what is and isn't possible. Don't make things too tight. Allow for treats. Understand the timing of one-off costs and how they are going to affect your cashflow. Some months are going to be tighter than others, depending on when big bills are paid. Plot this; get your head around it. You will feel in control when your money progress is in line with what you expect. Remember fluctuations in income and spending create volatility to your progress. Volatility of outcome is one of the main challenges to creating behavioural change.

Where do you want to be?

Your financial destination is not just where you want to be but what you want to achieve along the way. The journey can be broken down into short-, medium- and long-term goals that mark the road to your success.

Along the way to a comfortable retirement you may have other more specific goals. Although each person's path will vary, you must keep checking your progress against your road map to ensure you remain on track overall. In the absence of clearly defined goals, people become strangely loyal to performing daily acts of trivia (distractions that ultimately get you nowhere). Too often we focus on small things where their impact on the big picture is meaningless. Spend time determining what actions will give you the biggest bang for your buck. Typically I set two key actions every quarter that will unlock the most forward momentum for the client. Forward momentum is one of the most significant drivers to wealth creation. Forward momentum is propulsion, and it will get you to your goals faster.

It's not enough to take steps that may, someday, lead to a goal — each step must in itself be a goal and a step in the right direction. Make every step count so that you can achieve the perfect balance, getting ahead as fast as your circumstances allow.

Setting goals

Because a lot of people are intimidated by money, they fail to set goals for themselves and never change their financial outlook.

When encouraging my clients to set financial goals, or to think about the things they want to achieve, I ask them to list their goals for the next 12 months, the next two to five years, and beyond. The most common goals I find people have are set out in the table opposite.

With each client, we ensure that they achieve their immediate goals over the first 12 months and then refine their plan, where necessary, to achieve their medium- and long-term goals faster. The sooner all your goals are achieved, the sooner you can stop working!

Short term: next 12 months	Medium term: next 2–5 years	Long term: next 10+ years
· Feel in control of my finances · Develop a plan · Repay short-term and credit-card debt · Save more · Pay off my mortgage faster · Stop living pay day to pay day · Remove money worries from my relationship · Live a lifestyle I enjoy · Know my longer-term goals are in hand · Buy a property · Refinance · Understand my retirement number and what investment strategies could be effective in achieving it · Understand the window of time I need to act in to de-risk my retirement number · Build my financial resilience and money confidence	· Replace my car in X years, spending $X · Renovate/ upgrade my property, spending $X · Take a holiday in X years, spending $X · Buy an investment property · Protect my wealth · Start a family · Pay for a wedding	· Be mortgage-free · Save for retirement · Complete retirement planning · Buy an investment property · Buy a holiday home · Buy a boat · Take at least six months off work · Help kids onto the property ladder

This is a guide only: not everyone has the same goals or timeframes to work within. The timeframes to aim for will be unique to your financial situation and level of ambition.

Acknowledging obstacles

Developing a plan for success involves identifying obstacles that have prevented you from getting ahead in the past, such as your general attitude, lack of time, and ambivalence towards money or the role money plays in your relationship. Until you are aware of your weaknesses and how they create obstacles for you, you will not be able to overcome them.

Common obstacles I find people face include:

- not knowing what to aim for, so not bothering
- being unfamiliar with setting financial goals
- not knowing their financial capability
- not having a compelling enough reason to try
- frittering money away or spending a little bit more than they realise across a lot of expenses
- not knowing where they are going

- having good intentions, but being unable to sustain the results they want
- being on the back foot so they cannot correct any backwards movement
- disagreeing with their partner about money or having a different approach to money from their partner
- owing too much money
- being behind in payments to the IRD and incurring penalties
- having cashflow problems
- having nothing put aside for a rainy day — no savings, low financial resilience.

Strategies for success

The following simple tricks will help you to build better money habits and keep on track to your financial goals. Making habits pleasurable is a surefire way to make them stick. Another way to hack the habit-building process is to make it easy. By making our desired habits as easy as possible we reduce friction and increase the odds of them sticking.

- Separate out your weekly costs from all other costs.
- Payment convenience will translate to less savings, so learn to insert friction into your payment process.
- Always use cash or EFTPOS — avoid credit cards or digital options for your most frequent costs.
- Set a budget. Understand the timing of income, and the fluctuation of costs.
- Set savings, spending, mortgage or debt-reduction targets.
- Track your spending. A simple trick for making new habits stick is called habit tracking.
- Have a stretch target.
- Tweak your budget to make it sustainable.
- Measure your results. Reset the plan for the next three months. Rinse and repeat.
- Understand which actions unlock opportunities.
- Have a wealth/asset-building goal, outside of spending targets.
- Have a budget fluid enough to absorb curve balls and the timing of purchases.
- Share your goals with people. Surround yourself with people on a similar journey.

- Write your savings targets down on a Post-it Note. Pop it on the fridge and by the light switch in your room.
- Have an accountability partner.
- Celebrate progress!

Case study 1: high debt, no property

Natalie came to me at the age of 28 with high debts and no property. She was on a salary of $65,000 per annum before tax, and had a $47,000 debt from spending on herself. Natalie thought she had a great relationship with her bank because she could call up and ask for an extension on her credit card or personal loan and it would be available to access within 24 hours.

Natalie struggled to repay her debts, so she consolidated and refinanced with another bank, repeating this process twice. Each time she refinanced for slightly more and kept on spending. Her main vice was clothing — she always looked good, but she was going backwards.

She was given a stark reality check when she finally went to a budget advisor and they told her to declare herself bankrupt. She called me and wanted to know what to do. We met and worked through her spending.

For some people, bankruptcy is a legitimate option, although it is not usually the only option. Natalie *wanted* to repay her debts — she felt strongly about them being her responsibility. She didn't want to hide from the consequences of her actions, but she also didn't have the tools to address the problem.

We listed all her expenses and debts. At a push, we could clear her debts within 18 months if she was prepared to commit to a plan. The plan was tight and required very close monitoring to ensure she was making the best possible progress for her circumstances. It was important for her to see results quickly, otherwise she would lose momentum.

After listing every creditor, we prioritised her debts and estimated how much she could afford to repay each one. She then contacted every creditor, explained her situation and started making repayments. Not once did she default — she was ready and determined to sort things out once and for all. As her debts were repaid in order of priority, she had slightly more money to pay the remaining creditors. Whenever a debt was repaid, she contacted the remaining creditors and advised them she could afford to pay them at a higher rate. She kept this up for six months. She became known as someone who did what she said she was going to do. Instead of seeing her as a bad debtor, her creditors were viewing her more favourably.

Over the first 12 months her income increased slightly and her contract changed to receive commission payments. She asked me what she should do when she received her first commission payment. I told her to call her creditors and ask what they would accept as a full and final payment of their account. Surprisingly, one of her last creditors, to whom she owed $20,000, accepted $10,000 as full and final repayment of their account!

Just 15 months after meeting and starting to work with me, Natalie was debt-free and in control of her financial destiny. Now she is saving for a house.

I initially asked Natalie to commit to a strict budget for 12 weeks, to allow us to get some runs on the board. We slashed her clothing budget during this time and I asked her to make do with her existing wardrobe, or massage other costs down to allow her to spend money on clothes if she needed to. She stuck to the plan, though. She was determined. And when she saw the result after 12 weeks she was motivated to keep going (although I did increase her clothing budget after that, as I didn't want her to fall off the wagon and have a clothing binge!).

In general, some organisations may accept lower balances and waive penalties as soon as they know your intention to repay the debt. Most don't. They may in time, but not until you prove yourself. If you are in debt and struggling to get ahead because of economic abuse or setbacks then I encourage you to enlist the help of the amazing team at Good Shepherd. This is a charitable organisation designed to support and advocate for women who have suffered financial abuse or need some extra financial love. They have interest-free loans and financial-wellbeing coaches who help you take the necessary steps towards you getting debt-free. They also negotiate with your creditors on your behalf. They are amazing. Check them out at goodshepherd.org.nz.

Case study 2: high income, high debt, no property

One of my favourite clients, Alex, was earning a salary a little over $200,000. She flatted with friends and, despite her income, her living costs were fairly moderate. She was generous with others and occasionally generous with herself, describing her spending tendencies as 'fast and loose'. She was $60,000 in debt when I met her, and could comfortably afford her debt repayments. While she would have preferred to have no debt, she wasn't overly fazed by it or motivated to do much about it. I asked her what she wanted to achieve — she wasn't sure. She'd never set herself a financial goal before.

Alex wanted to get onto the property ladder but didn't think it could be achieved anytime soon, so she wasn't sure this was the right goal for her. I asked her the goal a different way. 'If we could get you into a property within the next 12 months, would that appeal to you?' 'Hell yes! But do we have a real chance at this, because I can't see how it can work,' she replied. I needed to build Alex's plan in reverse: to work out where we needed to be in 12 months, and how much we needed to have saved for a home deposit to be sufficient to secure a property. The byproduct of getting her property ready was that her debts would be paid off within five months. She was more than happy to now get cracking on following a spending plan, knowing that it was going to unlock a far greater goal.

Case study 3: buying a house

Roger and Renee were aged 31 and 29, respectively, and living in a de facto relationship when they first came to me. This was almost 15 years ago. Their combined after-tax income was $95,000 per annum. They had savings of $20,000, and although they used credit cards to pay for their lifestyle the bills were all paid in full each month.

They wanted to buy a house, but their savings were not quite enough to enter the housing market. As a result, they had started spending all their income each month and feeling ambivalent towards money.

Renee was the higher earner of the couple, and she was also the spender. By nature, Roger was a saver. They both wanted to become self-employed, but felt that this was not possible because of the likely financial impact. Roger thought that because he earned significantly less than Renee, he didn't have a right to question her spending. He felt disempowered as a result.

They wanted a house, but they didn't know what they needed to do to actually get the house they wanted or how long it would take. They were fearful that buying a house would mean their lifestyle would be significantly and detrimentally impacted.

After our first meeting, we identified $30,000 per annum that was being spent that didn't need to be. *Many people spend because they have no reason not to.* My job is as much about finding out their reason to try, the goal to hook them, as it is about achieving the goal. Roger and Renee soon learned they could live the lifestyle they enjoyed without that money being frittered away. Over the course of the first six months, they saved a further $15,000 and started looking for a property.

After a couple of months of what seemed like endless searching and attending lots of challenging auctions, they still hadn't managed to buy a property, and again became despondent. They lost their focus and decided a trip to New York was just what they needed, so off they went and spent half their house deposit. They loved their trip but on their return they realised they still wanted a house!

After that setback we reset the plan. It's important to accept that what's done is done, and not to bother focusing on what cannot be undone. Too often couples feel aggrieved by their spouse's financial behaviour and focus on this. I see little point: focus on what you can change, and make up the lost ground as quickly as you can.

Six months later, with a concerted effort and a combined pay rise of $15,000, they were even further ahead than before they had left for New York. They purchased their first home for a little under $400,000 (remember this was almost 15 years ago). They renovated and refurbished it, but these costs had been factored in right at the beginning so there were no financial surprises. When they announced they were getting married, the cost of their wedding was factored into the plan too, including the cost of a honeymoon in Thailand.

Roger is now self-employed. Before this transition, they worked to build sufficient headway on their mortgage to mitigate set-up costs and loss of income while he began to build his business. They optimised their mortgage by restructuring it to allow them to get ahead as fast as possible in their new circumstances while they continued to live a lifestyle they enjoy.

> A correctly structured mortgage, coupled with a dynamic plan, allows you to access your equity as you need it, but still ensures your long-term picture remains rosy. Remember, *a successful plan stretches you to your full potential and also adjusts to changes in circumstances.* If you are waiting for the perfect time to start a plan, it will never come — financial stability is earned not inherited, and the sooner you make a start the sooner you'll achieve it. Mortgages and plans must never be static.

An initial snapshot of Roger and Renee's mortgage structure showed they could be mortgage-free in six years, assuming they had no children. Five years into this plan, they remained on track to be mortgage-free within the next 12 months. No children were on the cards, but a home upgrade was likely, which simply meant we would refresh the plan, understand the new mortgage we had to work with and then systematically kill it.

When Roger and Renee finally purchased their first house, their lifestyle did not change; we simply replaced rent with mortgage payments and added in costs specifically related to property ownership. Because they had worked on their spending for some time they knew exactly what they needed to spend to have a lifestyle they liked. Without changing their discretionary spending, we simply channelled the surplus funds into repaying their mortgage faster.

More than 10 years later they did upgrade their home and they have welcomed two children. They have relocated cities and now have two investment properties under their belt. For them, financial success is about having options.

12. Building up — the next phase

When I work with clients in the building-up phase, I am trying to grow wealth. Although the extent and speed of the wealth creation differs for each client, I start with aiming to unlock $1 million of gain within the next 10 years.

Once you have mastered the art of creating a cash surplus by working to a budget, you need to use this money to make more money. Creating a cash surplus (step one) is probably the hardest of all the steps as for many it will require behavioural change, better money habits, better money management, better structures and more consistent effort. Few people drift towards a cash surplus.

Once a large enough surplus is created, we then move to growing wealth. This is step two. Creating wealth is a science.

To move from the Starting Out phase to the Building Up phase, you need to have at least $100,000 of equity, or own a property in a market where values are increasing. The lion's share of the clients who come to me are at this stage — that is, they have their home and they have their mortgage. Most know that they should be paying their mortgage off faster, but they struggle to do this as there seems to be no spare cash around to be used to repay debt faster.

To fix this, they need to learn or re-learn the key skill of the Starting Out phase: they need to master the art of creating a cash surplus, and then how to kill their mortgage. This becomes more challenging the older you get and the more you earn. (I tend to find older people are more set in their ways, while people with higher incomes naturally disengage from thinking about their money.) Don't think you have left your run too late to improve your outcomes. This is seldom the case. The shorter the runway, the higher the stakes. High stakes means you have to get it right the first time, and start moving forward quickly.

The short game hinges on creating a sustainable cash surplus, with the medium-term goal of paying off your mortgage faster and the longer game being retirement. For the most part, you will need to be mortgage-free by the time you stop working if you are going to have a shot at a comfortable retirement. But, while mortgage-free status is encouraged for retirement, this in isolation won't solve all your problems, as you can't eat your house when you retire — you are going to need more funds from somewhere.

Creating a cash surplus first, buying a property second, then killing the mortgage are the founding principles of a retirement plan. They are not particularly sexy, but they are critical to lasting progress. It is not until you are on the way to killing your mortgage that you can start to consider other strategies in order to get you mortgage-free faster again, or to get you to retirement safely. Whether it is saving more, buying an investment property, investing in shares or managed funds, or even starting a business, there are many and varied options for growing wealth. What suits you might feel uncomfortable to another, and what one person's financial situation can allow, another's might have no tolerance for. You need to understand your options and keep moving forward.

You need to know whether you will be mortgage-free by retirement. If you won't be, or are only just, then it's unlikely you'll have much time to physically save for retirement, as all your funds and energy will be going into getting your mortgage paid off first.

If this is your reality, you have four options: earn more, work for longer, spend less, or borrow against your property to buy another property. *Those are your options. There is no magic dust.* This is what you have to work with, although when you work with leverage it does feel pretty magical.

Investments

If you do have some saved funds, or are able to leverage against your property, looking at investments as an additional source of income is an option. The key is to focus on what you are trying to achieve. What problem do you need to solve, and what tools do you have available to help you solve it? Don't jump to a particular or preferred solution without first articulating the problem and considering all available options. Weigh up the options to understand their impact on your financial position.

A lot of financial advisors hate property. This could be because they can't charge you a fee if you buy property, so they make no money from you! Or it may be because they simply love shares and managed funds (investments on which they *do* earn a living).

Haters are gonna hate, but the reality is that if you have no real savings

— and most of us don't and won't — then leveraged property is likely your only investment option to close your retirement savings gap. If your retirement savings gap exceeds $300,000 (and for most of my clients, it does), then property is most likely your only option to close it out, without you having to take premature drastic action (like downsizing the family home tomorrow). This is because property is unique among investment options: it is recognised by the banks as something they are prepared to lend you money to buy. When you borrow to buy a property, you are 'leveraging' the bank's money for your benefit. You can take the bank's money and buy a property, and, provided the return outweighs the interest rate you are being charged, you can take advantage of the bank's offering for your own gain. (You can sometimes borrow to buy a business, although unless the business is an established brand with assests, the banks won't lend much, if anything. In some instances, you can borrow a small amount against some shares, but the bank will lend you less and the interest rate will be higher. Further, if the shares drop in value, you can be asked to repay some of the debt.) A leveraged property tends to outperform most other investment options. However, not all leveraged properties would be suitable to close out your retirement gap; more are lemons than not.

I believe shares and managed funds have their place, but the main disincentive of these types of investments is that *you need money to invest in them*. Many Kiwis do not have the money available to consider these types of investments, simply because they are spending everything they earn. While they might own their own home, it most likely has a mortgage against it and there is no spare cash for investment — and, even if they did have cash, I would suggest it went towards paying off their mortgage in the first instance.

Once you have mastered the creation of a cash surplus and have purchased your property, killing your mortgage is the next critical step to creating more options. Once you have no outgoings to the bank for mortgage repayments, your cash surplus will grow faster and you will then have the funds needed to consider all investment options.

There are some common mistakes people make with leverage (borrowing against their own home for investment), which need to be avoided if they are serious about getting ahead. Structuring your debt incorrectly is an unacceptable outcome when your home is exposed.

You need to be accumulating assets, whether they're in the form of a home, investment property, business or shares. However, if the objective is to grow wealth, I favour investment property, KiwiSaver and businesses (if you have the know-how) over a home, shares and managed funds. I understand the logic behind these investment vehicles and have applied it to my personal situation and those of many clients. That's not to say that shares and managed funds are bad investments; owning your home could also be defined as being an unproductive investment, usually costing you more than it should unless you use the equity in your home to your advantage. But shares are a different beast with a mind of their own. If you are experienced, you can make a solid return, but it takes a lot of knowledge and a tolerance for daily updates and an emotional market dictating the value of your investment.

I personally don't have the stomach for investing large amounts directly in shares, though I will later on discuss the advantages of this form of investment, as well as managed funds (see Chapter 23). Property, by comparison, is a tangible investment that you can readily borrow against, insure, acquire without real cash and has less volatility than other asset classes. These characteristics distinguish it from shares, and mean that, when coupled with the Kiwi hankering towards owning it, property holds a greater attraction.

Owning a business remains a popular way to create wealth, although it holds its own risks. A staggering 540,000 Kiwis are self-employed (sole traders) — despite high failure rates for start-up enterprises. Almost 45 per cent of self-employed people are over the age of 55. Becoming self-employed seems to hold more attraction as you get older and can be a viable way to keep yourself in the workforce, when being an employee may no longer be an option.

KiwiSaver is a great option for those who are employed, but in isolation it is unlikely to be sufficient to fund your retirement. Nevertheless, if you can afford to be in it, you should, but cap your contributions to the level your employer matches. If you are self-employed — so you are the only person making contributions — there isn't too much gain to be had, so only contribute enough to unlock the government's contribution.

Remember, it is not the smartest who get ahead, but the bravest. When you are trying to get ahead, you can't play not to lose; you have to play to win. It's imperative that you surround yourself with people you can learn from.

Opportunity is missed by most people because it is dressed in overalls and looks like work. —Thomas Edison

13. The magic of compound interest

People get excited about compound interest. It's said that Albert Einstein once declared it to be the most powerful force in the universe. It consists of putting money into an account and letting it earn interest from that moment on. The interest you then earn on the interest is added to the original pot of money, and then you earn interest on the new higher balance. It's kind of interest on top of interest.

Over the short term, and with low real interest rates, compound interest is not all that exciting. Real interest rates describe the rate that is earned on the investment after accounting for tax and inflation. Real returns are lower than nominal returns, which do not subtract tax and inflation. For example, if the nominal savings interest rate is 6 per cent, the tax rate is 33 per cent and inflation is 4 per cent, then the real return is 0 per cent. When inflation is high, most investments will have a nil or negative return. If the real return is close to zero, there is no real benefit from compound interest.

But, over longer time periods, with higher real returns, the results can be more impressive, although unlikely to be quite as exciting as our friend Albert suggested. This could be because inflation (the enemy of compound interest) didn't play as big a role back in the 1880s as it seems to now. More on that later.

Let's say you put $1,000 in the bank at 5 per cent interest per annum (compounded annually). At the end of the year you will have $1,050. If you leave the entire amount in the bank for another year at the same rate of interest, you will then have $1,103. In the second year, not only did you get interest on the original investment, but *you also got interest on the interest you earned the prior year*. This is when compound interest kicks in.

Compound interest is of relevance to anyone leaving their investment to grow over a long period of time. The $1,000 investment mentioned above, when invested for 40 years at 5 per cent, will end up being worth over

$7,000, without you putting in any more money! Although the calculation is correct, in practical terms the investment needs to grow at a faster rate than inflation to have created a genuine gain.

The following compound interest chart shows how the future value of an investment grows most spectacularly in its later years. In this example, half of the future value is earned in the last 10 years. This is the inverse of a mortgage-payment graph when half the principal is paid off in the last seven years of a 30-year term.

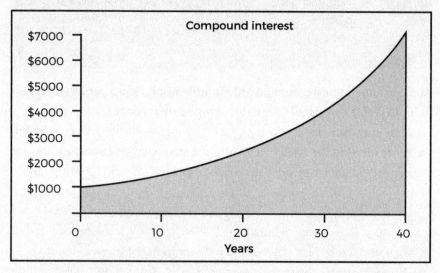

Mortgages follow the same principle, but in reverse. If you commit to the bank's predetermined mortgage length (25 or 30 years), you are not going to start making obvious dents in the loan balance until the last 10 years of the loan. The bank compounds the interest it charges you, so that you pay a lot more back to them than you first borrowed.

The longer the term, the more pronounced the effect of interest rates. At first glance it might be tempting to say that the difference between investing at 5 per cent and 6 per cent would not be significant. However, an increase of a single percentage point on an investment can result in a 46 per cent increase in the future value of that investment over a 40-year period. Again, while the maths is correct, we probably should ask how likely it is you will hold any investment for 40 years. When you shorten the timeframe, the results are nowhere near as exciting. For example, the 1 per cent difference in interest rates creates a 10 per cent difference over 10 years, lifting to 21 per cent over 20 years.

The frequency with which interest is applied to an investment account can also be important. This refers to how frequently it compounds, or adds interest to the investment. The more frequently the interest is paid, the better for savings growth. Most compound-interest projections assume that interest is added annually. But there are opportunities to earn interest daily, monthly or quarterly.

The following table, for the value of a $1000 investment after 40 years, compares the effect of compounding interest yearly, quarterly and monthly.

Interest rate	Interest paid yearly	Interest paid quarterly	Interest paid monthly
5%	$7,040	$7,298	$7,358
10%	$45,259	$51,978	$53,700

At 5 per cent, interest compounded monthly results in a 5 per cent increase in future value compared to interest compounded yearly.

Compound interest works nicely with savings — the longer you save for, the more exciting the result. Time and the frequency of compounding are the key ingredients. Consider the following examples (and ignoring tax).

Jim is 20 years old. He saves $1,000 per annum every year for the next 10 years (to accumulate $10,000). He then stops saving, but does not withdraw any money, leaving his savings in the bank account until he turns 65. His savings are earning interest at 5 per cent per annum. The interest earned is added to the savings made each year. When he turns 65, he has $69,380 sitting in his savings account.

Kathy is 35. She also starts saving $1,000 per annum. She continues this saving regime until she is 65, so over that 30-year period she has physically saved $30,000. Like Jim, the interest she is earning over time is added to her savings balance and she makes no withdrawals. She is also earning interest at 5 per cent per annum. When she turns 65, she has saved $66,439.

Kathy has saved $20,000 more than Jim, *but ends up with $2,941 less.* This highlights the benefit of starting earlier, so the investment can be held for longer. Without trying to be a Debbie Downer, can I also point out that if we overlay the impact of 5 per cent inflation, then while Jim and Kathy have done well — and in the case of Jim his saving balance may be genuinely higher — this balance will still only buy him $10,000 of goods in today's dollars, in 45 years' time.

The moral of this story is not to marry someone 15 years younger than you (although it might help — joke!), but instead to get started on sorting out your financial situation sooner rather than later.

Compound interest respects no man or woman, but is dictated by time. Have a look at the following examples below.

Saving $10 per week from the age of 20

Start saving $10 a week when you're 20, and by the time you're the age in the left-hand column you'll have saved the amount in the right-hand column. Look at how the power of compound interest makes your savings grow!

Age	Capital	Interest 2.5%	Total*
25	$2,600	$170	$2,770
30	$5,200	$700	$5,900
35	$7,800	$1,640	$9,440
40	$10,400	$3,050	$13,450
45	$13,000	$4,980	$17,980
50	$15,600	$7,510	$23,110
55	$18,200	$10,710	$28,910
60	$20,800	$14,680	$35,480

*Rounded to the nearest $10
Source: www.sorted.org.nz

Saving $50 per week from the age of 20

Now look at the same example, but saving $50 a week from the age of 20.

Age	Capital	Interest 2.5%	Total*
25	$13,000	$850	$13,850
30	$26,000	$3,500	$29,500
35	$39,000	$8,200	$47,200
40	$52,000	$15,250	$67,250
45	$65,000	$24,900	$89,900
50	$78,000	$37,550	$115,550
55	$91,000	$53,550	$144,550
60	$104,000	$73,400	$177,400

*Rounded to the nearest $50
Source: www.sorted.org.nz

What about inflation?

While the concept of compound interest is interesting, in real life instead of using the nominal return on an investment, you need to use the 'real' return, which is the net return after you have deducted inflation. So if the investment is paying 6 per cent, but inflation is at 4 per cent, the net return is 2 per cent. The net return is almost always lower than the nominal return. As I've noted earlier, inflation tends to erode any of the wonder of compound interest because, while a 6 per cent return compounded highlights drastic returns, a 2 per cent growth rate isn't overly exciting.

Where inflation does benefit you is with debt. It helps you to pay it off because the value of the debt remains constant, even though the asset is worth more and your income is higher (which means you can afford to repay the debt more easily). Typically inflation will shave 10 years off your mortgage over its lifetime. Let me illustrate.

Let's say you had $100,000 of money sitting under your bed. Inflation is at 4 per cent. If you did nothing with your money, you would still have $100,000 in dollar bills, but in 12 months' time, this would only buy $96,000 of goods, because the cost of goods has increased by the rate of inflation. We could say you've lost 4 per cent of your money because you didn't invest it in anything that would offset or surpass the cost of inflation.

If we had $100,000 in a mortgage, and all things being equal, with 4 per cent inflation that same year, the value of the mortgage would have lowered by 4 per cent. Yes on paper it still shows as $100,000, but this amount is worth less with inflation. This is more pronounced when you look back at your parents, who may have paid something like $30,000 for their home. At the time that would have felt like a lot of money. Let's say they never paid the mortgage off, opting to pay interest only for all of this time. Fast-forward 50 years, and the value of that mortgage, relative to the house value and the income you could now make, shows the impact of inflation.

Debt and inflation are a match made in heaven.

> **Compound interest is the eighth wonder of the world. He who understands it, earns it; he who doesn't, pays it. —Albert Einstein**

14. Buying your first home

Compound interest is all very well, but greater gains can be made from using leverage, and investing wisely in property. While I am sure that there are some people who like to see their wealth increase on paper, the main purpose of wealth is to allow you to live a lifestyle you enjoy — to live in a home you like, drive the car you want, provide for your family, take holidays when you want to and enjoy yourself during retirement. One of the key ways to prepare for retirement is to have purchased a home and repaid the mortgage well before you stop working.

The reason for this is twofold. If you don't own your own home, you have to pay rent, so you have an outgoing no matter what. Whether you pay rent to someone else or continue to pay off a mortgage, the money is still leaving your bank account. The beauty of being mortgage-free before retirement is that the money that was paying off the mortgage no longer leaves your bank account, allowing you to save more while you are still working. You will also spend less in your retirement, so any savings will last longer.

If you're like most first-time home buyers, you've probably listened to friends and family and looked to the media for advice, much of it encouraging you to buy a home. In New Zealand in particular, people love buying property. It accounts for half of the net wealth of New Zealand households. We have more money locked up in property than in all other asset classes put together, including superannuation, life insurance and shares.

House prices seem to keep increasing — especially in Auckland — yet salaries are not increasing at the same rate. This means it's going to get harder and harder to buy your first home. But as soon as you buy a property, you get on the property ladder and start to benefit from the increasing prices.

For some, the idea of buying their first property is intimidating, and the process of home ownership unfamiliar. The more you know about why you should own a home, and what to expect from home ownership, the less frightening the entire process will seem.

There are many benefits to owning property, some financial, some emotional. Although it's important to go into property ownership with your eyes open, there are clear reasons why getting on the property ladder is important.

Property tends to increase in value quicker than savings in the bank. However, properties are not easily converted into cash so, while they might increase in value, that doesn't mean you necessarily have access to this extra money like you would if it were in a savings account. You can increase the value of most properties independent of the property price cycle through small DIY initiatives. Instead of paying rent, you are paying down a mortgage. It is still an outgoing, but at the end of 20 or 30 years you are going to own something for yourself instead of creating profit for your landlord.

Psychologically, pride of ownership is one of the most important forces driving people to want to own their home. The property is yours to treat as you see fit, to express yourself with and to live the lifestyle you want, instead of being curtailed by your landlord. You can change the look and feel of the property according to your taste, without having to ask permission. Home ownership gives you and your family a sense of stability and security. It's making an investment in your future.

Why you need to get started now

The house-price-to-income multiple is an internationally recognised measure of housing affordability. It represents the ratio between median house price and median annual household income, and is otherwise known as the median multiple. The United Nations World Bank says this ratio is 'possibly the most important summary measure of housing market performance, indicating not only the degree to which housing is affordable by the population, but also the presence of market distortions'.

Based on the World Bank's official research work, it has become accepted that a median multiple of 3.0 or less (that is, median house prices are no more than three times the median annual household income) is a good marker for housing affordability.

Finance website interest.co.nz calculates regularly updated multiples, based on median house prices as reported by the Real Estate Institute of New Zealand. It calculates median household income as one full-time male median income, plus half of one female median income, both in the 30–34 age range, with the family's income topped up by Working For Families support.

While not definitive, when plugged into the median multiple formula, the model gives an insight into housing affordability across the country.

New Zealand house prices have massively increased in comparison to incomes since about 2001. Back in the early 1990s, the ratio was only around 4:1, which slowly increased until 1998 and then it simply took off — peaking at just under 8:1 at the height of the housing mania in late 2007, and again after the Covid sugar high in 2022 where it was almost 9:1. Nationally, affordability levels have since reduced to 6.6, which is slightly higher than the affordability in October 2018 of 6.33. There continues to be wide variations between suburbs and regions, with Auckland's North Shore sitting at a whopping 9:1, compared with Whanganui and Invercargill, which sit closer to 4:1. What this says is that, over the past 20 years, house-price growth has outstripped wage growth by a factor of 2:1. This is one of the reasons why it's important to own property — it only gets harder to climb onto the property ladder the longer you wait.

On one hand, I think it is unsustainable for property values to stay as high as they are, but until the cost of building a home and net migration reduce, and the supply increases, I cannot see how it will correct itself, in the Auckland market especially. That said, *never pay more than what a property is worth*, and if possible negotiate a discount up front so you can make an immediate equity gain.

New Zealand house-price-to-income multiples (January 2024)

	Population	Median house price	Median income	Median multiple		
				Feb 24	Feb 23	Feb 22
NZ total	5,335,000	$790,000	$115,508	6.84	7.10	8.75
Whangārei	98,300	$750,000	$112,495	6.67	6.69	8.00
Auckland – metro	1,717,500	$1,026,000	$120,951	8.48	8.85	11.30
– North Shore	225,800	$1,295,000	$128,217	10.10	10.27	12.45
– Waitākere	204,500	$915,000	$118,740	7.71	8.16	10.43
– Central	444,100	$1,160,000	$125,058	9.28	9.72	11.48
– Manukau	368,500	$960,000	$112,737	8.52	8.72	11.11
Hamilton	175,500	$750,000	$112,771	6.65	7.33	8.51
Tauranga	151,300	$901,500	$110,143	8.18	8.89	11.34
Rotorua	77,300	$630,000	$112,442	5.60	5.71	7.27

Continued overleaf

	Population	Median house price	Median income	Median multiple		
				Feb 24	Feb 23	Feb 22
Gisborne	50,700	$619,000	$101,601	6.09	6.06	7.99
Napier	88,000	$690,000	$106,633	6.47	6.74	8.84
Hastings	66,300	$729,000	$106,304	6.86	7.55	9.20
New Plymouth	86,100	$700,000	$105,802	6.62	6.42	7.82
Whanganui	48,100	$490,000	$100,847	4.86	4.76	6.07
Palmerston North	90,400	$635,000	$112,300	5.65	5.72	7.06
Wellington – metro	487,700	$800,000	$124,613	6.42	6.83	9.15
– Kāpiti Coast	57,000	$790,000	$109,036	7.25	8.39	8.78
– Porirua	61,000	$911,000	$119,317	7.64	7.81	9.12
– Upper Hutt	47,100	$618,900	$121,186	5.11	5.28	5.46
– Lower Hutt	111,800	$800,000	$122,432	6.53	6.34	8.80
– Wairarapa	40,800	$630,000	$88,814	7.09	6.41	9.55
– Wellington City	216,200	$876,500	$138,632	6.32	7.34	9.05
Nelson	54,600	$732,500	$107,318	6.83	6.83	8.69
Christchurch	394,700	$721,000	$111,926	6.44	6.46	7.42
Timaru	48,400	$525,000	$104,569	5.02	4.93	5.53
Dunedin	134,100	$590,000	$101,286	5.83	6.02	7.76
Queenstown-Lakes	47,400	$1,545,000	$84,318	18.32	17.71	18.33
Invercargill	57,100	$469,000	$106,047	4.42	4.34	5.04

Source: Interest.co.nz

15. Mortgage basics

If you're considering purchasing a home or an investment property in the near future you need to get up to speed on how to get a mortgage, from the pre-approval process through to how to use the mortgage to your advantage once you have bought your first home. If you already have a mortgage, you need to understand the fundamentals before I can show you how to optimise your mortgage for faster repayment.

Things to know

You will need a deposit of usually 20 per cent of the value of the property you want to buy, to qualify for a mortgage on that property. The size of the deposit can vary, depending on which bank is lending the money and the type of property you are buying. For some first-home buyers, you may need as little as 5 per cent of your future home's value as a deposit.

Remember, it is the deposit that allows you to apply for a mortgage with a bank. Whether you then get a mortgage will depend on your financial character. Assuming you pass this test, the last gate to pass through is servicing. Servicing is your ability to repay the mortgage. Your income and expenses will determine your capacity for lending, or how much the bank believes you could afford to repay. Your capacity determines the size of the mortgage you can get.

Deposit

The deposit can be funded from your own savings, KiwiSaver, a gift from someone (usually family), equity in another property (usually your family's) or a combination of all of the above. Where this money comes from doesn't seem to make too much difference to the bank. Provided you have a good savings history, are of good character, and have a high enough income to pass the bank's servicing test (that is, the bank is confident that you can make the repayments), the rest is pretty easy.

Financial character

Your financial character is a combination of your credit history, credit score, bank account conduct and number of debts. If you go into unarranged overdrafts, have late-payment fees or are charged penalties, this can imply your money management (in the eyes of the bank, at least) is too weak to qualify for a mortgage, or that they don't think that you are a safe bet, right now. Your financial character is not influenced by your income levels. I recall a client who earned more than $300,000, had a $100,000 deposit, but didn't initially qualify for a loan at a mainstream bank because their financial character was considered weak. Of course we were able to eventually turn this around, but it took time and considerable effort.

> **Tip:** Check with a credit company such as Veda Advantage Ltd (www.veda.co.nz) to see if there is anything unusual showing on your credit history. If you have any unpaid fines, pay them. If any charge is in dispute, get this remedied.

Capacity

Your capacity to borrow is the amount of lending the bank believes you could repay based on your household income and current spending. Excessive spending can dramatically dampen how much you can borrow. The bank tends to look at your spending for the previous 12 weeks to get an idea of your lifestyle cost, so you'll need to make an effort to get 'bank ready' by working on better money habits and getting improved saving rates for the 12 to 24 weeks leading up to the bank application. As a rough rule of thumb, every $2,500 you don't spend in a 12-week period unlocks another $100,000 of lending potential.

Provided your spending is 'in check', and you don't have lots of short-term debt, the bank will typically lend you up to six times your combined household income (before tax). So if you collectively earn $100,000 per annum, you would expect to be able to borrow $600,000. This is also described as the debt-to-income ratio.

Other debt (like car loans, credit cards and overdrafts) is a massive handbrake on your borrowing potential. For every $10,000 of debt, your borrowing capacity reduces by $40,000. Interestingly, your credit-card limit counts as debt in the eyes of the bank, even if you haven't spent it. Reducing credit-card limits prior to a bank application can be smart.

Don't assume there's a standard way of determining your income between all banks, because there isn't. Similarly, not all expenses are treated the same way. This difference in assessment can lead to big swings in lending potential from one bank to another. I had one client who qualified for $500,000 lending at one bank and $700,000 at another. The difference came down to how each bank treated the different types of income. For example, some banks won't acknowledge bonuses or child-support income. This means, if you receive $20,000 of child support each year but it isn't recognised as 'income' in the eyes of your bank, then that is $100,000–$120,000 of lending you can't access.

In the same way, most banks apply a different amount of discount to any rental income included in a lending application. Some banks ignore cash jobs, and discount self-employed income dramatically. This can translate to hundreds of thousands of dollars of lending that you could access at one bank, but not another. The best way to circumvent this is to chat with an experienced mortgage broker who will know the rules of the game and direct you to the best bank for your type of income. Make sure you understand the impact of the different options before making a call.

How much can you afford to borrow?

Banks are usually happy to lend you money as long as they are confident that you can afford the repayments. As a rough guide, assume you can borrow five to six times your gross household income. So if your household earned $200,000 per annum, you could expect to borrow $1 million to $1.2 million.

Banks will determine your ability to repay using their own calculators and internal policies. If you are self-employed, a single parent or someone who receives large bonuses each year, your lending ability could range quite dramatically between banks as not all banks acknowledge income the same way. Some banks test your repayment ability at a higher interest rate than others, which will mean, according to their calculations, you can't afford as much lending as another bank who uses a different test rate.

These lending calculators apply predetermined assumptions that might not correlate to your actual spending patterns. The banks build margins into the interest rates they use in these calculations to exaggerate interest repayments, and, as noted above, they tend to discount some income streams like rent, and disregard other legitimate types of income, such as child support. This can mean that, even if by your calculations you can afford to borrow a certain amount, the bank might disagree. Conversely, the bank's calculations might indicate that you can service a higher mortgage than your lifestyle really allows. That said, it's in the bank's interests that you are able to repay your mortgage, so you would expect they'll lend you only what they believe you can afford to repay (or for what they can insure their loans for).

> Use a mortgage broker to canvas the lending market for you.

To sumarise: to get a mortgage you need to have the following things:
- A deposit of up to 20 per cent of the property value. Banks usually have a small allotment of lending for customers who stump up with less than a 20 per cent deposit, but those people have to have strong financial character and a good reason for a low deposit, and they must pass the servicing tests.
- Good bank account conduct and a clean credit report.
- Solid and consistent employment. It is usually harder for self-employed people to get a mortgage, unless they have been in business for a few years and their financial statements show a strong and reliable profit.
- The ability to pay the mortgage based on the bank's calculators, which often use a higher interest rate than the current rates on offer, to build in a contingency for interest-rate fluctuations over time.
- It can help if you already bank with the bank you are seeking a mortgage from, but this is no longer a priority. Customer loyalty counts for little these days.

Let's assume you manage to jump through all of these hoops, and you get the mortgage you need to buy the home you want. Awesome. You now own a mortgage of say $800,000 – how are you supposed to structure this thing? I talk about this in detail in the next chapter, but for now, you need to understand the different types of mortgages available, and which mortgage best suits your circumstances.

Types of mortgage

There are many types of mortgage, each with its own interest rates, fees and flexibility. Each of these factors affects how much the loan will cost and how long it will take to pay off. Interest rates can be fixed, floating or a mix of both. There are also different repayment structures to choose from.

Let's unpack the terminology.

Mortgage term

The mortgage term refers to the length of time the loan will exist, or how long it will take you to repay it. The most common type of loan (table mortgage) has a term of 25–30 years. The longer the mortgage term, the lower the fixed monthly (or fortnightly) repayment. You can usually choose your mortgage term. As a rule, I prefer the longest mortgage term for my clients, which reduces their minimum fixed mortgage payments each month. I accompany this with an aggressive mortgage-repayment plan (discussed in the next chapter).

If you don't have a mortgage repayment plan, then a blunt but effective way of ensuring you are mortgage-free by retirement could be to lower your mortgage term to coincide with the number of years before you retire. So if you are aged 45, you might want to set your loan term to 20 years. This will increase your monthly repayment when compared to a 30-year mortgage. Be careful with this approach, though, as you can't easily re-access the 'extra' payments you have made to the bank and it negatively impacts your future lending potential. Weirdly, on the bank's servicing tests, you showing initiative by repaying your mortgage faster only shows as a higher fixed monthly commitment. The calculator doesn't delineate between the different types of commitments or if you paying more is actually a good thing for your financial situation. Instead, it concludes you have higher outgoings, which means there is less money available to service more debt. Further, these fixed higher repayments take up more of your cash surplus, which leaves you with less cash to cover you in for unplanned events.

Table loan

A table loan has set, regular repayments and a set date by which the loan will be paid off. The typical term is 25–30 years. The main advantage is the certainty of knowing what your payments will be (unless you are on a floating interest rate). Although table loans are the most common type of loan, they don't suit everyone. Fixed regular repayments might be difficult for people with irregular income.

If you could fix an interest rate for the loan term, your monthly repayments would be the same every month for the full term of the loan. Fluctuating interest rates are the reason for changes in the regular repayment amount.

With a table mortgage, the monthly payment remains the same but the principal portion of your principal-plus-interest payment increases slightly every month. It's lowest on your first payment and highest on your last payment. On average, every $100,000 paid in the first year of a table or amortised mortgage will reduce your principal owing by about $500. The rest of your repayments will simply cover the interest payable on the loan. Because the loan balance is reducing by such a small amount in the early years, the balance remains higher for longer. A table mortgage drip-feeds the reduction in mortgage balance to allow the bank to charge more interest for longer. Typically a bank will charge you 1.5–2 times what you borrowed in interest. So if you borrowed $300,000, then you can expect to repay this, and another $450,000 in interest costs. It's unbelievable.

Because the banks aren't that keen on you repaying your mortgage quickly, they don't always make it easy for you. The key to getting out of debt sooner is to pay more back to the bank faster. But how you do this is key. Simply increasing your repayments, which would generally be seen as a positive move, invariably leads to a perverse outcome for the borrower (but seldom for the bank). For example, increasing your repayments on your loan makes it harder to borrow more money in the future, because it has locked you into higher outgoings. When the bank is assessing your application they look at your total monthly commitments, not whether you are making more progress because of them. There are ways to get your cake and eat it too, but we have to be more strategic with how we structure your mortgage, or restructure it, in the event you have locked yourself into a shorter term.

Let me teach you the rules of the game, and how to win.

Should I fix or float?

When you take out a mortgage, you usually have the option of fixing the interest rate or letting it float. Typically, a fixed rate will be lower than the floating rate, although that is not always the case.

With a fixed-interest loan, the interest rate you pay is fixed for a period from six months to five years (some banks will allow you to fix for up to 10 years, but this is not common). At the end of the term, a fixed-interest loan should automatically move to the floating rate, with your monthly repayments changing to reflect the new rate. Be careful on this point, though. If the floating rate is lower than the fixed rate, not all banks will automatically reduce your repayments to reflect the lower interest rate, instead requiring you to sign off on the new repayment amount. Unsurprisingly, though, if the floating rate is higher than the fixed rate you have been paying, they will automatically increase your repayments to reflect this.

It's possible with some banks to negotiate a new fixed-interest loan up to six weeks prior to the expiry of the existing fixed term without incurring any break costs or penalties.

The key benefit to fixing your loan is that you know exactly what your monthly or fortnightly repayments will be, making it easier to budget. *Do not underestimate the power of certainty.* Certainty covers a multitude of budgeting sins. Having a fixed term means the repayment amount does not change during the period of your fixed term, irrespective of what's happening in the global economy or changes to domestic interest rates. Normally, if market interest rates are rising, you can lock in lower rates for longer periods. Fixed rates tend to be lower than the floating rate (normally by 1–1.5 per cent).

The main disadvantage of a fixed rate is that you cannot easily repay the principal faster than you are scheduled to without incurring penalties, or the amount you can repay is preset by the bank. What's more, if you were to pay the principal back at a higher rate, in an emergency you won't be able to easily access any funds voluntarily applied to the mortgage. That said, most New Zealanders don't have surplus funds to invest in their mortgage anyway, so not being able to pay the loan back faster is no real disadvantage.

Floating rates, on the other hand, are variable and can change regularly, often without warning. Banks can raise or lower rates at their discretion, although this is usually dictated by wider market changes. Interest-rate changes affect your repayments, meaning that your repayment amount will increase if rates are rising, and decrease if rates fall. If you don't foresee fluctuations, or no buffer exists in your budget to cover these movements, the ramifications can be huge.

The key benefit of floating rates is that, if you are one of the few people in a position to repay your mortgage faster than your current mortgage repayments dictate, you are able to repay the loan more quickly without incurring any penalties from the bank.

It's also possible to split your loan into different amounts on fixed or floating rates. This lets you make extra repayments without penalty on the floating-rate portion, while paying lower rates on the fixed portion. This might seem like a good idea, but most people are not in a position to make extra mortgage repayments, so there's no point having a floating mortgage with a higher interest rate for the sake of being able to repay the loan without penalty.

Tip: If you are going to split your loans to allow you to repay the debt faster without penalty, or locking yourself to fixed higher repayments, limit your floating portion to the size of your annual cash surplus, as you should be able to repay this over the course of the year. There is no point having any more borrowings on a floating rate than what you can afford to repay.

If you want to repay your mortgage faster without worsening your financial resilience, then you need to be able to re-access the extra payments made, through a more detailed mortgage structure.

Tip: If you are going to pay off a loan with savings or your cash surplus, set the loan up as a revolving credit facility, so you can access the additional money you are putting towards the debt if you need it in the future. This could be used to build up your financial resilience, or be put towards investments.

How long should the term be?

I believe you should maximise the length of your mortgage term, then find a way to voluntarily repay it faster as funds are available to you (see Chapter 16). Taking out a 30-year mortgage at a fixed interest rate is generally the safest bet, especially if you expect to live in your house for more than five years. This keeps your fixed obligations low, which should allow you to build up your cash surplus. The plan is to then channel the cash surplus against the mortgage, but via a different mortgage (revolving credit) that allows you to re-access the funds in the future as needed.

The exception to this rule is if you are over 50. If this is the case, the length of your mortgage term should be connected to the time until you plan to retire, provided you are on track with your retirement savings. This means if you are 50 your mortgage should be for no more than 15 years, to ensure that you are on track for repayment by retirement. If you are not on track for your retirement savings, then you might need to re-access some of the equity in your home, and that is easier to do the lower your mortgage repayments (the longer the term). For some clients who are on short loan terms, but still need to grow wealth before retirement, I have restructured their lending and extended their term, just to allow them to borrow the deposit for an investment property.

How long you fix your loan for will depend on your situation, what interest rates are doing generally and your goals. If you intend to stay in your house for the next few years, and interest rates are increasing, it makes sense to lock in a lower interest rate for as long as you can afford.

However, if you intend to sell your home in 18 months, there is little sense in fixing for longer than this, as you may be exposed to break costs or penalties when you eventually sell the house and repay the mortgage.

> When interest rates are dropping, fix for shorter periods of time. When interest rates are increasing, consider fixing for longer.

How frequently should I make payments?

Mortgage payments can be weekly, fortnightly or monthly. In general, people should match their payment frequency with their income frequency. So, if you are paid weekly, pay your mortgage weekly. If you are paid fortnightly, set up your mortgage payments to be made fortnightly, and so on.

Some people believe a secret saving can be made by making payments weekly or fortnightly versus monthly. Yes, you can pay off your mortgage faster if you make payments fortnightly rather than monthly, because you pay more back to the bank each year by paying fortnightly than monthly (there are 12 months in each year, but 26 fortnights). It stands to reason that, if you pay the mortgage back faster, you will be mortgage-free sooner. The extra fortnightly payments do reduce your debt a bit faster, although saving to pay that extra fortnightly payment can be stressful, and isn't the option I tend to encourage my clients to take.

When working with clients, I place little importance on the frequency of payment, instead focusing on channelling all surplus money into paying off the principal faster (via revolving credit).

Mortgage types that come with a warning

Mortgage offset and revolving-credit mortgages are two valid ways of repaying your mortgage faster. In reality, though, without clarity around your mortgage repayment plan, these types of mortgage encourage any tendency you have to overspend, which ironically derails any promised progress. They do have benefits, but until you learn to master your own money behaviour, and have a clear mortgage repayment plan, their use should come with strong warnings.

Revolving-credit mortgages

Revolving-credit — or *revolting*-credit, as I like to call them — mortgages are a licence for disguised overspending and an increase in your mortgage balance over time. A revolving-credit mortgage is like a giant overdraft that charges interest at the standard floating rate. Banks encourage you to put all your money into the revolving-credit account, then put living costs each month onto your credit card. You pay off the credit card in full each cycle, therefore paying no interest on these purchases. The money you would normally be spending on bills sits in your revolving-credit account until it pays off the credit card at the end of the month, minimising the amount of interest you have to pay on your mortgage. The banks will argue that technically you have saved interest, and this argument is technically true.

But let's dig down a bit. If your average annual living costs (excluding mortgage payments) are $60,000, that means that $5,000 in costs is being charged to a credit card each month, without incurring interest, for up to 60 days. If the $5,000 could remain against your mortgage (temporarily lowering the mortgage balance, so less interest is charged on the balance), then that will save you the interest that would have been charged ($5,000 x 7 per cent interest rate, divided by 12 months). This creates an interest saving of $29 per month. In reality — and the reality is more important than the technicality — you are likely to spend $29 per month more than you realise by the simple fact that you are using your credit card all the time and have no real transparency on your spending.

Most people who have a revolving-credit mortgage do not pay it off within the expected timeframe. Most inadvertently spend more money than they would have otherwise, and lack the transparency to record their progress. The balance on a revolving-credit account, when used in the traditional fashion, tends to fluctuate, which makes measuring your progress nigh on impossible. (The easiest way to gauge progress is to look at your balance today, and the balance exactly 12 months ago. The difference between the two is how much progress — or lack thereof — you have made.)

I have many issues with revolving credit, the biggie being that you can be going backwards, eating into your credit balance and technically sinking financially, but it all seems so painless. It encourages you to be removed from your behaviour, and this is what we need to circumvent. That said, if you can master your money habits and get your savings under control, there is space for revolving credit in your mortgage plan. However, for a revolving-credit mortgage to work successfully, you need clarity. I encourage my clients to use the revolving credit as their 'progress account', where we track their overall progress, see the mortgage reducing and know that we could re-access the funds if an emergency required. But for it to work well, we need to add some friction. So we ditch the credit card – or at the very least, don't have it linked to this account. In fact, try to minimise any transactions that come from your revolving-credit account.

Because this type of mortgage uses a floating rate, the benefit of paying the mortgage down faster without penalty is greater than on a fixed rate. This means people are exposing themselves to a higher interest rate in exchange for the ability to repay debt faster. However, in most instances they aren't actually doing this because they don't have any money left over after they've paid their living costs for the month. In this situation the only one who wins is the bank.

> **Tip:** Pay close attention to your revolving credit — it should be reducing consistently each month. If it isn't, consider restructuring the debt and fixing the mortgage to lower your interest costs to help increase your savings rate.

However, if you can implement a clear money framework and evidence of faster debt repayment, then a revolving-credit mortgage does bring some undisputed advantages.

Its biggest advantage is your ability to re-access any funds you have put against it. For example, if you had a cash surplus of $20,000 you could transfer this against your overdraft balance and be able to access it again the next day if you needed to. With a traditional fixed-term mortgage, if you wanted to make a $20,000 lump-sum payment, you might be faced with break costs. Furthermore, if you needed to re-access the funds the next day because of an emergency, you would typically have to complete another mortgage application to verify to the bank that you were still a good credit risk. This could prove challenging if your curve-ball event was being made redundant from your job.

Obviously this flexibility can work against you if you are not operating within a clear financial framework. However, if you are disciplined, it can allow you to throw everything you have at your mortgage, knowing that if you have a major curve ball, you can easily re-access the funds. (See more on page 177 about using a revolving-credit mortgage to your advantage.)

Offset mortgages

Offset mortgages are another mortgage structure that allows you to save interest on your balances if you have savings sitting with the same bank. The offset savings lower the mortgage balance and you are only charged interest on the reduced balance. For example, if you had a $400,000 mortgage and $100,000 sitting in a savings account, the savings balance would be offset against the mortgage to reduce the mortgage balance to $300,000.

It's a bit odd that with an offset mortgage, you still make the same monthly payment to the bank for the $400,000 loan. The fact you have less interest charged because of your savings balance just means that a greater proportion of the monthly payment is repaying the principal. While this is a positive outcome, in many instances you would benefit more from having the monthly mortgage repayment lowered to reflect the interest saving you have realised.

Offset mortgages, like revolving-credit mortgages, can be used to your advantage, but in most instances they result in a false sense of progress, a lack of transparency and at times a higher overall cost.

Should I break my mortgage?

When interest rates are trending down, the only people who benefit are those on a floating interest rate. If you are unlucky enough to be fixed on a high interest rate when current rates are low, it can be tempting to break your existing contract and take out a new mortgage at today's rate. While this is possible, there is often a penalty to pay for breaking the contract early. Interestingly, break costs only apply if the interest rate is lower than what you are fixed for, not if it is higher.

Break costs are designed to act as a deterrent to breaking your loan early. They aim to neutralise any gain that you might make if you changed from one interest rate to a lower one. The penalty is prepaid to offset any future reductions in interest charged for the remaining term of the initial contract, and is calculated using a fixed formula described in very small print in your mortgage documents. The calculated fee is based on the size of the mortgage being broken and how far the comparative interest rates have fallen since the loan was first fixed, combined with how many months remain until the fixed-interest period was supposed to end.

Although it sounds complicated, the fee roughly equates to $1000 per $100,000 borrowed for every 1 per cent fall in rates, and for every year of its remaining fixed-rate term. So, if interest rates fall by 3 per cent, a customer with a $200,000 mortgage on a five-year fixed rate with two years still to go will face a penalty fee of around $12,000 — ouch!

However, there is one exception to this rule. If you're going to break your contract and pay the penalty, you can still make a financial gain if you are able to contract at a lower rate than that used in the penalty calculation. This can be achieved if you fix for a different term. So, instead of fixing for five years (on which the break cost was first calculated), you fix for a shorter period, like three years if the three-year interest rate is lower than the five-year interest rate. In calculating the penalty, the bank will usually compare your fixed-rate term with today's rate for the *original fixed-rate period*.

For example, if you have a $400,000 mortgage and have fixed your interest rate for five years at 8 per cent, and you are three years into the contract (with two years remaining), the calculations, assuming today's five-year rate is 6 per cent, might look like this:

The difference in the five-year interest rate = 2%
There are two years left to run on the $400,000 loan
$400,000 × 0.02 × two years = $16,000

Interest charged per year on $400,000 loan:

8% = $32,000
6% = $24,000
Annual difference = $8000

So, based on the calculations above, if you were to break your mortgage you would pay $16,000 in break costs. However, each year for the next two years, you would pay $8,000 less in interest costs, so over time you are actually no worse off.

However, nowhere in your bank documents does it say that you have to re-fix your mortgage for the same term if you break your original contract. So if rates were looking favourable on a one-, two- or three-year term you might consider changing the interest term, to save more over the next two years.

For example, say the rate for a three-year term was only 5 per cent. The penalty for breaking your contract remains $16,000. But, if your new mortgage is fixed at 5 per cent for three years, your interest charge would be $20,000 per annum (compared to the $32,000 it was originally, at 8 per cent). So you will save $12,000 a year over the next two years. Overall, you would gain from breaking your original mortgage. Yes, it will cost you $16,000 initially, but you will save $24,000 in interest costs over the next two years, putting you $6000 in the black overall.

> Remember, although the bank uses the equivalent fixed-term rate to calculate the break cost, you are not obliged to re-fix for the same term at the lower rate. Financial gains can be made if you re-fix at a lower rate than was used to calculate the penalty, or if you go to a floating rate that is less than the rate you were fixed on. You can also break your mortgage and keep it on the floating rate, and wait out further reductions in the official cash rate (OCR), before refixing. This will cap the break cost but allow your interest savings to be higher again.

Generally, banks do not charge break costs if you are breaking a contract to go onto a higher rate by comparison. But this may also be a way to make savings. For example, if you were fixed for five years at 7 per cent and today's five-year rate was 8 per cent, but the two-year rate was 5 per cent, you could break your contract and not be charged a penalty (as the bank will compare the same-term fixed rate), and then fix for two years at 5%, making a saving.

Remember that if you are going to break your mortgage you will be required to pay the break cost up front, either with cash or by increasing your mortgage balance by the amount of the break cost. The interest saving is earned over time, so there is a delay in the benefit that will be derived.

No one is immune to high interest rates

At some point during your mortgage, interest rates are going to be high and you are likely to struggle to keep up with the payments. Those unlucky enough to have had a mortgage in the mid- to late 1980s will remember the crippling interest rates in excess of 20 per cent. If your fixed-rate loan expires when the market is offering high rates, you might not have the option of floating your mortgage and waiting for lower average rates to emerge.

I am not necessarily suggesting rates will go as high as 20 per cent, but in the years preceding the GFC fixed rates were in excess of 10 per cent and floating rates hit 12 per cent. Many people could not afford the option of floating their mortgages and exposing themselves to higher rates, especially when the word on the street was that the floating rates were not likely to come down anytime soon. They had no option but to fix, so as to gain what little respite they could from the slightly lower fixed interest rates.

The impact of this decision affected people well after the GFC ended. I had clients who were fixed for five years at a rate in excess of 8.75 per cent, because this was the only rate they could afford at the time. They didn't have the option of breaking their loans to enjoy the floating rates and lower repayments, as they did not have enough equity to pay the break cost. What soon followed was rate drop after rate drop all the way down to historically low lending rates (prior to Covid). While the rest of us enjoyed these low interest rates, they had to ride out the storm of unfortunate timing.

Refinancing your mortgage

There are times when you can get a better mortgage deal at a different bank. Perhaps it's because mortgage rates differ between banks, the equity in your property has increased, or your income or your type of property is recognised more favourably at a different bank. Whatever the reason, you can make clear, tangible and persuasive financial gains when refinancing for the right reasons.

It makes sense to refinance your mortgage if your bank is not assisting you — for example, if interest rates are lower at a different bank and the cost of penalties to change banks is less than the future interest saving, or if your bank is not prepared to consolidate debt and as a result you are paying a higher average interest rate, or move you onto interest-only terms if your situation requires it. Note, too, that some banks offer special interest-rate discounts to people working in certain industries (such as government employees) or organisations, or conversely might increase interest rates if you have low equity.

I know a lot of people do not like their bank, but most banks are the same. It's worth shopping around from time to time, but don't expect to get radically improved service by going to another bank — this is seldom the case.

> **Tip:** Check with your HR department to find out if your employer has a special relationship with a bank which you might be able to capitalise on.

My mortgage story

My husband and I purchased our first property for $350,000 in the early 2000s. It was a two-bedroom townhouse, and we needed a mortgage of $300,000. The interest rate was 8 per cent, so we were going to be paying back just under three times what we'd borrowed over the 30 years of the mortgage — including $490,000 in interest.

We knew we needed to get on the property ladder, and although the mortgage payments were slightly higher than our rent at the time I could see the merit in owning property. I also understood that I couldn't own property without the bank's investment, but $490,000 seemed a lot to pay for the privilege of being loaned the money. Some 15 years on, that same property is now worth $800,000.

Each year our repayments paid off more and more of the principal, but initially the slow rate of principal reduction can be demoralising. This is emphasised by the annual letter from the bank confirming how much you have paid over the previous 12 months, and how little your mortgage has reduced. For example, after the first 12 months of our mortgage we had repaid $26,000 to the bank, yet the principal had reduced by only $2,300. Talk about depressing!

I always assumed that in year 15 — the halfway point in the life of our 30-year mortgage — our monthly repayments would be evenly split between paying interest and paying off the principal. But this was not the case. *For a 30-year mortgage, you only start paying more principal than interest, within your monthly payment, from year 24.* Using this example, we would pay the bank $565,000 over the first 24 years of our mortgage, but our principal balance would only reduce by $138,000.

I wanted to pay my mortgage off faster, but I didn't want to commit to a shorter term, as I couldn't guarantee that we'd be able to afford the increased repayments indefinitely, and nor did I want my mortgage dictating the lifestyle I wanted to live. I still wanted to take a holiday every year, and replace my car. I also knew I wanted a family at some point. The prospect of going down to one income for a time definitely meant we couldn't afford fixed higher repayments. I wanted flexibility but I wasn't sure how to get this without paying yet more money to the bank. This conundrum made me want to understand how mortgages worked. But because no one spoke about money honestly or openly, it was hard to get a sense of whether I was the only one experiencing this frustration. I couldn't understand why financial advisors failed to give actual financial advice, unless they were selling a product, and the financial advice they gave seemed to be conflicted because they were selling a product. It also became clear that I was less likely to achieve financial success simply because I was earning good money, which was pretty much the opposite of what we are taught growing up. We are told to live within our means, which I was kind of doing (although not particularly well), but it still wasn't enough. So then what?

It was in looking behind the curtain, and learning the rules of the game, that I got a sense of how stacked the system is in favour of the banks and financial institutions. I wanted to share what I'd learnt with people and show them the path forward that can work for them no matter where they are starting from. This eventually took the form of enable.me — financial personal trainers.

16. Kill your mortgage!

I try to get my clients mortgage-free in under 10 years. Faster if I can, but 10 years is my starting point. For my impatient, ambitious or older clients, 10 years may still be too long, so wherever possible I want to accompany the mortgage strategy with a wealth-creation strategy that achieves faster results.

Let's start with your mortgage-repayment strategy. Here are the five things that will make the most impact to getting mortgage-free fast.

Maximise your cash surplus	Understand your repayment capability	Structure your mortgage for your capability	Have targets that are measured and adjusted quarterly	Build momentum

Maximise your cash surplus

The amount of money you have 'left over' is your engine room to progress. Take time to remove all inefficiencies, so you can save faster. The faster you save, the faster you can pay down your debt. Chapter 3 is your starting point for how to maximise your cash surplus.

Understand your repayment capability

Your repayment capability will depend on your annual household income and debt levels (this is called your income:debt ratio). This capability assessment provides the benchmark for how quickly you could get mortgage-free if you were to adopt my repayment methodology.

Income:debt ratio — how quickly could you repay your mortgage?

1:4   8 years
1:5   10–12 years
1:6   think about downsizing your property
1:7   buy an investment property instead of a home

If your household income is $150,000, and your mortgage is $570,000, your income:debt ratio would be 3.8 ($570,000/$150,000), and my starting point would be to get you mortgage-free in a little under eight years. We then have to overlay the nuances of your situation, which might push the target out slightly, or bring it in. These nuances will set the pace at which you will repay the mortgage, and when you'll hit key milestones. These milestones impact the way we need to structure the mortgage.

It's crucial to get this part right. The timing of your income and expenses will help us set mini-goals to support bigger milestones. We'll then track your performance against these mini-goals, because seeing progress against targets is how you'll lift and shift your mindset. Stacked achievements help you believe you can keep going. Belief coupled with a strong mindset is key for the next phase, because a five- or 10-year plan is still a long time for you to fend off complacency.

> Complacency is the cousin of fritter.

Whenever you attack any big goal, in any area of life, you have to believe the outcome is possible otherwise you will sabotage your effort right from the get-go. So if you want to invest in your financial future, go to a financial advisor who can assess your capability and have them show you what you could achieve if you had the right structure, methodology and support.

Structure your mortgage for your capability

Back to the example above: if we can get you mortgage-free in eight years, this becomes your big financial goal. To achieve this goal we then work out how to structure the mortgage, repay it and measure progress. If we do this right, we pick up momentum. Forward momentum is one of your greatest financial assets.

The power of calculus

Dr Jamie Sneddon, from the University of Auckland, helped me to understand the maths behind how banks structure debt, and how I needed to restructure my mortgage to repay it as fast as my situation would allow, while living a lifestyle I could enjoy.

Jamie and I (mainly him, to be fair) used algebra and calculus to determine the exact amount of debt each person should have floating and fixed to ensure the fastest repayment of debt and the corresponding maximum interest saving. The formula takes into account things like the nuances of a client's situation, current interest rates, one-off costs and the amount of cash surplus to determine the 'how' of debt repayment.

This patented formula, which is eight pages long, makes one key assumption: *that you actually have money left over at the end of the week, month or year after paying any one-off costs — for example, holidays or car replacements — and that these surplus funds can be channelled into repaying debt faster.* It doesn't assume that you will save evenly over the course of the year, because that is unlikely, even for the best of us — but that overall you will in fact save your targeted amount.

At the time I didn't have a cash surplus — credit cards were my buffer for random, one-off costs and there were times when I couldn't repay my credit card in full. As it turned out, my husband and I were frittering away close to $20,000 every year, and spending more as our incomes increased. I don't know exactly where all the money went but I do own a lot of shoes!

Once we had a general idea of where our money was going we found $20,000 we could save — and therefore channel into our mortgage — without affecting our happiness and lifestyle, and without relying on a juicy pay rise or bonus. We found that we could be mortgage-free in nine years and save $368,000 in interest costs. (In actual fact, we repaid our mortgage even faster than that because of pay rises and because we picked up momentum.)

The graph opposite shows our initial mortgage balance of $300,000 and the speed at which it was reducing. If we had stuck to the standard bank repayments, you can see we would have been mortgage-free in 30 years. Channelling our new-found surplus of $20,000 per annum into our mortgage repayment, we were able to reduce the term to just nine years.

Repaying your mortgage as fast as your lifestyle allows is usually the best strategy to grow wealth because you are creating an interest saving by becoming mortgage-free faster. Once mortgage-free, you are then able to save more, because as you are no longer making mortgage payments, there is more money left over. So, there is an interest cost saving (roughly the size of your mortgage in interest savings), as well as being able to physically save more. A double winner. You can then land the hat-trick if you use the equity you have created, by paying off the mortgage faster, to grow your wealth, usually in the form of an investment property.

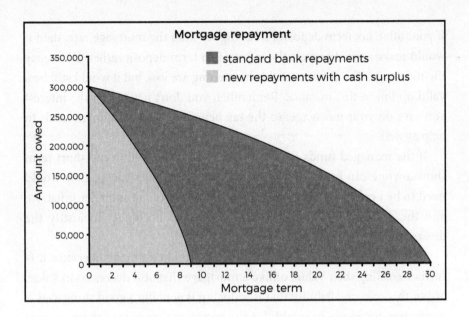

I am often asked if it makes more sense to repay debt or to save and invest the money into something else. It's a good question that should be asked more often. Like any good question, the answer will depend on your situation, but as a rough rule of thumb I apply the following assumptions and logic:

- You are not aligned to any product or investment product.
- You want the money to work as hard as possible for you.
- You want the return to be as certain and consistent as possible.
- You don't want to lose your money.

You need to compare the investments fairly, by reflecting inflation and tax.

Against these assumptions, you then go for the investment that will make your money work the hardest, at the lowest risk in the short term (or greatest certainty). This list below isn't exhaustive, but it gives you a guide.

Investment type	Before-tax return	After-tax return at 30% tax rate	Less inflation at 4%	Certainty/consistency of return in short term
Term deposit	5%	3.5%	-0.5%	High
Mortgage	7%	7%	7%	High
Managed fund	6%	4.2%	0.2%	Low-medium
Shares	10%	7%	3%	Low

If your after-tax term deposit rate is higher than the mortgage rate, then it would make sense to invest the money in a term deposit rather than repay the mortgage. The chances of this happening are low, but it would still be a valid option in this instance. Remember, you don't pay tax on the interest you save on your mortgage, so the tax benefit of debt repayment tends to help as well.

If the managed funds or shares are performing well in the short term (how anyone can know this ahead of time is anyone's guess), they would need to be performing at a much higher rate before tax and after inflation, and the certainty of the return would need to be higher to justify the diversification.

Inflation should also be deducted from the investments, because it is further eroding their value, unlike a mortgage that also decreases in value, but in this case any liability that is reducing is actually a good thing as it is creating more equity or wealth for the owner as the value of the mortgage is going down in today's dollars.

Because of the after-tax and inflation comparisons, repaying your mortgage debt will usually emerge as the best performing strategy. The exceptions to this are if the mortgage rate is super low (say 2 per cent), where you could get your money working harder if you invested it in another asset class, or if your employer was incentivising you to invest in an employee share scheme or a preferential superannuation scheme. In this case, if your increased contributions are matched by the employer, then this is in effect a 100 per cent return on your money. This will usually be better than repaying your mortgage faster, provided you can afford the increased cash payments that the scheme might require.

In another example, if you had a guaranteed risk-free return on an investment or term deposit of 12 per cent gross — 7 per cent after tax (excluding inflation) — then saving would be a valid substitute to repaying debt. However, it is unlikely such an investment exists (with the exception of KiwiSaver), and if it did it would be unlikely that the return would be no-risk and guaranteed. This means that debt repayment is nearly always the preferred choice.

The key, though, is *not to force money towards your mortgage*. Instead, live a lifestyle you enjoy, understand the rhythm by which you can spend and save, and then capture the money left over and channel any surplus towards the mortgage. If you do it correctly you won't feel like you're on a budget. Yes, you will be more conscious of your spending, but it won't feel too tight. Basic psychology suggests that if it feels effortless, and you are seeing results, then this is when you'll get into a sense of flow and your plan will become sustainable. If you don't have a sustainable cash surplus, then all your energy needs to be channelled into fixing this first.

In this example, not only would we be debt-free in a minimum of nine years, but we would also have saved a lot of money that would otherwise have been paid to the bank. Our fixed outgoings also drastically reduce (often up to 50 per cent) when we became debt-free. Once this happens, saving and investing for retirement of course become easier, without mortgage repayments being a barrier to getting ahead.

This assumes you don't have any lifestyle creep emerging once you have repaid your mortgage. Too many of my mortgage-free clients failed to then save at the same rate they were paying off their mortgage. This was partly because they found it easier to pay off debt than save (a common characteristic for spenders), and partly to do with the psychology of achieving one goal, so now they feel they can relax.

Now is the time to do some honest reflection. Do you save? If you don't, then you are going to benefit from targeted one-on-one assistance to diagnose what you are capable of, because it won't be clear to you based on your progress to date.

Structuring your mortgage

The bank's default mortgage term is usually 25 or 30 years. In a perfect world, you should set the term to the longest allowed, aiming to be mortgage-free by retirement. For example, if you are aged 35, you should get a 30-year mortgage. If you are 55, ideally your mortgage should have no more than 10 years remaining.

This is where ideology and reality meet. We know that only 40 per cent of Kiwis are on track to be mortgage-free by retirement. So yes, for 40 per cent of us, shortening the mortgage term could happen without causing much inconvenience. But for the majority, shortening the mortgage term (which means increasing your repayments) would be the fastest way for you to default on your mortgage, which doesn't serve you at all.

If you know you're not on track to be mortgage-free by retirement, or you want to have more than a mortgage-free home in retirement, then you're going to have to grow wealth in addition to attempting to pay the mortgage off faster. If it's then determined, usually by the size of your retirement savings gap, that buying an investment property is the best way for you to grow wealth, then how you structure your mortgage becomes more important than ever. In many instances you'll need to extend your fixed term to lower your fixed repayments, to allow you to borrow more money to buy the investment property. This strategy is not without risk, so needs to be planned carefully and executed clinically to give you the best of both worlds.

Your objective should always be to repay the mortgage at a faster pace than the default fixed term with the bank, but you want this to be at your discretion, not the bank's. The problem with locking in a shortened term with the bank is that you are obliged to make the (higher) repayments consistently, and should you fail or default on a payment — even with legitimate reasons — you will have to pay default fees and get poor account conduct on your record (which could work against you if you want to refinance); worse, you could be deemed to have broken your mortgage agreement, which might incur a break fee. Worse still, you impair your ability to borrow for an investment property in the future.

Even if I believe a client could be mortgage-free within a five-year period, the journey is seldom smooth. In fact, if I were to drill down on their five-year target, it would have ups and downs each month and each quarter. This might all come out in the wash and not compromise the five-year objective, but it does highlight the difficulty in guaranteeing a smooth repayment. Volatility is one of the main reasons people don't achieve their potential — because they fail to get an accurate read on their progress, such as mistaking timing gains as being ahead of schedule, and faltering when they haven't made progress even when their effort hasn't waned. This volatility exists before life throws you the curve balls that could really derail your plan to get ahead.

Volatility in spending and income patterns, and life's unexpected curve balls, require us to have flexibility and financial resilience. This sits in your ability to re-access your savings and being able to hold your line, even if a Mack Truck event tries to push you over. If you really get into financial trouble, it's on you to have enough resilience to get through it. This is where your mortgage structure can help.

A client's operational cashflow (normal living costs) plus their one-off costs affect their ability to repay debt and the rate of debt repayment. When determining how to structure a client's mortgage, I break it down into yearly chunks. Within each chunk I set quarterly and monthly goals. The objective is for the client to repay the chunk of debt as quickly as possible while still living to their financial plan and maintaining the lifestyle they want. I tend to place a portion of their debt on a revolving-credit mortgage, a chunk fixed for one year, another for two years and so on up to three or sometimes five years.

I use a revolving-credit facility because it provides flexibility (which improves resilience), a floating interest rate (which tends to be a bit higher than a fixed rate — not so good), the ability to repay debt without penalty (good), but a whole lot of temptation (not so good). I want to take the good from this type of mortgage, but ring-fence the bad. The easiest way to do this is to use it as an account against which you can measure your overall progress by repaying the overdraft, but you can't have EFTPOS or credit-card access to this account.

Remember a floating rate is usually higher than a fixed rate — so if we are going to have a portion of the mortgage on a floating rate, we need to be sure that we will save more than it is going to cost us to have this type of mortgage. If the benefit doesn't outweigh the cost, then we wouldn't have a portion of the mortgage on a floating rate. I measure progress against targets every 12 weeks, and reset the target for the next 12 weeks based on the expected timing of when income and expenses could hit.

I cannot stress enough how crucial it is to measure and reset the spending plan to ensure progress is being achieved at the pace you need to achieve the results you want.

Here's the thing about a floating mortgage: if you are systematically repaying it over the year, the interest is charged on the reducing balance. While the rate is the same, because it is being applied to a reducing balance, the interest cost is reducing with each payment. If you add up the interest charged for the year (on the reducing balance), then the effective interest rate is usually about 50 per cent of the floating interest rate. The key is to consistently reduce this balance to ensure your effective interest rate is lower than the advertised floating rate. I normally give my clients 12 weeks to get the results. If we haven't seen results, then I will be looking to restructure the debt, removing the floating portion of the mortgage.

Have targets that are measured and adjusted quarterly

Once you have the structure right, you need to determine the speed of progress, and set mini-goals to track your performance against.

Understanding the timing of your income and expenses for the year, quarter and month will tell you how quickly you can make progress during that period. Before you set any money goal, you have to understand where you are at in your money cycle. Progress is about both keeping your head down (working hard) and your head up (paying attention). Progress is about focus, not frenzy. You have to know what you need to hit and then check you are still heading in the right direction by regular accountability sessions.

Build momentum

As you stack your wins, this magical thing happens: you start to build momentum. This is when your effort remains constant, but the progress stretches further each time. As you stick to the plan, it gets easier. You get fitter and go faster. As you pay down the mortgage, your mortgage balance drops and the payments reduce, which allows you to save more to pay off the debt even faster. The system is finally working to propel you forward.

This is when a coach is invaluable and often is the difference in you achieving your goal, and doing it well. Last year my husband and I watched a funny, inspiring movie called *Brittany Runs a Marathon*. It was about an unfit, out-of-shape woman who trained and ran a marathon. Afterwards I looked over at my husband and asked if he wanted to run one too. He said, 'Why not?' Five minutes later we were registered to run the New York Marathon.

One minute after that, I googled 'from coach potato to marathon runner'. The internet served me up a plan to get me marathon-ready. I started with a hiss and a roar. Well not really — I could only run for one minute — but I was committed. I stuck with the plan for a good six weeks and reached 20 minutes of running, then I missed a session because of bad weather. Then I missed two, and before I knew it I hadn't run for a fortnight. I then bought a book about women running marathons, because apparently we run differently and have different challenges to men. This felt like a comfortable reason for falling off the wagon, but now I was off on the right plan for me. Much like I had with my internet plan, I started with a hiss and a roar, then I petered out. I got further than before, but there was still a gap between where I was and what was needed to run a marathon. This is when I got my running coach. They designed a plan for me. Each week they would check in; some weeks I'd done well, others I hadn't. But they kept me going. They didn't let me quit, they kept shuffling me forward. My plan was tailored for me, and was different to my husband's.

Having a running coach gave me structure, accountability, support and quick resets so that I never drifted or dropped anchor. Sometimes it was difficult, but they kept me going. The same is said for a leadership coach, a nutritionist, a lifestyle coach or a financial personal trainer.

Invest in yourself and surround yourself with the right people to help you lift to your capability. If you want to sustain this lift for however long it takes, then your support system will be more important than ever.

And yes, I did run the marathon. And yes, I crushed it.

How long will it take to kill your mortgage?

When I work with my clients, I determine what their financial capability is with regards to mortgage repayment. I then break this down to quarterly and annual mortgage-repayment goals. I then measure their progress against the set goals, keeping them accountable to their goals and capability. As a minimum, my goal is to have my clients on track to be mortgage-free in 10 years. I illustrate four clients' scenarios in the following pages. These examples focus on paying down a mortgage before growing wealth, but most of my clients actually pay down the mortgage and grow wealth at the same time. I talk about this in Part Three of this book.

Case study 1

A married couple, both in their mid-forties. They had a mortgage of $375,000 that had not significantly reduced in five years despite their incomes increasing; in fact, their mortgage had increased through mortgage top-ups. These clients were sick of making no progress, despite having a combined income of just over $120,000. The husband had just been promoted at work and had received a $20,000 pay rise that they were scared was going to be frittered away unless they took some constructive steps to do things differently. They described themselves as spenders and had previously been going backwards, but they never really felt like they were sinking because they had access to credit cards and, if times got too challenging, they would top up their mortgage to right all wrongs. Their non-negotiables were upgrading their car and going on a family holiday to Europe in two years.

My initial projections suggested they could be mortgage-free in nine years, saving around $388,000 in interest. This assumed that their projected cash surplus of around $29,000 was real — and we could capture it before they inadvertently spent it.

At the time of writing, these clients are currently nine months into their first year and $500 ahead of schedule. They are excited to be making the progress on the following graph real.

Each year their progress will be more dramatic, as the interest they were once being charged on the principal that has now been repaid will increase their cash surplus and allow them to pay off even more debt the next year, and so forth. For example, if they paid off $100,000, they would save $6,000 in interest costs each year. Without having to pay out this money, or put in any more savings effort, their surplus will become $6,000 higher, allowing them to pay off even more principal the following year.

All things running smoothly, they should be mortgage-free by their early fifties, therefore allowing them 11 years of saving for retirement without having a mortgage to pay off. Initial analysis suggests that they should be able to save in excess of $550,000 in the 11 years between being mortgage-free and retiring. On the assumption that they can reduce their lifestyle costs by around $5,000 per annum in retirement, they could fund their lifestyle until age 89. Of course, how they invest their retirement savings is the next piece of the puzzle to work through — but as a starter, knowing they are on track to be mortgage-free by retirement is key.

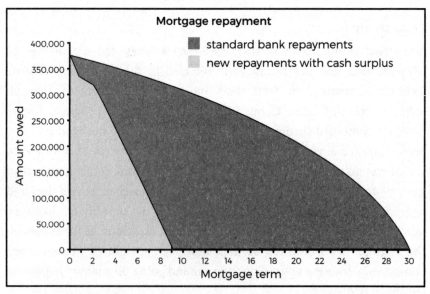

Case study 2

A self-employed couple in their mid-forties with a higher mortgage and higher disposable income than the couple in case study 1. They had a mortgage of $550,000 and a combined income exceeding $200,000, with a strong cash position. Their businesses were very profitable but they spent this money 'living the dream'. In fact, they frittered away $80,000 per annum!

They seemed to be more focused on putting as many personal costs through their business as possible to increase tax deductions than they were on determining if the expenses were necessary in the first place. This meant that they frittered away money both personally and in the business. There was no clarity around what they were capable of, what they needed to do and, perhaps most importantly, whether the result would be compelling enough to get them to try.

If they were ready to work to a tighter framework and be accountable for their spending, I believed we could structure their debt better, save more in tax and, most importantly, capture the money that was being frittered. The combination of these forces showed their mortgage could be paid off in a little over four years.

These clients are now three years into their programme. They have recently become mortgage-free — 15 months ahead of schedule.

The power of clarity, transparency and accountability came into play for them to fast-track their success. But their plan doesn't stop there. The next stage is using the next 15 years to sort out their retirement and, if we do a good job, to also give them the option of retiring early.

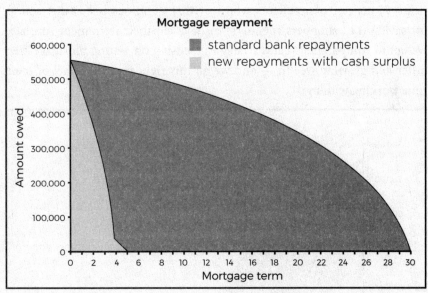

Case study 3

A single lady in her early fifties, earning $75,000. She had a mortgage of around $275,000 and no clear strategy for retirement, but appreciated that the first necessary step was to spend less and pay off her mortgage faster. She had probably known for some time that she needed to do something, but in her own words she had only recently found herself 'ready to do something'.

When I first met this client she had no history of saving. She wasn't a shopper per se, but more a mindless spender. She succumbed to a general lack of direction and had no plan of attack. She admitted that she didn't think she earned enough to make any real inroads on her mortgage, which was strange — she earned plenty, but she just spent it all. I determined that if I could find the money that she was frittering and get her excited about what was possible, we should be able to restructure her mortgage so she could be mortgage-free in seven years, instead of 15, saving her $88,000 in interest. Most importantly, though, she would have eight extra years to save for her retirement without mortgage payments.

This client is now 18 months into her plan and $2,500 ahead of schedule. This progress was made by an unexpected pay rise and a delay in replacing her car.

Crucially, we now know that she can stick to the plan to make this level of mortgage repayment work — which means we will be able to run retirement wealth strategies alongside her mortgage-repayment goals. For nearly 75 per cent of my clients, who are either ambitious, need a distraction for saving (i.e., shoppers/spenders) or have left their retirement run late, we opt to run parallel wealth strategies focusing on getting mortgage-free faster *and* growing wealth — and we do this right from the start of their time working with me.

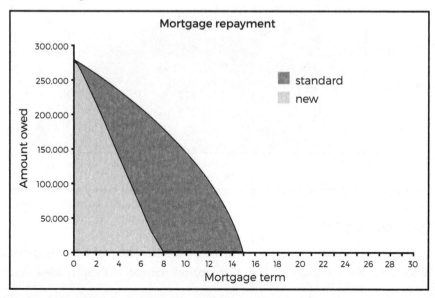

Case study 4

Tom and Donald were both 43 years old when they first came to me. Tom was a company director and Donald was a teacher. Their annual combined income from salaries was $200,000, and their total debt was $550,000. They owned their home and two investment properties — but one of those properties was leaky.

They were running two separate 'money lives': Tom was more of a saver and Donald was more of a 'save up to buy' personality. Donald would save hard, but always with the intention of eventually spending all his savings. Things had become quite tense in their relationship because of money issues — they never seemed to have quite enough and were starting to resent their mortgage mountain.

They understood they needed money to reach their goals in life, but they didn't understand how to use money well. They had read all the get-rich-quick and invest-in-property books and dived into buying their first rental property back in 2000. They felt they were doing the right thing but there was never enough money to get on top of the large mortgage, household costs and credit-card bills. Even though they were experiencing high levels of financial stress, they bought their own home in their early thirties, but found they still could not get ahead. They were asset-rich, but they were paying interest-only on all their mortgages and felt the assets weren't really theirs — they were owned by the bank.

They received a reality check a few years later when they discovered the first rental property they had bought was a leaky building. The repair bill could have been as much as $150,000 and would need to be paid over the next five years. Who would lend them that money? How could they afford to pay interest on an even larger mortgage? Was this a sign they should sell the property? They had also just lost some savings in a failed investment, so they were pretty jittery, and their money issues were causing them more stress than ever. This is when they called me. I worked through a plan and discussed the implications with them.

Essentially, they were spending too much on their day-to-day costs, while not doing everything they could to minimise their tax liability and maximise their savings rate. They were 'comfortably inefficient'. They had no cohesion in their finances or financial goals. They had been frittering away a lot of money — over $40,000 per annum.

Initially they had $550,000 of debt that was going to take them at least 30 years to repay. (I say 'at least 30 years', as the mortgages were interest only, which suggests they were never going to be repaid.) They felt that they were struggling to keep up with their current mortgage repayments, so the likelihood of paying off their mortgage faster was not viable until there was money left over.

My first projections, which assumed we would get in control of the money and restructure their mortgage quickly, suggested they could repay all their debt in less than eight years, even after factoring in holidays and car replacements. A key part of optimising their financial position involved the following steps:

- They allowed me to restructure and optimise their mortgage.
- They would have only one credit card and use this primarily for bill payments.
- If they used the credit card for non-bill payments, then it needed to be repaid within 24 hours of its use – keeping it at a zero balance.
- They would only ever use cash/EFTPOS for their most frequent costs (food and fuel).
- They would know their saving target for the next 90 days. They would write this down and pop it on the fridge.
- They would track their spending weekly, and on a set day determine how they had gone for the week. They would need to take 15 minutes to reflect on their savings rate for the week, upcoming expenses and mortgage payments.
- They would have an accountability meeting with me every 12 weeks to make sure they were keeping to the baseline momentum (hitting savings, spending and mortgage repayment targets) needed to get them mortgage-free in their projected timeframe.
- If curve ball or opportunity occurred, they had to contact me within 48 hours. This served two points. Firstly, when something has gone wrong, knowing you can offload to someone is really important and allows you to keep your head in the game. Knowing that the curve ball will impact their savings rate allows me to reset the plan and to adjust targets immediately. This allows the client to know that whatever they are aiming for is still achievable and strengthens their mindset.
- They allowed me to optimise their KiwiSaver contributions and investment.
- They allowed me to review and structure their affairs for tax efficiencies.

After 18 months, they had cleared their hire-purchase debt, cleared their credit-card debt and paid $155,000 principal off their mortgage. Most of the accelerated mortgage repayments were the result of new savings they had accrued by sticking to their new budget programme, coupled with a slightly improved tax position and some pay rises. Money was now left over at the end of the week, and that surplus, although quite small to start with, consistently built over the course of time and was systematically applied to the mortgage.

Together Tom and Donald have changed the way they use and manage their money. Not only are their finances in better shape, but their money behaviours have improved and their money mindsets are stronger. They have affordable life insurance and a day-to-day budget, plus their bills are all budgeted for and paid automatically each month.

It gets even better. In the past five years they have enjoyed many overseas trips — one to California, one to Europe and too many to count to Hawai'i — all budgeted and paid for as they went. They still can't quite believe how they did this with so little money stress! And their leaky home is now being fixed.

Most importantly, they are ahead of their scheduled progress, which means they are on track to repay the mortgage 18 months sooner than the eight years initially projected. It is one thing to project an outcome — it is quite another to monitor progress and be accountable to achieving the projection. I still meet with them every 12 weeks to refine their plan, make allowances for new expenses and keep them motivated and on track.

They were initially nervous about giving up their freedom to spend money how and when they wanted. Now that they have learned how to create a budget and stick to it, they have also discovered that the key to killing a mortgage is to fast-track how you pay off the principal. The interest rate is a cost for having the mortgage but, to be honest, the actual interest rate you are paying is not that important. It is more important how quickly you can pay off the principal.

Tom and Donald are no longer afraid of money or its impact on their relationship. They still love to spend but they factor this into their plan, so there is no guilt attached. Money is no longer a key issue in their relationship and they no longer run separate money lives. They actually work better together as a couple now with a set budget and defined money goals.

Tip: Reducing debt as fast as possible is one of the most effective ways to reduce stress. Above all, it allows you more choice about how you live your life.

If you want to reduce your mortgage faster than your mortgage plan suggests you could, then you will have to accompany your mortgage plan with a wealth creation strategy. In Tom and Donald's situation, if they had asked me to get them mortgage-free in five years (rather than seven), I would need to have created another $100,000 in five years (outside of their improved saving rate and mortgage reduction plan) that could be cashed in and applied to the mortgage, so they could be mortgage-free. Creating wealth while paying off your mortgage is possible and often a great idea if done correctly.

Once you have got the basics right, and your foundation is strong, then your wealth strategy, which is when the money starts to work harder, is the rocket fuel needed for lift-off.

PART THREE

Wealth creation

17. Wealth-creation options

Growing wealth gives you options. For most, wealth brings a sense of freedom: freedom to retire at 65 or earlier, to help your kids onto the property ladder sooner, or to be able to live in your home for longer without downsizing. All of which brings a feeling of security.

Most Kiwis aren't on track to be mortgage-free by retirement. Practically, even their best savings efforts will not create enough savings to give them the retirement they want. Most people are going to need to grow wealth, in addition to managing their money better.

If you are going to grow wealth, big questions immediately follow. Before thinking about the wealth-creation options available to you, you need to understand how much wealth you need to create, and by when. Knowing this will naturally rule out some investment strategies that just can't deliver what you need.

My number one rule with financial planning (and life generally, if I'm being honest) is that if we're going to put effort into solving a problem, we need to be clear on what the problem is (how big it is) and how long we have to solve it (when it needs to give us the payback). If you aren't managing your money well, and if your mortgage is taking too long to pay off, then your problem is going to be bigger than if everything was as efficient as possible. So before calculating the size of your retirement gap, first get everything as lean as possible, otherwise you will overstate the problem. I take my time with clients to determine if we can reduce the size of the problem by managing money better, and getting mortgage-free faster, as these things are largely within our control.

Remember, wealth creation works differently depending on where you are at in your financial journey. If we need to grow wealth, because we have a savings gap, then we are going to focus on leverage. If we have a short runway then we are going to focus on liquidity; and if we have enough assets to see us right, then we will focus on diversifying the asset base to hold value. Each stage has a different objective, and a different strategy to support that objective. You must get clear on your objective before you can determine the right strategy to apply.

Reducing the size of the problem

If you're not on track to kill your mortgage by retirement, you need to determine whether you could earn more money, either by negotiating a pay rise, developing a business or taking on extra work — or, if none of these options are viable, you *must* spend less. If spending less isn't possible because your budget is already at austerity levels, you need to consider whether you can downsize your home, or if you can leverage off (borrow against) the equity in your property to buy another property. Those are your only options. Some people need to do all three.

If you are on track to be mortgage-free, but you fail to save or do not save enough for your retirement, then the same three options apply to you. For the majority of Kiwis in this position, earning more won't seem viable, and spending less will feel restrictive, which means they are left with being able to leverage against their property.

If your retirement savings gap is more than $300,000, then you're going to need to use leverage to help close it. You'll need to use the equity in your home, or available cash, as a deposit for another investment property. The bank could lend you up to 100 per cent of this next property's value — and miraculously you will keep all of the gain (or loss) attached to this property. The challenge is to be able to hold the property long enough to get the likely gain. This means you have to hold the property for a full economic cycle (up to 10 years), and there will usually be at least one recession within the cycle. To be able to hold the property, you will rent it out. The rent you receive will cover a lot of the expenses (interest and so on), but it is unlikely to cover all of them, so you'll need to be able to fund the weekly shortfall.

When you buy a property, you want it to give you the most probable gain, as quickly as possible and at the lowest holding cost. In this regard, not all properties are created equal. I take a hard line on which properties will work and which won't, because we often have one shot at getting this right. But if we can get all three points, then we hit the trifecta. We also have to then balance the property-acquisition strategy with an aggressive holding strategy. There's no point buying well if you can't afford to hold the property for long enough to get the gain. Most people don't get the first step right (setting the right criteria), and almost all fail to de-risk the investment with an actionable hold strategy.

For example, let's say you are 55. You have a mortgage and you are on track to have it repaid in 15 years. This assumes that you are working for the next 15 years (until 70), which might be a stretch, but let's stick with this assumption for now. Even if you did work until 70 to get mortgage-free, once you are mortgage-free you could live off your KiwiSaver for a bit, but it will likely only cover you for the first few years of retirement. So as it stands, you could probably fund yourself until 75 and then you'll have no money. If we wanted to have enough savings to last until age 90, then we would need a whole lot more money.

Before you panic, we can get a clear plan of attack on how we can repay your mortgage faster. Let's say we can get you mortgage-free by 62. This gives you three years of saving for retirement without a mortgage, and the ability to retire at 65. With three years of accumulated savings, together with your KiwiSaver, we can fund your lifestyle until you are aged 78, say. Let's assume that the gap between ages 78 and 90 is $350,000. Under this scenario the problem we need to solve is getting you mortgage-free by 62 and simultaneously building $350,000 of wealth. We don't need to access the extra wealth for a while, probably around age 70 (so another 15 years), but it would be great if we could see it when we retire, which is 10 years away. Therefore, the problem for this client is to find/build/grow $350,000 of wealth, in addition to getting mortgage-free, within the next 10 years.

While I discuss all investment options in the following pages, the lion's share of the more traditional investments (shares, managed funds, etc.) are not usually appropriate while you're still trying to kill your mortgage. As my grandmother says, there is a time and a place for everything. This is also true for the types of investment you hold at different stages of your life.

Objective	Wealth strategy	Ease of entry
Grow wealth	Residential investment property using leverage (a mortgage)	Normally need access to a minimum of $50,000 of savings/equity
Liquidity	Non-property assets, which includes managed funds, shares and savings	No minimum investment
Diversify	Property and non-property assets. Property assets might not need a mortgage, and could extend to include commercial property	

A leveraged property typically outperforms all other investments by a minimum of 250 per cent over a 10-year period. But it's not the property itself that's amazing, it's the effects of leverage that make it such a great investment — and that you can benefit even if you have no savings to invest.

Levels of risk

Before you jump in and buy any old property, let's make sure you aren't sleepwalking towards a lemon investment. We start by determining the problem we need to solve, and then get clear on the property criteria needed to solve it.

There's no such thing as no risk when it comes to investing your money. It's said that investing at a conservative term-deposit rate is the safest form of wealth creation or investment. This assumes the financial institution — usually a bank — has sufficient income to pay your deposit back to you when asked. This would be the case in most instances, but if that bank gets into financial difficulty, it will now fall to deposit holders to be the first line of defence, before the government (a.k.a. the taxpayer) will look to bail it out. In New Zealand we don't yet have a deposit guarantee scheme; embarrassingly we are the last OECD county without one. But one is coming. From 2025, deposit holders will have their first $100,000 of savings protected/guaranteed. This guarantee will likely cost the deposit holder a fee or reduce the interest rate they receive as the cost of the guarantee would likely be passed on to the customer. You may think it's unlikely that a New Zealand bank would need to be bailed out, but BNZ has had to be bailed out twice in its history, most recently in the past 40 years.

Putting the Global Financial Crisis (GFC) or Covid to one side, the inherent disadvantage of keeping your money in the bank is that the returns are often lower than the inflation rate. This makes sense, because it is assumed there is little risk of default by the bank. This higher certainty of payment is another way of saying the payback is less risky. The more certain the return, the lower the risk. The lower the risk, the lower the return.

For many people, even if the returns from the bank keep up with inflation, they are still not enough to meet their financial goals, so they need to look at other investments. *The key to investing wisely is understanding what you are investing in, why you have chosen this investment type and what you are expecting it to give you in return.* Because New Zealanders seem to have one of the lowest levels of financial literacy in the developed world, we are attracted to what we understand even if it doesn't solve the problem.

Property tends to tick this box. Looking back over time, the typical family home with a reasonable section has consistently increased in value in most cases. We also like the fact that a house and section is a physical asset. It is appealing that even if the market crashes you will still own the asset — provided you keep paying the mortgage.

The same cannot be said for investment in businesses and financial institutions, as many people learned the hard way after the GFC and Covid — many businesses and banks were not around for people to collect their money.

What's more, you can insure a house. So even when natural disasters strike, such as the Christchurch earthquakes, you have ring-fenced and protected your wealth. Although, as we've recently learned from the earthquakes or floods, even with insurance you're not always guaranteed a quick or easy pay-out!

Kiwis tend to like property because they understand it. But this is where they make their first mistake. They assume that any property is going to solve their problem, which is seldom the case. In fact, as retirement gaps get larger, and financial conditions get harder to navigate, it is less likely you will find the right property by default. To this end, not all properties increase in value at the same rate. Some properties that do not possess any land — for example, apartments or leasehold buildings — may not increase in value at all. Townhouses (attached properties) tend to increase at a lower rate than stand-alone properties. Different regions increase at different rates. In general, a typical family home in a good area near good schools can expect an increase in value over time. This increase is greater than any gain you could earn by investing your money in a bank, yet it's not perceived as being significantly more risky. In fact, people who don't need to borrow much to purchase the property (because of existing savings) can often get a better cash return on the property from receiving rent (and deducting expenses) than from leaving the money in the bank earning interest. Not only do they improve their cashflow, but they are positioning themselves to get capital gain on the property over time. You definitely don't get a capital gain from leaving your money in the bank.

Low-risk options such as term deposits can be a great way to *store* wealth but are not usually recommended as a way to *grow* wealth. In fact I cannot recall one person who has become rich by leaving their money in the bank. Money left in a bank will actually decrease in value over time; unless the interest rate exceeds the inflation rate, the capital is dropping in value.

If you are serious about getting ahead, then you need to engage a two-pronged attack: first, create a cash surplus, then make an investment.

What are the options?

Investment options include:

- paying down your mortgage faster (this saves you from paying interest)
- KiwiSaver
- savings/term deposits
- residential investment property (with a mortgage, or without)
- commercial property
- business
- shares
- ETF (exchange traded fund)
- managed funds
- gold/metals
- cryptocurrencies
- art.

The two most popular wealth-creation options in New Zealand are owning an investment property or building a business. Not all of the options listed above will be right for you, but it's important to understand how whichever tactic you choose to grow your wealth works. You must understand the risks and be comfortable that you have taken all necessary steps to mitigate your financial exposure. I call this 'protecting your financial flank'. Don't plan for the good days, prepare for the bad days.

Unfortunately, many of those lucky enough to have money to invest are too easily persuaded to invest in a product endorsed by a famous or friendly face, without looking more closely at what they are actually betting on. In some instances, an investment might look worthwhile on the surface, but scratch a little deeper and you will see that the risks involved are so high its success is little more than a gamble. And we wonder why investments collapse and people get burnt.

You need to understand the principles of building wealth if you want to build and keep it. The first principle is that wealth seldom comes to those who adopt a get-rich-quick mentality. Growing wealth is a science. Understand the problem you are trying to solve first, then understand what investment options can solve that problem for you. Of the options available to you, which will give you the most probable outcome at the lowest cost and within the timeframe you need? As you overlay the criteria of what will work, fewer and fewer options will remain. Leave your personal preferences at the door until you understand all viable options and their implications to your situation (short-, medium- and long-term impacts). This will help you form a considered view before deciding what path to take.

When people get wealth quickly, it often leaves them just as quickly. I continue to work with two first-division Lotto winners who, prior to working with me, each received over $1 million of winings, yet within five years had little to show for it. Of the people who come into money, whether through Lotto, athlete contracts, a large payout or even an inheritance, a good chunk of these will lose their windfall within a few years. According to *USA Today*, nearly one-third of lottery winners go bankrupt within three to five years of winning, with more avoiding bankruptcy but not having much to show for their winnings as time passes. Forbes.com quoted 80 per cent of retired NFL players go broke within their first three years out of the League. While there can be contributing factors to their financial demise, divorce being one of them, if you have not been trained to manage your money well, having more money will usually make you lazier. Easy come, easy go.

The next principle is to protect your financial flank. Your cash surplus helps do this – and also being able to access funds if needed. This is where the revolving-credit facility comes in handy. Together the cash surplus and rainy-day fund are your shield of protection if bad luck strikes at any point. If you need a tax rebate to make an investment work financially then you probably can't afford it.

A good investment in my view has two components: income (in excess of inflation) and capital growth. Capital growth is fundamental to increasing wealth. You could invest in any of the wealth-creation options listed in this chapter, but, unless you understand your risks, there's a good chance the investment won't give you the return you need, in the time you need it.

I appreciate the liquidity of cash, but I don't like the fact that it doesn't grow. I like the ease of share transactions, but I don't have much stomach for the market's volatility — I hate that you can lose everything you invested because a company fails and in some instances the commentators never saw it coming (as in the GFC or the 1987 sharemarket crash). It's often said that being a successful investor is not about getting it right first time, but merely about minimising the number of mistakes you make. The best way to avoid these mistakes is by being armed with the right information.

18. Leverage

Leverage is best described as buying an asset using borrowed funds in the belief that the income from the asset (the asset's appreciation) will be more than the cost of the borrowing. Almost always there will be a risk that the cost of the borrowed funds will be larger than the income earned, that the capital gain (in addition to income) could take longer to arrive, or that the value of the asset will fall before increasing in value.

Basically, leverage is using the bank's money to buy another asset. Banks see standard residential property as a fairly safe investment. As a rule, they are prepared to lend or 'gear' up to 80 per cent of the value of a 'new' investment property, and less (up to 65 per cent) for an existing property.

For a property to be new, it can be purchased 'off the plans', so not yet built, or completed but not yet lived in — provided it was completed less than six months earlier, or anywhere in between. For most, buying the property will mean you have to take a loan from the bank. Yes, you have to pay for this loan — or your rental income is supposed to pay for it — but, as the asset increases in value, you are the one who enjoys the spoils with comparatively little money invested — provided you invested in the right property. Property is seen as more secure than shares, with banks willing to lend up to twice as much against property. As a rule of thumb, a leveraged property could outperform unleveraged shares by 350 per cent.

At face value, shares might have a better return than property, but this calculates the return on the money you have invested. For example, let's say you invested $100,000 in shares with a 10 per cent return each year. If you invested the same money into managed funds you might get a 6 per cent return, and if you invested the money into property you might get a 7 per cent return (net income plus capital gain). Based on this logic, shares look like the better investment.

But you wouldn't buy a $100,000 property. Instead, you would take that $100,000 and ask the bank to loan you $400,000, which means you can buy a $500,000 investment. This investment goes up by 7 per cent, which on $500,000 is an increase of $35,000. A 10 per cent return on $100,000 is $10,000. For the same cash amount invested, your $100,000 can work 3.5 times harder with property than with shares.

The leverage available with property investment is one of the reasons it is my preferred medium for wealth creation. You can sort of leverage shares, but not nearly to the same extent as property, and for most of us leveraging shares isn't even an option because we don't own enough shares, or the right shares, to be able to borrow against them. Further, the interest rate you pay to leverage shares tends to be higher than the interest rate on property, and the term (or length of the loan) is much shorter than the 30 years you can get on property.

The sharemarket is more volatile than the property market, going up and down daily. This volatility means the bank can suddenly require you to put more equity into the shares (i.e., repay some of the loan) to keep the debt level in check (relative to the value of the assets). So while it is technically possible to leverage off a share portfolio, the risks, costs and barriers make it unrealistic for the average investor to benefit in any meaningful way.

Instead, for most residential property deals, even if the property does drop in value for a time, the banks don't pay too much attention to its unrealised loss (provided you aren't trading the property). Banks tend to consider any drops to be relatively short-lived (say for 12–18 months). Provided your level of borrowings isn't too high and you are keeping up with your repayments, then you are free to jog on. If your borrowings are high (say $2 million plus), which is usually measured by whether the bank has assigned you a private banker, then the bank will offer you more support, but also pay more attention to the performance of your assets, including property. My advice is to keep a low profile and be strategic by spreading out your borrowings between banks, moving to another bank when your total debt exceeds the $2 million threshold. On that note, also try and minimise the cross-securing of assets for prolonged periods, wherever possible.

> **Tip:** Take steps to uncouple your home from investment lending, as quickly as practicable.

Negative gearing means the amount of rent you receive is insufficient to cover the total costs to run the property (interest, rates, insurance, property management, accounting, etc.) so you have to top up the shortfall. A negatively geared property means the property is running at a cash loss that the owner has to personally cover. Typically the owner will get a tax credit for any top-up made, but this is ring-fenced until the property becomes cashflow-positive and will offset against any future tax you would otherwise pay. If you have followed my investment criteria and are borrowing close to 100 per cent of the property's value, a property is likely to break even from year six or seven, so tax credits won't benefit you until this point. While the tax benefits in isolation should never be the reason for taking on an investment, they are a nice little cherry on top. This cherry was removed by the last government, who also added some arsenic to the mix by removing the tax-deductibility of interest costs. This has been repealed by the new government but could change again in the future. So check with your accountant to understand any tax impact. You always want the investment to stack up without factoring in any tax benefits.

If the government were serious about taking the heat out of the property market, they would remove all tax benefits for property investors, tax capital gains, and place a higher tax on people who own land but aren't developing it. Even if these taxes were introduced at current tax rates, with the benefit of leverage, the investment return can still far exceed other (non-leveraged) investment options.

Leverage in action

Let me illustrate how leverage can work for you. Let's say you are buying an investment property for $600,000. In the three scenarios below, you have different levels of deposit, meaning the amount of money you intend to borrow from the bank will vary.

Deposit	Bank borrowing	Purchase price
$600,000 (no gearing)	Nil	$600,000
$300,000 (50%)	$300,000 (50%)	$600,000
$120,000 (20%)	$480,000 (80%)	$600,000

Putting the cashflow of the property to one side, let's assume the property goes up in value by 6 per cent every year. In the space of 10 years the property will be worth around $1,075,000, irrespective of the level of money you invested initially. But the equity that you will have gained will be drastically more if you used leveraged funds.

If this property is purchased outright with no funding, you will achieve a return on your investment of 79 per cent over 10 years. (If the capital growth was 7 per cent per annum, you would achieve a 97% return.) This is a solid return on the money you have invested.

But if you decided to borrow 50 per cent of the purchase price from the bank, using $300,000 of your own money and borrowing the rest, this would mean your initial equity in the property would have been lower, as the bank would have owned $300,000 or half of its upfront value. But the bank's exposure is limited to the funds borrowed ($300,000), so the return on your investment is actually higher, at 158%. This share of the investment is yours.

What's more, if you had used 80 per cent gearing you would only have had to put in $120,000 of your own equity up front, which when coupled with leverage would have given you a 395% return on your initial investment.

This effect is magnified over time, as shown by the chart on the opposite page.

> **Tip:** The property market doesn't move in a straight, upward line, but in cycles. At the start of a cycle, interest rates can be high, and affordability and credit is tight. Towards the end of the cycle, credit frees up, interest rates are lowered and it is easier to get loans.
>
> While the property market is seen as less volatile than shares, the value of property can still drop at some points in the cycle. This drop tends to coincide with negative economic factors and worsening lending conditions. Historically this drop could last for a year or so, before the property values correct themselves and start to move up again. It is often immediately after this economic contraction (recession) that an economic correction/boom starts — which is where the majority of growth from the cycle is usually found. It's critical that you can weather the recession, so you can enjoy the sunshine of growth.

Effect of leverage on return on investment

Year	Starting value	Return	Ending value	% funded by debt		
				0%	20%	50%
		6%		Return on investment		
1	600,000	36,000	636,000	6%	30%	12%
2	636,000	38,160	674,160	12%	62%	25%
3	674,160	40,450	714,610	19%	96%	38%
4	714,610	42,877	757,486	26%	131%	52%
5	757,486	45,449	802,935	34%	169%	68%
6	802,935	48,176	851,111	42%	209%	84%
7	851,111	51,067	902,178	50%	252%	101%
8	902,178	54,131	956,309	59%	297%	119%
9	956,309	57,379	1,013,687	69%	345%	138%
10	1,013,687	60,821	1,074,509	79%	395%	158%
11	1,074,509	64,471	1,138,979	90%	449%	180%
12	1,138,979	68,339	1,207,318	101%	506%	202%
13	1,207,318	72,439	1,279,757	113%	566%	227%
14	1,279,757	76,785	1,356,542	126%	630%	252%
15	1,356,542	81,393	1,437,935	140%	698%	279%
16	1,437,935	86,276	1,524,211	154%	770%	308%

What if you don't have the cash deposit for an investment property?

You don't always need to have a cash deposit, provided you have equity in your home that the bank is prepared to recognise. For example, if your home is worth $800,000 and you have a $500,000 mortgage, you have $300,000 equity. The bank will usually be prepared to lend you up to 80 per cent of your home's value. This means that it would lend you $640,000 as a total mortgage, or $140,000 more than your current mortgage. So, while you have $300,000 equity in your property, only $140,000 is available to be productive. Productive equity is equity the bank will lend against, that you can get working for you, and that you can invest.

You could use that $140,000 to buy a tiny property in a small town (it is more likely to be a carpark than a house as I am not sure any property would sell for $140,000), owning the investment outright, or you could use this equity as a deposit on a higher-value investment property. Using the power of leverage, this $140,000 would constitute a 20 per cent deposit, with the bank willing to lend you another $560,000 to allow you to buy an investment property up to the value of $700,000.

If you are using equity in your home as the deposit for an investment property, the banks will always prefer to cross-secure the properties. To avoid this, increase the mortgage on your home up to a level so that you can take out the needed 20 per cent deposit for the investment property secured against your home. Then, with this deposit, obtain a pre-approval from another bank for the 80 per cent of the investment property's value to complete your purchase. Doing it this way limits the exposure of your home to the deposit portion and de-risks your lending structure so you do not have an over-reliance on one bank and you limit any exposure to your home. In some instances, especially when equity or servicing is tight, it may be easier to stay with one bank for all lending. In this scenario the bank cross-secures the home against the investment property and vice versa. When the investment property increases in value, look to refinance this lending with another bank, to limit the exposure to your home.

When you have a lot of mortgage debt, it can be tricky to work out which mortgage to repay first. As a rule, I prioritise debt repayment as follows:

- Pay off the home mortgage first. This debt is unproductive and there are no tax benefits to keeping this debt. Pay it off and save interest costs.
- If the investment property deposit is secured against the home, I will then focus on paying off this debt. If both properties are cross-secured, I will try and pay down enough debt for the investment property to be refinanced to another bank, leaving the home protected.
- Once I have unencumbered the home, I look to repay more of the investment property debt, but only to the point that the rent can cover all the property costs (including interest). This is when the property moves from being negatively geared to 'washing its own face', or breaking even on a weekly basis. Hitting this milestone is a key component of any wealth strategy, as you have essentially de-risked your ability to hold the property. It no longer costs you anything, so you can hold it for as long as you need to get the gain.
- Once the property is cashflow-neutral, you can either pay off the investment property mortgage, buy another property or redirect

your savings into another asset (like term deposits, managed funds, shares or commercial property). If you have enough wealth to close your savings gap, then you might consider diversifying your investments at this point. If you don't, then you will need to double down on your growth strategy.

To minimise your exposure to property-cycle drops and the resulting need to find money that doesn't readily exist, consider limiting your debt to $2 million at any one bank. This usually means no more than two to three investment properties with the one bank.

19. Why invest in property?

Reserve Bank analysis has previously concluded that the highest-yielding asset class in New Zealand (after farms) is residential property, when compared to other types of investment. Not all of us are able to pop out and buy ourselves a farm. So, for the rest of us, the next best option is residential investment property. In fact, if you add rent received to the capital gains, residential property is bearing down on, and at times out-performing, equities (shares), usually with a lower level of risk and more predictable gains.

This is before we overlay the benefit of leverage. When we bring leverage into the mix, residential property will outperform shares and managed funds over the long run by around 300 per cent. This isn't to say that shares are not a viable investment alternative. But there remains a pull towards residential property, and its appeal is not unique to New Zealand. Billionaire Andrew Carnegie famously said that 90 per cent of all millionaires make their money through real estate, and that more money has been made in real estate than all industrial investments combined. While this may have been true in his day, I'm not sure the statistic is running quite so high today.

What I can say, though, is that a good number continue to make their money from property. This is especially true if your income doesn't tip the scales, as you become more reliant on your money working harder rather than simply earning more money. For most of us, though, being wealthy isn't the goal; we merely want to be able to retire at 65.

In New Zealand, just over one-third of properties are owned as an investment by 'Mum and Dad' landlords. But most ordinary people don't go near the property market because they find property investment confusing or are scared off by media headlines. They don't understand the rules of the game, or the problem they are trying to solve, so they choose to do nothing.

In my view, understanding the rules of property is a lot easier than understanding the rules of shares. In New Zealand, property has some unique characteristics which differentiate it from other wealth-creation vehicles. These benefits can dramatically increase your wealth over time. But the time needed can be lengthy, and not all returns are the same. Like anything, gains also come with risks, which should be clearly understood to allow them to then be mitigated. Like most investments, property can produce an income (rent), and it will grow in value over time (usually). But the two characteristics that distinguish property from other asset classes are the options to leverage your asset (experience significantly higher returns relative to the money you have invested) and the ability to insure it.

Before you drift towards property, remember, not all properties are created equal, and not all properties make a good investment. Different components drive a property's rate of growth, the timeframe you are expected to hold the property for and the holding cost you need to cover before you see the growth. Also, being able to ride out a property cycle, no matter how long or volatile, is a critical component to successful property investment.

Understanding the property market

Before you invest in property you need to understand the philosophy of the rental market, how it works and why residential property can be a good investment. You need to recognise the signs of a lemon, be clear on the problem you are trying to solve, and understand the factors that directly influence the property market.

The key drivers of property prices are:

- interest rates
- location of property
- type of property and number of bedrooms
- age of property
- lending rules
- population growth
- new housing consents
- build prices
- rental market growth (excess or shortage of properties in the area)
- affordability of rent to tenants
- tax policies
- affordability of weekly cash top-up, to the property owner
- global factors.

The fundamental assumption with real estate is that, the longer you hang onto a property, the more it'll be worth. To that end, property is about two things: the rate of return, and time. Property is supposed to increase in value over time and, if you take a long-range view, this is usually the case. But the value of property does not increase by the same amount year after year. The gain is not linear — it goes up and down, and sometimes it even stays still. Property investors need to ensure they can hold the property through the bad times in order to realise its capital-gain potential in the good times. Never forget that spring comes after winter, dawn after night. The economic cycle is the same. You must be able to hold on through these times if you want to enjoy the full fruits of your labour.

But what drives property values, and how come some properties increase in value at a faster rate than others?

Property prices are driven by the basic economic notion of supply and demand. If there is a limited supply of property or an oversupply of borrowing power, then prices increase. If there is an excess supply of property or a tightening of lending conditions, then prices are likely to stall or fall, although many people simply hold onto their properties during this time to prevent realising any loss. Interest rates (the cost of capital) and bank lending policies tend to influence property values the most — especially if foreign buyers are not allowed to invest in the country. As a rough rule of thumb, I tend to say for every 1 per cent drop in interest rates you can expect property prices to increase by 10 per cent. This slide goes the other way as well: as interest rates increase, you can expect property growth to stall and possibly fall. Understanding where we are at in the economic cycle helps us understand the supply and cost of capital, to help anticipate the timing of property gains. Conceptually this makes sense, but you also need to understand what drives the supply and demand of property, not just the supply of capital.

Demand is ultimately driven by the number of people needing a house to live in. This is driven by net migration, internal migration (between cities) and organic population growth. Net migration is the difference between people coming to New Zealand for a long period of time (immigrants) and people leaving. We are currently experiencing a net annual migration in excess of 100,000 — the highest on record in New Zealand. This equates to a new person arriving every five minutes. While migration has peaked, it is likely to remain strong for some time. And the more people that arrive, the more properties that are needed. The majority of immigrants flock to the big cities as this is where the job opportunities tend to be. This also fuels internal migration.

In conjunction with net migration, you also have organic population growth, which takes into account births, deaths and increasing lifespans. With people living longer and baby boomers ageing, it is estimated that soon more than 20 per cent of our population will be over 65.

When considering what areas to invest in, not all locations are created equal. Just because the wider population is increasing doesn't mean the value of properties in your town will increase at the same rate. You need to understand where the increased population is going to be based, what the property supply is like for the projected growth, and if there is already a shortage of investment properties available in the area selected. Then you need to look at the property prices. If a property doubles in value every 10 years (a rough guide), cheaper properties will have less capital gain, even if they grow at the same pace. So buying a property in Invercargill, despite it being cheaper than a property in Auckland, and despite it having a similar historical growth rate, might not result in the same ammount of gain within the same timeframe because the average house price in Invercargill is $600,000 compared with $1 million in Auckland. At face value, if both properties doubled in value, you are still $400,000 better off for having invested in Auckland.

But remember, capital gain is as much about your ability to hold on long enough to realise the gain you were trying to make, as it is about buying the property you think will give you a capital gain. So, in this example, while you could stand to make $400,000 more on the Auckland property, the likelihood of you being able to hold on to get the gain is much lower. This is because property yields (what a property rents for relative to the purchase price) start to reduce as a property gets more expensive. In turn, this means that your weekly top-up is much higher. The top-up on the Auckland property may be $600 per week, compared to the Invercargill property which might be, say, $150 per week. We would need to first deduct this higher cost from the gain — so yes, you make $400,000 more, but it is costing you $30,000 per annum in top-ups. While the top-up reduces over time as rents increase, the Auckland property might still cost you $200,000 in top-ups over a 10-year period. The incremental net gain is therefore $200,000. It's still a lot, but not as high as we first thought. Then we have to overlay the likelihood of you being able to afford the top-up. It's a lot easier to afford $150 per week than $600 per week. So while the Invercargill property may produce less gain when sold, the probability of you actually realising it is much higher. Not to mention that it is easier to borrow $600,000 from the bank than $1,000,000.

Statistics New Zealand prepares calculations on the projected population growth of different council areas up to 2048. Within the regional population projections, it highlights the top three areas for growth proportionate to the current population. The following table shows what these areas were as at October 2022.

	Average annual % growth*	Amount of projected population increase
Auckland	0.80%	459,100
Waikato	1.00%	163,500
Canterbury	0.80%	159,900

*Using medium projections

Therefore, demand for properties is expected to be highest in these areas.

A high demand for properties is good, but this in itself does not make investing in these areas a sure thing; it simply increases the odds in your favour. Personally, I prefer not to invest in smaller areas that depend on one industry or employer, such as a sawmill or meat works. If the industry falters or goes through a bad patch, this directly affects house prices. Jobs are lost and families need to move to find work. I like to know the area has a hospital and ideally a port or a university. I'm also interested in what investments the council and government are making in the local infrastructure.

Once you have determined the areas likely to have higher demand due to forecasted population growth, you then need to find out how quickly those areas can meet that demand with an increase in supply. That is, how quickly can developers access more land to build more houses. Some councils are better at addressing this than others. For instance, Waikato has plenty of flat land and seems to add subdivisions in the blink of an eye — compared to Auckland, at least. This means that, while Waikato is tipped to have significant population growth, its ability to meet this demand is higher than Auckland's. Using economic principles, this suggests that property values might not increase to the same extent because the market is able to correct itself more quickly, and meet demand with supply. (The positive side of this is that the market doesn't get as heated, and the gains become more genuine.)

The easiest way to see this is to check the number of new housing consents being granted. When consent numbers are high then the supply is up, which means that property values could stall or not increase as much if not matched by demand. If consents are low, it means the area might be under-building or not keeping up with the demand. It could also mean that there is no demand for that region, although that is less likely. The following graph shows a supply:demand imbalance with a shortfall in new properties to offset immigration levels.

At a macro level, we have annually averaged 40,000 new building consents since 2018, and post-Covid we are seeing record immigration. It doesn't take much to work out that with that many people arriving we are creating a widening housing deficit.

Many social issues are created by a lack of supply of properties. Practically, when demand exceeds supply, people still need to find shelter somewhere. Camping-ground and motel bookings increase, homes get overcrowded and there is a general increase in homelessness.

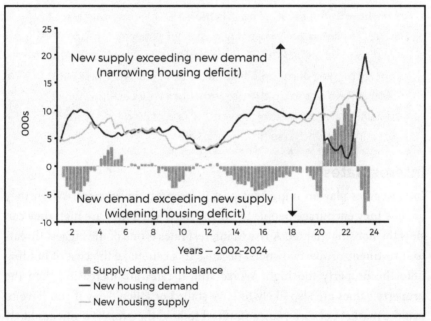

Source: Stats NZ, Macrobond, ANZ Research

While these are serious issues, the general lack of housing can also be an opportunity for people wanting to fast-track their savings by taking on boarders or flatmates. If you are a landlord, it means you can increase your rents due to high demand, or at the very least be more selective with your tenants.

> **Tip:** One of the great things about residential investment property is the ease with which you can find tenants. If there is a shortage of tenants because property supply exceeds demand, then it will likely mean you need to drop the rent in order to attract tenants. In this way you limit your potential exposure to the amount of rent that could be forsaken in order to get a tenant. Newer and warmer properties are usually easier to let, so their vacancy rate is lower.
>
> For example, if you rented out your property for $500 per week, but your tenant moved out and you couldn't find another one willing to pay the same amount, you could drop the rent to $480, and you might find a tenant more easily. In this way you have lost money, but it is only $20 a week, rather than $500.

> **Tip:** Where possible, I try to have a buffer (normally a separate line of credit with the bank) of no less than $10,000, but ideally up to $50,000, which usually covers two years of property top-ups. This way, if you had a Mack Truck event and couldn't work, and if the property market slumped at the same time (just your luck), you wouldn't have to top up the property from your cashflow while you wait for the market to correct. The line of credit is a form of protection from adverse timing pressures.

Interest rates

Interest rates play an important part in property investment. When they are low they encourage people to borrow, and when they are high they can slow the housing market. A rise in interest rates is one of the biggest threats to investment-property owners, because this can make the cost of holding onto the property too high. Worse still, if rates are increasing then the property values are also likely to have stalled or fallen — so if you have to exit the market because you can't afford to hold the property, you are likely exiting at the worse time.

As you probably know, the Reserve Bank is charged with managing inflation. Using monetary policy, the Reserve Bank increases or decreases the supply of money in the economy with changes to the official cash rate (OCR; the interest rate set for bank-to-bank lending) and legislation.

If reducing interest rates does not stimulate the economy, then the Reserve Bank's next option is to lend money to our banks at super low interest rates or to print money, known as *quantitative easing* or QE (see below). When you print money, you devalue the dollar, which is great for exporters but not so good for importers.

Conversely, comparatively good interest rates can attract overseas investors who believe they can get a better return investing their money in a New Zealand bank than they might get back home. This then pushes up demand for the New Zealand dollar, which in turn slaps exporters in the face, lowers our gross domestic product (GDP) and decreases the supply of money because our exporters are not making as much, which puts downward pressure on inflation. To increase the supply of money, credit needs to be offered at an attractive rate. The Reserve Bank can lower the OCR so bank lending is cheaper. A lower OCR pushes retail interest rates back down.

I go into this detail here because I consider the mortgage interest rate one of the greatest risks to any leveraged property investor. If you can hold a property indefinitely (15–20 years plus), it doesn't matter what the market is doing in the short term because eventually it should right itself. Interest rates are the biggest obstacle to this outcome, as higher mortgage rates may reduce affordability and therefore how long you can hang onto an investment property.

As I write this in 2024, do I think the Reserve Bank will increase interest rates? Probably not anytime soon. I think as inflation gets under control, rates will reduce. Over a full economic cycle, it's likely they could move up again, but I don't expect them to radically increase beyond their current levels within the next few years. Higher rates, relative to our international trading partners, will likely result in a stronger currency than historical averages, and will further increase the damage to our exporters and possibly grind the economy to a halt. For our interest rates to seriously increase it would have to be due to a major increase in inflationary expectations, which are fuelled by a significant improvement in the global economy. While this is possible and some inflation is definitely more desirable than deflation, I think it's unlikely for some years.

Why interest rates won't rise anytime soon (quantitative easing explained)

Governments and central banks around the world like there to be just enough growth in an economy — not so much that it could lead to inflation getting out of control, but not so little that there is stagnation. Their aim is the so-called 'Goldilocks economy' — not too hot, not too cold. In this, the New Zealand Reserve Bank is no different. Currently we are 'too hot, but cooling'.

One of the main tools central banks use to control growth is raising or lowering interest rates. Lower interest rates encourage people or companies to spend money rather than save. If they are spending more, then more jobs are created, which in turn boosts the economy.

But when interest rates are almost at zero and government stimulus packages are not viable, then central banks need to adopt different tactics to kick-start economic growth — such as pumping money directly into the economy. This process is known as quantitative easing or QE. The Bank of Japan deployed QE in the 1990s and our government adopted a version of this during Covid.

The central bank buys assets, usually bonds from investors such as banks or pension funds, with money it has 'printed' — or created electronically these days. It sounds a little uneventful, but it has serious effects.

Spending this 'new' money increases the amount of cash in the financial system, encouraging financial institutions to lend more to businesses and individuals. This in turn should allow people to invest and spend more, hopefully increasing growth.

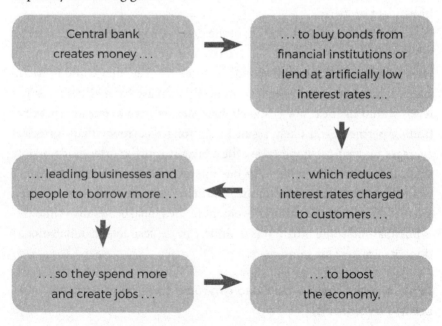

While in theory it can work, the long-term effects of QE are yet to be felt. One of the immediate problems is that QE pushes up the market price of government bonds. If a bond price increases, this reduces the return or yield paid out to investors. In other words, investors have to pay more to get the same income. This means that some pension schemes have shown deficits in recent years.

The main fear of QE is the upwards pressure on prices as more money joins the system. We experienced this first-hand in New Zealand during Covid, when the banks loosened all lending and asset prices jumped in value. While this temporary sugar rush was fun, asset values corrected themselves relatively quickly, but the correction was still jarring. Most sugar rushes lead to inflation, which may be a lesser evil than an out-and-out depression. That's the theory at least.

We have also seen that when a country stops printing money, the recovery they have been trying to kick-start is often put on hold, or the economy even worsens. This effect is shown by the fact that sharemarkets often fall when it is announced or speculated that a quantitative-easing programme will be brought to an end.

Tax-deductibility

When you are in business, you're allowed to incur expenses, provided they relate to the business or its ability to earn income. These expenses reduce profit, and tax is charged on the business's profit. If the business makes a loss, you earn a tax credit or a tax rebate, depending on the type of ownership of the business.

The same occurs when you own an investment property. To all intents and purposes, you are considered to be in the business of owning property. Therefore, the rental income you earn will be taxed. However, you can reduce this taxable income by offsetting property-related costs (rates, maintenance, body corporate fees, management fees, repairs, accounting, insurance and, most importantly, interest) from the rental income received. Many properties, if leveraged with a mortgage and other property-related costs, make a loss. This means you don't have to pay tax on the income received, but instead pay tax on the overall profit after expenses, which is usually zero. For a time, just before Covid, changes to the tax rules were introduced reducing the tax-deductibility of some interest costs. By design, the impact of this change was a higher tax bill for some property investors. While the next government has taken measures to walk back these changes and make interest tax-deductible again, it still highlights mechanisms available to any government.

Often when people buy their first home, they build up equity through repaying debt in conjunction with capital gain. When they decide to upgrade their property, some consider keeping their first home and converting it to an investment property. While this might seem to make sense, I don't recommend this, as the numbers don't tend to work out as well as they could when compared with other options. Always make sure you understand the different options available, and the impact of each option on your cashflow and wealth potential, before you make a call on what will work best for you.

> **Tip:** Don't mix your drinks when it comes to your investment strategy. Just because you already own your home, doesn't mean that this would make it a high-performing investment property. This also extends to a family bach that you are trying to present as a quasi-investment property because you rent it out occasionally.

Many people assume that the costs of borrowing the extra money to buy a new home can be loaded against the investment property and become tax-deductible. *They cannot.* The only way to legitimately push more debt against the investment property is to sell the property to a new entity (either a company or a trust). Both have legal and tax implications, so don't act without discussing it with a qualified accountant or lawyer.

For example: a client had paid off her first home (worth $1 million) and then met the love of her life. Together they wanted to buy a family home. She wanted to keep her original property and rent it out.

The family home they wanted to buy was going to cost $1.2 million. My client's new partner was bringing $250,000 towards the purchase price. This meant that they needed to raise a loan of $950,000. The banks were happy to do this because the couple were excellent borrowers due to their high incomes and strong equity.

My client was able to rent out her original property for $700 per week. She assumed she could transfer the $950,000 of new borrowings (relating to the new home) against her old home (the rental) and the interest costs could be offset against the rental income so that she wouldn't have to pay tax on the rental income, especially given the mortgage was cross-secured against both properties.

However, she was unable to offset the interest costs against her rental income because she hadn't structured the transaction correctly. This resulted in an additional $10,000 per annum tax bill that could have been avoided if she had structured things correctly from the start. Although she rented out her original property, receiving $700 per week in rent, she then had to pay tax on this income because there was no debt against the investment property — all the new borrowing was legally sitting against the new family home.

The only way to push the debt against the investment property was to sell the property to a new entity, such as a company or a trust. A look-through company is often used to own investment properties. It is a standard company that has a special tax code so that the tax implications are the responsibility of its shareholders. For example, if the company has tax to pay and the company can't afford it, the shareholders will have to pay it at their marginal tax rate.

The bright-line property rule

The bright-line property rule means if you sell a residential property within certain timeframes, you might have to pay income tax on any gains (that would be considered capital gains if not for the bright-line rule).

The bright-line period has historically differed between new and existing properties. New builds have a shorter bright-line period than existing properties. At the time of writing, proposed tax changes suggest the bright-line period will be reduced to two years, with no distinction made based on the age of the property.

If you are buying 'off plan', the bright-line period starts when you go unconditional on a contract, provided you don't change the purchasing entity. If you do nominate a new entity to own the property at settlement, this will reset the bright-line start date to the date of the entity nomination.

How to get a great deal

When buying a property, what you are prepared to pay for it should be limited by how productive it is or can become. Initially this means you should pay attention to how much rent you will receive for the investment you are making. Commercial property, by comparison, is easier to value as its value is typically based on the investment's productivity. The more productive (rent/yield) the commercial property, the higher its value. I encourage you to apply a similar logic when trying to determine how productive a residential property is, and by default what it is worth.

A property's rental income will determine its yield. Annualise the rent, then divide by 4 per cent to get a sense of the property's value relative to how hard it works for you. I only consider properties where the asking price is in line with or lower than the suggested value.

Example: a property rents for $700 per week. Annually, this is $36,400. I want this property to give me a yield of no less than 4 per cent, which means I can pay no more than $910,000 for it (calculated as $36,400/.04).

Some situations will require a higher yield to justify the money invested, perhaps because you could get your money earning a similar return elsewhere. Let's say I needed a 5 per cent yield to justify investing in this property – then I would pay no more than $728,000 for it ($36,400/.05). I would set this as the ceiling price I would pay. If I managed to get it for this value then I would consider it a good investment. No property is bad per se, but many can be overvalued for how productive they can be.

Investment properties can sell below their value when the vendor needs to sell down quickly. The timing pressure might come from their bank or shareholders requiring them to sell more properties by a particular date. If you are lucky enough to be in the right place at the right time, you might get yourself a bargain — although you would want to move quickly. Similarly, if there is only one or two properties left in a development the vendor may be more willing to accept a discounted offer so they can move onto their next development. Buying early in a subdivision can be another way to bank some capital gain quickly — not because you are buying the property at a discount per se, but because the developer tends to increase the purchase price at each stage of the development. If you get in at the early stages, you could benefit from this gain.

Cashflow versus capital growth

When considering a property, you need to look at both its net *cashflow* (what income it will generate, i.e., rent less expenses), and its likely *capital gain*. Combining these amounts together will give you a feel for how well the property will perform over time.

Most properties don't earn quite enough rent to pay for all the costs associated with owning them. This means that you will have to top up the difference weekly by physically paying the difference. Over time the rent should increase, which means your top-up will reduce with new properties (with a yield greater than 4 per cent), often breaking even from year seven onwards. This weekly top-up needs to be reflected in your personal budget and ideally should account for no more than 50 per cent, but ideally closer to 30 per cent, of your weekly surplus.

Why would you be prepared to top up a property? Well, because you believe that over time the value of the top-up will be superseded by a capital gain when you eventually decide to sell the property. Conceptually this makes sense, but it's not always the case (see page 224).

While all investment properties will have some cashflow attached to them in the form of rent received, not all properties are cashflow-positive. High capital-growth areas usually mean lower cashflow, and high cashflow normally means lower capital growth. To be a high-cashflow property, the property needs to have enough income coming in to pay the mortgage and all the other property-related expenses (insurance, rates, maintenance, etc.). These types of property tend to be in lower socio-economic parts of town, mid to outer suburbs and in smaller towns outside of the big cities, or be dual-income (two income streams from the same property).

Let's illustrate the difference between property prices and returns. In a low socio-economic suburb such as Ōtara in South Auckland, properties don't cost nearly as much as they do a few suburbs down the road in, say, Māngere. But rents are not proportionately lower. A three-bedroom property in Ōtara might cost $705,000, whereas the same size property in Māngere might cost $1.1 million. The rental income might be $650 per week in Ōtara, compared to $700 per week in Māngere.

Let's say you borrowed the full purchase price of your investment properties. If you used debt to buy the Ōtara property, your interest payments would be $42,300 per annum, versus $66,000 in Māngere (based on a 6 per cent interest rate). This means that it costs $23,700 less per annum to own a property in Ōtara, even factoring in the lower rent ($2,600 less per annum). From a cashflow perspective, you are $21,100 better off each year if you buy in Ōtara over Māngere.

If you want a cashflow property like the Ōtara property in this example, it usually means that you won't have to top up the property to cover costs, because it stands on its own two feet. This is great if your cashflow is tight, but it is usually at the expense of long-term capital gain, which is where you make the real money. Cashflow and capital gain tend to be mutually exclusive.

This is where it gets a bit confusing. When real estate agents and even financial advisors look at the cashflow of a property, they use a term called *yield*. This is the gross income that a property earns. But it doesn't take into account the property-related expenses (excluding interest), which can be anywhere from $7,500 to $15,000, depending on the property (including repairs and maintenance, property-management costs, insurance, rates and body-corporate charges). This means the often-quoted 'gross yield' can be misleading, as it doesn't highlight the true cash cost of the property. You need to understand the property's *net yield* to determine if it will in fact be a cashflow-positive property.

Looking back at the Ōtara property in the example, it has a 4.8 per cent gross yield (the income divided by the price paid) or rental income of $33,800 per annum, but let's say it incurs costs of $10,000 each year for rates, insurance, accounting, etc. If you factor in these costs, the net yield is 3.4 per cent. If you don't have a mortgage, this return is still OK — slightly lower than current bank interest rates, but a stable income with a capital gain to come (which term deposits don't offer). But if you have a mortgage against this property, fixed at 6 per cent, then you'll be making a -2.6 per cent return. You would want to be sure the property is going to give you the capital gain to justify the top-up.

> **Tip:** If you are borrowing 100 per cent of a property's value, it's unlikely to be cashflow-positive from the start. If you are buying a true cashflow-positive property that has no real capital gain prospects, it needs to give you a net yield exceeding 10 per cent, otherwise the income you make may not be high enough to offset the capital growth you are forfeiting.

So, if cashflow properties don't go up in value as much as properties in better areas, why do people buy them? Some people buy them because they think they'll make money from them eventually. But because the capital gain can be so woeful for these properties, I'd prefer to tighten my spending to save the cash injection the property would have given me.

In New Zealand, unless you are a full-time property investor with a huge portfolio or have really low gearing, the income you make from an investment property is usually offset by the costs of owning the property. But, if you can hold onto it indefinitely, you can make some pretty awesome capital gains (provided you buy within the property criteria that are right for your situation), and it is these capital gains that create the juicy return. In the past five years, property values have doubled in some suburbs in Auckland. I am not saying this will continue, but if you happened to own a property in one of these suburbs, your equity may have increased by $300,000 or more in the past five years, just because you held onto it.

Investment property costings calculator		
	($)	($)
Purchase price	705,000	1,100,000
Weekly rent	650	700
Annual rent	33,800	36,400
Less interest (–6%)	–42,300	–66,000
Less other costs (e.g., rates, insurance, accounting, repairs, property manager)	–10,000	–10,000
Net income / loss	–18,500	–39,600
Weekly top-up needed (–) / Income (+)	–355	–761
Tax credit (33%)	6,105	13,068
Net annual return	–12,395	–26,532

Now some would argue that it doesn't matter, because if you sell your home you have to buy in the same market, so you are no better off. This is true. But what if you had an investment property *and* a home? You keep your home, but you sell your investment property. Referring to the example above, if you sold the investment property you would have pocketed $300,000. Crazy . . . but true.

Here's the hook, though. Rent doesn't always keep pace with increases in property values, as evidenced by comparing properties in Ōtara and Māngere. In our example, the property in Māngere cost $395,000 more, or was 57 per cent more costly than the one in Ōtara, but the rent was only 7 per cent higher.

Some people would be able to afford the weekly top-up of $761, so for them it would make sense to avoid the hassle of owning a property in a lower socio-economic area and head straight to where the higher capital gains are likely to be made. You just have to accept that you will have to top up the cashflow until interest rates reduce, rent increases or you pay off enough debt to lower your mortgage cost.

Let's say it takes 15 years for the Māngere property to go up in value, and let's assume that instead of doubling in value, which is what a property cycle suggests, it increases by only 75 per cent. This means that you would have paid $761 × 52 weeks × 15 years of payments, or $593,580 in total. So, at the very least, the property would need to increase in value by $593,580 over that 15 years for you to have not gone backwards (for the purposes of this illustration I am ignoring inflation). This is an increase in value of just over 1 per cent per annum, or 4 per cent per annum if you want to factor in inflation at 3 per cent. This seems like a fair assumption (provided you have purchased in an area with population growth).

But not everyone can afford the top-up, and some people commit to buying the property anyway, usually with devastating consequences. Or they buy a cashflow property, thinking that at least they are on the property ladder. But I disagree. Buying a dud property will not do anyone any good. A dud is a dud is a dud.

People sometimes think that they will be able to live off the rental income generated by the property in retirement. But in most instances there is still going to be a mortgage against the property, which the rent will be paying. So while the property might no longer require a weekly top-up, it's still unlikely to pay you much income each week while it still has a mortgage. The only way you could turn this type of property into a suitable investment for retirement would be by paying off the mortgage before you retire. For most investors, they run out of runway to do this (their income stops). One workaround would be to attempt to buy two investment properties and eventually sell one of the properties to give you the proceeds to repay the mortgage on the remaining property. At this point you would start to get rental income to help fund your retirement.

> **Tip:** Understand your property criteria. What growth rate do you need, what timeframe do you need to realise the gain, and how much can you afford to top up the property each week from your cashflow?

When setting your criteria for a property purchase, consider the following:
- What is the maximum purchase price?
- What growth rate are you hoping to achieve?
- What regions should you consider?
- What type of property are you looking for (stand-alone, townhouse, apartment)?
- How many bedrooms and bathrooms?
- What yield are you looking for?
- What top-up can you afford to pay?
- When do you need to own the property by?
- What type of financing options can you consider?
- If buying new, do you want to buy off the plan, under construction or completed?
- When would you prefer to settle (immediately, or into the future)?

I narrow properties down on these criteria for my clients, as this removes about 98 per cent of possible properties. I then ask my property team to reduce this list to their top three shortlisted properties so we can work through the merits of each one.

The exception

There is one reason why you would buy a high-cashflow, low-capital-gain property, and that is to use it as a stepping stone to getting the capital-gain property you really need.

Some years ago, I had a client who owned four properties in low socio-economic suburbs in the Bay of Plenty. These properties were cashflow positive, with the rent high enough to cover the mortgage. She had invested some of her own money and used the bank's money to buy the properties. Her property portfolio was worth $500,000 (this was almost 15 years ago), but most of this was still owed to the bank. She wasn't paying off the mortgages; they were on interest only. Yes, she was managing to hold the properties, but the properties' values hadn't increased by virtue of the type of property she had purchased.

When she came to see me, she was quite proud of herself, because her income was low in comparison to some of my clients yet she owned four properties. I asked her about the purpose of her investments, and she said to make money in the property market. I told her (politely) that she was going about it the wrong way. She needed to use the cashflow from her investment properties to buy a property in a strong capital-gain area. This capital-gain property would likely require a top-up, because the rent wouldn't cover all of the property costs. Based on the cashflow from her other properties, however, she could afford to top up a property by $150 per week.

When you use cashflow properties to facilitate buying a capital-gain property, you build what business coach Brad Sugars has called the 'Property Wealth Wheel', pictured on page 220. The wheel includes at least one property that is expected to go up in value and is negatively geared, or needs a big weekly top-up. But, instead of simply topping up the negatively geared property with your own money (which is my preferred option), Sugars endorses having four to five cashflow properties to produce enough income to cover the shortfall of the negatively geared property — this means you don't need to use any of your own money to make it work. Remember, a cashflow-positive property doesn't normally have much capital growth attached to it — so you are choosing to trade off future growth potential for the cash it can give you. With this cash, you combine it with your other properties to cover the top-up of the negatively geared, or high-growth property. Technically this is true, but there can be a lot of work owning six properties, and if only one of the properties was going to give you the gain that you wanted, my view is we should focus on getting you straight to that property without the fuss of the others.

Property Wealth Wheel

Source: Bradley Sugars, *The Real Estate Coach*

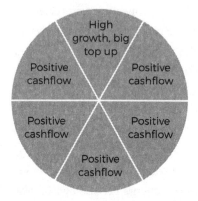

The problem with having a lot of cashflow properties is that they still don't tend to go up in value particularly fast, if at all, and now you have the headache of owning five or six of them. But its easy for me to say, 'Just buy a negatively geared, higher capital growth property, and be done with it.' How do you do that when you don't have much equity to start, or are struggling to come up with the deposit you need to buy the capital growth property? This is where a tighter spending regimen or even a delayed settlement might come in handy, as it gives you more time to save. Getting more creative, you might join forces with a friend or syndicate to own the property together.

Alternatively, if you already own property and are wanting to release some equity, think about how you can increase the value of your portfolio to release the equity. You might be able to improve the property and have this improvement recognised in a registered valuation, which the bank will lend against. But for many, the bank is the barrier to them accessing the equity in their existing properties, and they will need to sell down the property to get access to their usable equity because the bank rules might not allow them to otherwise get access to the funds.

Tip: Small renovations can increase a property's value. Adding a bedroom or a small bathroom can increase a property's value dramatically. But don't spend more than 10 per cent of the purchase price on renovations, or you may be over-capitalising. Many of my clients are already time-poor and the idea of having to add value to their investments is a turn-off, so we tend to buy new (or nearly new), where the numbers work from the start and no effort needs to be put into renovating. Most importantly, the bank require a smaller deposit on a new property, and settlement can be deferred to give you more time to save.

Managing mortgages on investment properties

As a rule, you want to leverage as much as possible — borrow from the bank as much as you can, provided you can afford to repay it and you are buying a productive asset. But if you buy the wrong property or fail to balance your property portfolio, you will run out of money to invest or, worse, have insufficient funds to pay the top-up on the mortgage and then be forced to sell the property (often at the wrong time of the cycle).

When you take out a mortgage, whether it is for a home or an investment property, you will have the option of paying off the principal (principal and interest) or just the interest (interest only). Many people will advise you to never pay off your investment property debt, opting to have the mortgage payments set to interest only. They are almost right, but not quite. Yes, keep your repayments on interest only so that your fixed outgoings are minimised. If you have excess savings (with the lower fixed outgoings), then you are in a position to channel your surplus into paying off your mortgages. If you still have a home mortgage, pay this off first as it is unproductive debt. If you are already mortgage-free, then you could channel the surplus savings into another investment (property or alternative), or instead start repaying the mortgage on the investment property. If you are going to repay the investment property mortgage, keep the payments set to interest only but optimise the structure of the mortgage so the extra payments are voluntary and you can re-access the money should you need to.

Some might ask why you would bother to pay off your investment-property debt, since it is usually tax-deductible. This is a fair question, I suppose. The interest you pay on an investment property is tax-deductible, sure, but *this deductibility means only that it costs you less, not that it is free.* If you have a $300,000 mortgage at 6 per cent, you're going to pay $18,000 in interest every year. If this property was a rental, you could claim back that cost and receive a tax credit of $5,940 (based on a 33 per cent tax rate). This means that the property's interest cost was $12,060, or the tax-effective interest rate was 4 per cent. So while the interest cost might be lower on an investment property by virtue of the tax benefits, it's still not free.

Basic financial management suggests you should pay off all debt, paying the most expensive debt first. If you had a mortgage on your home at 6 per cent and a mortgage on an investment property at a tax-effective rate of 4 per cent (or 6 per cent before the tax benefit), then you would pay off your home mortgage first. You could channel the surplus funds that would start to accumulate once you have paid off your home mortgage against your investment property; for every dollar repaid you would get a 4 cents saving in interest (after tax). This is a guaranteed 4 per cent net return. As discussed earlier, a net return, or real return, is the return *after* tax and inflation. Investments often show their return before tax and inflation, so a 4 per cent real return is the equivalent of a 10 per cent gross or nominal return (a 10 per cent gross return, less 30 per cent tax, gives a 7 per cent after-tax return, less inflation at 3 per cent is the equivalent of a 4 per cent return after tax and inflation). If you could find an alternative investment that was going to give you a guaranteed return of around 10 per cent before tax and inflation, then you might opt to invest in the alternative investment. But in the absence of such a return, you would normally be better off paying off investment debt, despite the debt being tax-deductible.

While investment property can stack up as an investment option, the property market has booms and dips. If you can ride out these fluctuations, you should be OK. It's easy to ride out a property cycle if a property isn't costing you anything to hold, or if you are not having to top it up. As noted earlier, the easiest way to balance a property's cashflow is to reduce the debt or mortgage to a level where the rent covers all costs. Paying down the mortgage requires careful structuring.

> **Tip:** Try to pay down your investment debt to the level where the rent covers all costs and you do not have to top it up. Only do this once you are mortgage-free on your home. This is a key part of any good hold strategy. This way, even if the property cycle takes longer to complete, it is of no immediate concern to you because the property isn't costing you anything to hold. Opt to have your investment property mortgage on interest only.

Tax structures

Kiwis have historically fallen prey to the tax incentives attached to a property investment. These incentives no longer exist in their historical form, so if you are trying to buy a property to immediately lower your personal tax bill, you will be in for a nasty surprise. It's true: for every dollar you use to top up an investment property's shortfall, you will receive a tax credit for this loss. This credit now carries forward to offset against the property's future profits, typically from year seven onwards. So for the first six or seven years, while you top up the property's cashflow each week, you build a tax credit. This credit sits there until the property becomes profitable, and then is credited against the tax you would then have to pay. Provided you hold the property long enough, the credit will eventually become of value. This is a change from the old rules, where the credit could be cashed in each year provided you owned the property in the right tax structure.

You have three general ownership options for an investment property:

1. personally (or in partnership)
2. in a trust
3. in a company (including a look-through company or LTC; see below).

Each option has different advantages and disadvantages.

Owning the property in your own name tends to be the easiest option. It doesn't cost anything to set up, because 'you' already exist. If you own the property jointly with your spouse or partner, then it may be deemed a partnership, but this in itself is nothing of real consequence. The problem with personal ownership is that, if something goes wrong with the property, you are personally accountable, and any personal assets you own could be exposed.

Owning a property in a trust is another option. This is a little more cumbersome to set up and could cost around $5000. Trust ownership makes sense if your property portfolio is profitable, or soon to be profitable, although I would limit the assets owned by the trust to the investment property only. I suggest holding your family home in a separate trust so if something goes wrong with the investment property your personal wealth will not be exposed.

The third ownership option is via a company. This company can be a normal company, or have a special tax exemption applied, whereby the profits or losses of the company are passed out to the shareholders, instead of being held in the company and taxed at the company's tax rate. This type of company where the tax credits pass to shareholders is known as a look-through company (LTC).

One of the key benefits of look-through company ownership is that profits are taxed at the marginal tax rate of each shareholder. This allows you to allocate shares to the lowest income earner, to reduce tax in the future.

As with all structures, there are little hooks that catch out the novice investor. Speak to an accountant who specialises in tax structures so they can help you to determine which structure will work best for you.

How to avoid the most common mistakes

Buying a good investment property is based on finding a property that fits set financial criteria. People who get burnt either buy the wrong property, pay too much, over-capitalise or have a top-up that is too high to be sustainable. Their due diligence tends to assume that the property will increase in value before their cashflow runs out, but this is often not the case.

The most common mistakes property purchasers make are:
- not buying new or near-new
- not paying attention to the yield
- paying too much for a property relative to the cashflow/rent the property can pay out
- assuming that all properties make good investments
- spending too much on renovations
- managing the rental property themselves
- not considering the long-term repair costs
- investing in overseas markets
- buying in areas that are unlikely to have capital gain.

To avoid the pitfalls listed above, follow these rules when choosing a property.
- Understand your property criteria. This is the most important component.
- Plan for the property cycle to take longer than it has done previously. Of course we hope it won't, but plan your cashflow so that if it does, you will still be OK.
- Use an interest rate of 7 per cent to calculate repayments, which is the long-term average rate. If your mortgage is likely to be repaid within five years, then use the OCR rate plus 2 per cent.
- Limit your weekly top-up to a maximum of 50 per cent of your weekly cash surplus, with a target of 30 per cent.
- Where you can, buy a new build to limit repairs and maintenance requirements.

- Buy in an area that is poised for capital growth.
- Assume a three-week vacancy every year so no rent in that time.
- Have someone manage the property for you.
- Ideally, look for a property with someone who is experienced in what constitutes a good investment.
- Buy properties built with permanent materials (brick, tile, concrete, wood).
- Buy near public transport and schools, in an area where the council and government are investing.
- Ideally buy in an area with tertiary institutions, a port and/or a hospital.

The biggest problem with buying a single investment property is the lack of diversification. This could be hedged by buying a second property in a different area, so that you can continue to benefit from leverage. If leverage isn't the driver to your investment strategy, you could achieve greater diversification by investing in a property portfolio via a managed fund (see page 256).

What if I end up with a lemon?

If you are moving forward, it's fairly common to occasionally take a wrong turn or make a misstep and end up buying something you shouldn't have. It might make sense at the time, but, before you know it, it's no longer giving you what it needs to, and it now feels like a lemon. The lemon could be a property, a business or any other investment.

It happens to many of us, and what may start off as a great investment can deteriorate into a dud due to a change of circumstances, market conditions, changing financing rules, poor planning on your part or just plain bad luck. Twenty years ago, many sensible citizens purchased properties made of plaster. The council approved these buildings, they seemed like a good buy, but when the rain came the buildings started to leak. The people who bought those properties could have taken all the precautions in the world and they still would have ended up with a lemon.

Some say it's possible to turn a lemon into lemonade. I'm not sure it's worth it; understanding when to cut your losses, and what to do after you cut your losses, is more helpful than hoping the situation will turn itself around. In many instances, the best thing to do is to focus on making up ground with an alternative strategy, rather than waste your time trying to recoup your losses. I have seen too many people holding onto a dud investment that has cost them a lot of money — I'm not sure whether this is out of obstinancy or pride, but they're not willing to get rid of the property until it has recouped the money that has been spent on it.

I had a couple of clients who bought a lifestyle block and rented it out. It made a $30,000 loss annually, which they were funding from their cashflow. They continued to top up this property for five years. They were prepared to do this because they eventually wanted to move on to the lifestyle block. They believed that it would go up in value and that, over time, the capital gain would be greater than their holding costs. But, most importantly, they could easily afford the top-up as their disposable income was very high.

This was all fine and dandy until the Global Financial Crisis hit. In response to the GFC, their income took a dive and one spouse was made redundant. The idea of having a lifestyle block, which had been a considered purchase holding so much promise, became a noose round their neck. They wanted to sell it, but the property had actually decreased in value by $50,000 from when they had bought it. If they decided to sell it, they would be out of pocket by a total of $200,000 (five years of $30,000 top-ups plus the $50,000 decrease in value). It was at this point that they came to me.

As I saw it, they had four options: hold onto the lifestyle block; do something to it to add value; sell it and call it a day; or sell it and replace it with another investment. The idea of holding onto it was not financially viable and there was no equity to develop it, which meant they had to sell it. But how do you swallow that bitter pill? The only way was to demonstrate to them the financial difference between doing nothing and selling the property. Perhaps most importantly, they needed to determine how they were then going to make up the ground they had lost. *It's OK to take a financial hit, but you then need to have a strategy to get ahead faster.*

Whether your properties are sucking you dry or your business is on the brink, before you take any drastic action you need to be open to ideas on how the situation could be improved, including walking away from the investment. It's best to engage an expert to help you understand your options because these are emotionally charged discussions that are hard to navigate when you carry guilt, resentment or blame. Money will likely need to be spent, whether you are developing the property or selling it. Don't default to throwing good money after bad; if you have spent a lot of money on something over the years, don't conclude it needs to repay you before you get rid of it. This is sometimes the worst possible logic to apply.

20. Owning your own business

Owning your own business can be a great way to create wealth. In fact, it's one of the most popular wealth-creation assets for Kiwis (ahead of shares, managed funds and property). Perhaps that's because New Zealand is considered the easiest place in the world to start a business and is in the top three countries in the world to do business, so people are drawn to start new businesses here — despite high levels of failure.

While starting a business can be a quick exercise, taking it from start-up to profit usually takes longer, and is harder than a newbie might think. In their research, a Better for Business survey showed that Kiwis start their own businesses for a multitude of personal and financial reasons. Most simply wanted to earn enough to live on (91 per cent), to become their own boss (89 per cent), and to have a better lifestyle (89 per cent). Two-thirds of business owners also wanted to contribute positively to society through their business offering, and almost one-third were motivated to provide financial support to a social or charitable cause. The prospect of financial independence, the ability to accumulate assets, and the potential for long-term stability are all factors that motivate people to take the leap into entrepreneurship.

Interestingly, while the desire to 'be your own boss' is one of the top motivators in starting a business, it's also the least likely to stick as the business continues. Two other starting motivations that drop away as the business continues are 'business activity is a passion' and 'building a good personal reputation'.

Businesses seldom make the money you think within the time you expect. Moving from the business idea through to profit usually takes more time, cost and effort than you could imagine, and often fails to make the money you first projected in the timeframe you wanted. That said, starting a business and, more importantly, *building* a business remains one of the most common ways of growing wealth for Kiwis.

Approximately 13 per cent of the New Zealand workforce is self-employed. Interestingly, just over half of these people are aged 45 or older. As the need increases for people to work for longer in life, businesses are expected to become a more popular way to do this. Approximately 70 per cent of self-employed people contract their personal services to someone else (contracting themselves out, or freelancing). They don't have employees and they aren't building up a business to sell. They *are* the business. When they stop working, the income stops coming.

However, 'being in business' means you are earning income while you sleep; it means your business has a value that you could sell.

Intertwining business and personal finances

I work with a lot of self-employed clients who are running a business (with employees). Although the business is technically a separate entity, it is often run as an extension of their personal situation, with their business and personal finances intertwined. Often the owner puts personal costs through the business, and fails to pay themselves a consistent salary, which makes it hard to get a read on how profitable the business is, or to be able to make progress personally. Profits and cashflow aren't usually consistent from month to month, which can sometimes makes it feel impossible to build a business plan. So they don't. They still manage to get by, but it's stressful at times. For all the hours they work, their overall progress relative to effort is weaker than it should be.

This is when they turn up in my office, frustrated with their lack of cashflow, wealth and progress. The first thing I do is separate out the business performance from their personal spending. I am not interested in what costs can be made tax-deductible (well, not at this stage). I'm more interested in what their life costs, and how profitable the business is if it is to pay the owner what they need.

Often here's where we run into our first hurdle. All the intertwining of payments disguises the inefficiencies of both the business operation and the household. We work out where the issues sit and we solve them. As a rule of thumb, the more complicated the tax and ownership structure, the more likely the client isn't making much progress, because it's impossible to get line of sight on where the problems and opportunities sit.

Building a business

Building a business is hard. I know, because I've done it, a few times. I've had those 3 a.m. wakeups when you worry about cashflow, when you're frustrated by staff under-performance or just mad at yourself. I've made staff redundant; even when it was the right thing for them and the business, I still felt guilty. I went years before I paid myself a salary, reinvesting everything I earned back into the business to help it grow. For the first few years of my business, after the kids went to sleep I would switch my laptop back on and work past midnight, every night. I existed on little sleep, lots of sugar and sheer grit. 'This is what you trained for' was a mantra spoken to me by my mentor. Or in the quiet hours of the morning, in my head I heard my grandmother whispering, 'You're from pioneer stock, my girl, you've got this.'

It was hard. Exciting. Terrifying. Lonely. But mainly hard. As you'll know by now, I'm fond of Mike Tyson's quote: 'Everyone has a plan until they get punched in the mouth.' Nothing is truer when you are in business. You hope for the best, but there is always someone or something ready to punch you in the face. Sometimes you might deserve it, but usually you don't. I listen to people who say they want to be passionate about what they do. To be honest, I roll my eyes and think, it's easy to be passionate about something when you are ideating about it. Check in with business owners who are in the trenches fighting for their income, fighting to pay their staff and wanting to be at home every night with their family. Passion may have been a motivator to starting your business, but unless that passion is quickly met with profit, it won't carry you far.

Building a business requires an investment of time and capital (money invested). You don't usually get the money you invested back within the first couple of years. Instead, you're trying to grow the business profit to a point where it can pay you a regular salary, so you can live comfortably. The longer you can survive without having to take money out of the business, usually the better the chance of the business's survival. For this reason, getting your personal situation optimised before starting a business is key. Many business owners don't get their original money invested paid back to them until they sell the business.

In its infancy, you'll need to leave the profits of the business in the business so it can be reinvested to fuel growth, such as paying for advertising, buying more stock and recruiting more staff. Delaying the payment of profits (dividends) to the owner can put pressure on their personal situation, and it can all be for nothing if the owner doesn't know how to grow the business effectively. If your business isn't growing by at least 10 per cent year on year, then you need a specialist to help lift your performance. In my business,

I aimed for 50 per cent growth year on year. This is why I would always encourage you to work with a business expert or group of experts (such as an accountant, business coach, mentor, advisory board or governance board). Look for someone experienced, who has successfully grown their own business and knows what you need to focus on, in what order, to get the best results quickly.

Surviving tight cashflow

Data from small-business accountancy firm Xero shows 95 per cent of Kiwi small businesses experience at least one month of negative cashflow each year, and that the average small business struggles with negative cashflow for a third of the year.

Negative cashflow is when the expenses or costs paid out for the month are higher than the income received. It's to do with the cash actually banked, not the invoices raised. Many businesses make great sales each month, well above their expenses, but if their customers fail to pay on time, that puts tremendous pressure on the business. Many big businesses fail to pay small businesses on time; in 2022 Xero found that almost half of all invoices owed to small businesses were paid late.

When your customer doesn't pay on time, cash in can be a whole let less than what you expected. This shortfall has to be funded somehow, preferably from business savings.

These business savings are called 'working capital', which is the money you are supposed to set aside in the business bank account to help you weather the year ahead. However, the main problem for most small businesses is they don't have much working capital. Their coffers are empty before the bad weather approaches. If they are a big business, they might be able to go to the bank for a loan to tide them over. But when you're a small business, this is almost impossible. Banks don't want to help you on a good day, and they definitely don't want to help you on a bad one.

What are you supposed to do if you have no working capital or funding? Initially, most owners resort to not paying themselves. The same Xero survey found that 46 per cent of New Zealand's business owners and 60 per cent of sole traders weren't paying themselves as the current economic climate puts the squeeze on them financially. But most people can't do this for long when they have a mortgage to pay and mouths to feed.

Months of negative cashflow will impact your anxiety levels, stop you sleeping and empty your safety net. Any rainy-day funds are used up. God help you if you have a provisional tax payment due at the same time. It can feel like you are drowning, because you are. I work very closely with my clients and their accountants (if they are any good) to help navigate these conditions.

Business failure

For all the opportunity starting a business offers, most people fail to get from it what they hoped. Many people become self-employed to earn more money, only to end up paying themselves less. In reality they are still 'working for the man' — it's just that the man is themselves! Often the promise of flexitime turns into working long hours for a fraction of what they could have earned if they were working for someone else. While they might have started the business with hope, excitement and a vision to create something better for themselves and their family, it usually doesn't translate to this.

Running a successful small business is incredibly difficult and not for the weary. Few people have the skill, structure, funding, stamina and grit to survive over the long term. Depending on which statistics you look at, the general consensus is that 50 to 70 per cent of businesses in New Zealand will fail within the first five years. First-movers (people with a bold new idea or product to take to the market) fail more often than those looking to build or improve an existing idea or product. Being first is seldom an advantage.

Too many small-business owners fail in business. What causes these failures can vary dramatically, but the most common causes of failure stem from:

- negative cashflow
- lack of working capital — which means if a debtor is late in paying you, you feel it, and you can absorb only so much of this before the lights go out
- poor cashflow management
- lack of capital to invest in growth — it is really hard to access funding; banks don't want to help and you aren't interested in or have a business ready for investors
- profit growing too slowly
- wrong business model or wrong pricing
- fixed costs creeping up
- not knowing the financial pulse of the business — just the basics (break-even, profit, and what you need to pay yourself to survive)

and how you are tracking against these numbers
- not minimising your personal spending, which then puts pressure on the business to fund your lifestyle
- burdening the business with personal costs
- intermingling business and personal costs so you have no clarity on how well each is doing
- focusing on tax savings at the expense of progress
- having no clear strategy to grow profit.

Dealing with tax

Tax is a necessity of living in the Western world. It can single-handedly wipe out a small business if you don't manage the business's finances well.

Keeping it simple, you pay tax on your business profit. The problem is that, all too often, the money is not sitting in the bank account when you need to pay the tax. There are two main reasons for this:

1. Tax is calculated on the business profit, but business profit doesn't recognise if you are yet to be paid for your sales, nor does it take into account when you buy assets that are not expensed through the business. Many small-business owners tend to intermingle personal costs with the business, which depletes business resources to fund their lifestyle.
2. Tax is paid in instalments that do not align with when you actually receive payment for goods.

There may also be poor cashflow in the business. That is, just because the business has made a profit does not mean that the money is physically sitting in the bank. It could already be spent (not good) or it might still be waiting to come in (payment from clients). In this second situation you need to collect from your debtors. Push hard to reduce the amount of money that customers owe you, because you will have to pay tax on the money even if you haven't received it yet.

Minimising tax

Leading up to year-end:
- try to keep stock levels low (purchase after year-end)
- delay sales
- write off bad debts in your accounts
- write back income that has not yet been earned.

In order to minimise your tax going forward:

- Push private debt into the company up to the value of your shareholder current account. There is a bit to legitimately unlocking this benefit, so please work closely with your accountant and financial advisor. The upshot is that the interest on this new business loan is now paid for by the business and is a tax-deductible cost to the business.
- Use legitimate structures to better manage and minimise your tax.
- Ensure you have maximised your home-office claim and claimed mileage for your travel.
- Form an independent opinion of what tax you would expect to pay and use this as a mental measure against what your accountant has prepared, then get them to explain (in plain English) any discrepancies.
- Run your personal affairs separately from your business. Mixing the two will mean you will be less aware as to how well you are really doing, and usually results in missed tax write-offs because your accountant prefers to take a more conservative view.

If you have tax arrears, you need a plan to pay these off. Don't bury your head in the sand — it is costing you more than you realise in terms of money, stress and a sense of hopelessness.

Things to watch out for

Just because you paid for a cost through the business doesn't mean that your accountant is deducting it. I had a client who had paid $30,000 of legitimate business costs through their business bank account and presumed that their accountant had deducted them. The accountant incorrectly made a call that the costs weren't tax-deductible. This meant the business profit was overstated and the tax was higher than what she should have paid.

> **Tip:** Print out your drawings account, as these costs are not currently sitting as a business cost. Review each item to see if you can spot any costs that are genuine business costs. Tell your accountant so they can correct the financial statements and tax returns.

Most accountants tell you what you have done for the year — not what you need to do — so I would encourage you to get separate advice on how to take your business forward and how to reduce your tax.

You are in business because you are good at what you do. However, being good at what you do does not mean that you can necessarily run your business the best way, minimise your tax or make as much money as you should. It makes sense to get professional help.

> **Tip:** Paying provisional tax is one of the biggest cashflow drags on a small business. Use Taxi (discussed overleaf) to buy you access to a funding line. This buffers your cashflow, improving the financial resilience of your business.

Help is coming

Cashflow management is hard. It's made harder when you haven't been able to access funding to tide you over until you get paid by your customer. I get it. It's rough. But help is on the way, and it's coming in the most unlikely form.

All small businesses need to be able to survive when cash is tight, right? This cashflow squeeze is usually exacerbated by provisional tax payments, which is tax paid in advance against next year's profit. You usually pay provisional tax in three instalments each year (January, May and August). If you pay late, you also pay penalties and sometimes use-of-money interest (UOMI). So for many making these payments is sacrosanct.

Provisional tax payments have been set up to help you manage your tax liabilities. The Inland Revenue Department (IRD) estimates the tax you have to pay from the prior year's earnings and adds 5 per cent, and splits it into three payments, with a wash-up payment at the end of the year if you haven't paid enough. Whether or not you're on track to earn the same as the year before isn't considered relevant.

The IRD takes the view that it will sort itself out in the wash, and if you have overpaid tax it will be refunded to you, so overall you won't be out of pocket. Which is true. But timing is everything, especially if you're going backwards. For the sinking business, it would have been better to not have to pawn the family jewels in order to make a provisional tax payment that was going to be refunded 12 months later.

When you make your provisional tax payments, the tax isn't due yet, because you haven't yet filed the tax return. And you haven't filed your tax return because the year is still in full flight. But you are doing what you are told, and avoiding late payment penalties, and getting the provisional tax bill paid on time. What you probably don't realise is the tax is sitting in a holding account with the government-owned Public Trust, who hold it for the IRD until it is due to be paid, which is after you have filed your tax return that confirms the tax amount owed. Because it is sitting in no-man's land until you file your tax return, it doesn't earn interest for you, and it's not earning interest for the IRD. Seems kind of weird, but stick with me.

There will be times in your business where you could have survived more comfortably if you didn't have to pay your provisional tax in full, or right away. A little bit of grace would have made a whole lot of difference. This is where Taxi comes in, to help you smooth your cashflow.

Full disclosure: I have been working with Taxi, testing their product and working with my clients as early adopters of the service. If you pay your tax through them to you meet your IRD tax obligations, then you can re-access a portion of the payments made. As you make future tax payments you get access to more capital. It allows you to keep your business moving, and the IRD happy. When you draw against the funds you have deposited, it acts like an overdraft or short-term loan (that you need to repay), borrowed against your provisional tax payments. It's linked to your IRD account and Public Trust. Although you might only need the use of the funds for a month or two, you have up to nine months to repay them. Which, for many in business, is more than enough grace.

For one of my clients it gave them the ability to keep up to date with their tax payments, and also pay for new signage immediately, instead of saving for another three months. Capital investment was no longer delayed for tax payments. For another, it gave them funds to complete a property purchase as they were slightly short on their saved deposit. They could have chosen to not pay their provisional tax in order to fund their property purchase, and incur penalties and interest. This way they got the best of both worlds at a fraction of the price. Another client was able to pay themselves their normal wage while they waited for a big customer to pay their bill. If they hadn't had access to Taxi, they would have either gone without, or delayed paying their tax bill, and this would have come at a higher cost. Another client used their Taxi account to negotiate prompt payment discounts, in excess of the overdraft rate charged. Timing makes all the difference when cashflow is tight. Taxi gives you funding to buy you time.

I am not going to lie, I love it. It's clever, easy to use and has been a game changer for my small-business clients. I especially love that it is a New Zealand business. Like everything, it comes with precautions, and should only be used if you are supported by your financial advisor or accountant.

At the very least, I now encourage all my clients to pay their provisional tax via Taxi, if for no other reason than to give them the option of a funding line in the future, should they need it. If they don't use it, then no harm done. But if they need it, it can be a lifesaver. It doesn't require an application process — the funds are ready for you and you can make a withdrawal at any point. You don't need to give a personal guarantee, and the interest rate charged if you do use the funding line is half what you would pay to the bank in the unlikely event they did give you a bank overdraft.

Some will never need the facility, but some might. Having it set up means no matter when you are punched in the face, you will be able to handle it.

Business life cycles

When you are in business, you need to be aware of your industry's life cycle and your business's life cycle. Only when you understand where your industry is can you determine the best strategy for your business. When you are clear about where your business is at in its life cycle, you can determine which of the many suggestions for improving your business are actually relevant. For example, many books tell you the key to success in business is for you to work *on* the business not *in* the business. At a conceptual level this is correct, but if your business is in its infancy, with a lack of systems and an 'all hands to the pump' mentality, delegation to others so you can work on growing the business is both premature and impossible.

> **Tip:** A business is five times more likely to fail if its growth is less than annual GDP growth. To be successful you need to sustain performance over a long period of time.

I have had many clients over the years with their hearts set on owning a business. Many have little to no financial literacy or experience in running a business, but dream of being their own boss. Anyone who owns their own successful business knows that being your own boss can be completely overrated (much like pregnancy, in my opinion), yet, if done right, owning a business can have huge financial benefits.

Depending on whether you are buying a business or starting one, the strategies for growth, profit and success will differ. I will address each separately in the following chapters.

21. Buying a business

A new client of mine bought into a business and paid what I thought was a lot of money for a dead duck. They were now struggling to make the business work. In short, she had paid too much for the business, and that cost was now causing her a financial haemorrhage because the business wasn't performing as it was supposed to. This meant she had to inject more of her own money into the business to keep it afloat while she worked out what she was going to do.

I asked my client if she had received any advice before buying the business and her answer was 'No, not really.' She pretty much let the seller jot a few notes down on the back of an envelope and took that as gospel. She checked out the business operations and then put in an offer based on her gut. If she'd been my client at that point I wouldn't have let her buy it, but all too often people only ask for help once they are already in trouble.

New Zealanders like to be their own boss. We like buying franchises or businesses and 'having a go'. We tend to trust other people too much, and too often don't understand the numbers of a business. We take the seller at face value. Too many people lack a commercial lens and make big financial moves like buying a business without getting a second opinion from someone who is qualified to give them an unbiased view. We are a DIY nation and this usually extends to financial advice as well.

How much should you pay?

The biggest setback to business success is paying too much for the business in the first place, then not retaining enough working capital to invest in its growth. Much like an overvalued house, just because you paid more than it was worth doesn't mean that the person you eventually sell to will do the same. If they are sensible, do their due diligence and have a smart accountant, they will only pay the market value, meaning the person who over-capitalised is the one who suffers — you.

I've found that the main reason people pay too much for a business is that they don't know how to value it — and, to be perfectly honest, most accountants don't know how to do this either. An accountant can apply a methodology to it, but you as the buyer need to understand what you are buying, what it is really costing you and what you are likely to get out the other end when you sell. *Always buy a business assuming you will sell it at some point.* Like negotiating to buy real estate, it's not what someone is prepared to sell the property for that is the issue. The issue is how much are you prepared to pay for it.

People often pay too much because it is easy for the vendor to manipulate a business's financial statements in order to show the purchaser what the vendor wants them to see, not what the purchaser needs to see. If I have a client looking to buy a business I run through a list of questions with them to help them with their due diligence. (Due diligence is the process of testing whether what the seller is saying is in fact correct; see page 242.) Not surprisingly, none of the following questions take into account what your gut is telling you, which disturbingly seems to be the most commonly used reason for going ahead with a purchase! Ask yourself the following questions.

1. How much (roughly) are you investing? What will this cost you in interest, or in interest you are not earning on money that could have been invested elsewhere? This needs to be deducted from the profit.

2. If you weren't working in the business yourself, what would you need to pay someone to do your job? This salary overhead needs to be deducted from the profit. Is the business still profitable?

3. Does the salary/wages cost in the profit-and-loss statement include money paid to the owner?

4. Do you think you can grow the business?

5. In your normal day job, what salary would you have been paid? Could you realistically replace this salary with business drawings and profits?

6. What return are you getting from your initial investment? Will the business pay at least 30 per cent of your investment back to you each year?

Before you buy a business, the vendor will give you a copy of their profit-and-loss statement and the business's balance sheet (what the business owns, usually stock). They will have set a purchase price. Anything above the value of the tangible assets and liabilities of the business you are buying is considered goodwill. Goodwill is a term to describe the intangible assets of the business that have value but are not reflected on the balance sheet. Goodwill can include the business brand, website, systems and processes, strategic alliances, software and licences. For example, if a business has an effective way of generating leads, this is an internal process that won't have a value on the balance sheet but is still an asset. If it has a database, operating manuals, internal systems or trademarks, these are all intellectual assets, but are not reflected in the financial records. The amount you pay for goodwill reflects the value of these intangible assets. So the real question is: what value are you prepared to put on the goodwill, over and above the tangible assets?

Another way to work out how much to pay for a business is looking at how many years you are prepared to take to pay off your initial investment. This involves ascertaining what *profit multiple* you are prepared to use to value the business.

If the vendor has used a profit multiple of three, it means they have multiplied the business's current annual profit (after tax) by three to arrive at a value which they are comfortable to sell the business for. This means it will take the purchaser three years before their initial investment is repaid. Pay attention to whether they are using the before-tax or after-tax profit number in their calculations, as this will shift the payback period. If it is after-tax profit, then whatever multiple they apply will be how many years before you are repaid. If it's before tax, it is going to take you 28 per cent longer again, so a multiple of three (which is three years), is divided by 72 per cent (1 less the company tax rate of 28 cents) to give us 4.2 years to pay off the original investment (assuming the business remains profitable at the same level) before you will be able to re-access the profits for your own use. In the meantime you can pay yourself a salary if you are working in the business, but this cost would be included in the expenses.

This is where so many purchasers go wrong. They base their calculations on the profit that the seller is showing and do not factor in other specific costs to determine a more accurate profit as it relates to them.

> **Tip:** Aim to get the business paying you a 30 per cent return on your initial investment. So if you paid $200,000 for the business, you would want it to pay you $60,000 profit each year plus your salary to run the business.

Understand that when the vendor is showing a profit, they're likely to have made it seem higher than what it really is. They might be working in the business but not paying themselves a salary, or paying themselves a lower-than-market salary, so the wages costs are artificially low. Secondly, they may show the *profit before tax*. And, thirdly, they won't have factored in the interest that you need to pay to invest in the business.

Paring this down to the essentials: if you are investing in a business, you are using your own money (or the bank's) to buy it. This money has a cost. By that I mean the business has to give you a return greater than what you could have earned on this money if you had put it in the bank, or if you are borrowing the funds the business needs to give you a return greater than the interest rate you're paying on the loan (the cost of funds).

Next, if you are going to work in the business, it needs to give you a salary to reflect the time you are investing in it or, more accurately, to reflect that because you're working in the business, you're not able to work for someone else, which is costing you a salary/income. (Personally, I believe that if you are buying a business you need to be prepared to work in it full-time. You need to be at the coalface to understand the intricacies of a business, especially when your own money is involved.) The business needs to pay you what it would pay someone else to do the same job (the market value of the role).

On top of all this, the business is also going to occupy your mind. You will be eating and breathing it for the foreseeable future. This means that you are not going to be free to live the balanced life you want (not in the short term, anyway). If the business grows, it's probably your money that will make this happen. If the business doesn't have enough money to pay wages, it will be you staying up at night worrying about it. If someone is unable to do their job, it will be you who steps in or finds the solution. What price do you put on this? What is a fair payment to recognise the risk you are taking on as the business owner?

Before you involve an accountant and start the due-diligence process, you need to determine at a core level whether what the vendor is asking is something you are prepared to pay. If the two values will never meet, then you are better to save yourself the time, effort and cost of doing due diligence and back out now.

You will need to get a good handle on the numbers early on. You don't need to be an accountant, but you do need to be able to understand some basic arithmetic. As an example, let's say you are considering buying a small business which is selling for $200,000, which includes $50,000 of stock. It's showing a profit of $50,000 after tax ($69,000 before tax). The owner of the business has been working part-time in it but has not been taking a salary.

At face value, you are buying stock of $50,000 and paying $150,000 for the business. This is a profit multiple of three — it will take you a little over four years to pay off your initial investment. However, this is only the starting point. Let's say you need to borrow $200,000 at 6 per cent to buy the business. That results in $12,000 in interest costs per annum. What's more, if you were to pay someone to work in the business to replace the owner, let's say this would cost you $15,000 per annum. This means you need to factor in a further $27,000 of costs (before tax). This means the profit will reduce to $31,000 after tax. This increases the profit multiple to five, meaning that it will take you 6.5 years to pay off the business, or it will be five years before you can take the profits of the business as your own. This also assumes that the business will be able to keep running at its current level for five years as a minimum. Is that a realistic proposition for your situation?

Let's assume the numbers do work for you, even though the profit is lower than what the vendor is advertising (when applied to your situation). The next thing you need to understand is the cashflow. People new to business think that the profit and cashflow of the business are interchangeable. They are not. The *profit* of the business is what your tax liability is calculated on. This can have little correlation to the cashflow of the business, which is *how much money you have in the bank at any one time*. Cashflow is king. Cashflow is what pays your salary, and it is how you pay your staff and tax and other obligations.

When you know how, manipulating the profit of a business is fairly easy. As an owner, you should be more interested in the cashflow of the business. Cashflow is the best indicator of business performance. It is a window on the business's soul.

> **Tip:** If you are new to business, pay more attention to the cashflow of the business and let your accountant worry about the profit.

Next, and again before you involve an accountant, you need to be thinking about how you might improve the profit position of the business. Realistically, is there an opportunity to increase sales or decrease expenses? What opportunities are at your disposal to grow the profit? If you plan to sell the business in five years, what could you do to make it worth more to the next buyer so you can receive a higher price?

For income to increase, one or both of the following need to happen:

1. You get more customers.
2. You increase the price of your product or service.

Your profit forecast needs to detail how you are going to achieve either of the things above, otherwise it is a target, not a budget.

> **Tip:** If the business is going through a high-growth period or phase, the cashflow improvements aren't usually felt for about 12 months. If you have had to invest in the business to fund the growth, the lag to profit lift will feel like an eternity. This means you'll have a high profit on paper, but no money in the bank to pay a physical dividend.

It's only when you have worked through the preliminary steps listed in the previous pages, and in doing so are happy in principle that it could work, that you can conclude that, based on the information provided, you are comfortable that the business might be a good investment. It's at that point that you start testing whether the numbers provided are true or not. This is when you start the due-diligence process.

Due diligence

The due-diligence process is a formal process you go through to verify that what the vendor is saying is true. Sure, they have provided you with a profit-and-loss statement, but is this sourced from their actual business performance or are they fabricating a spreadsheet and plucking numbers from thin air to make the business look better than it is? Always assume the latter and work through the data to prove yourself wrong.

Due diligence takes a three-pronged approach, incorporating the following elements:

1. financial — verifying the profit-and-loss
2. legal — verifying the balance sheet (does the business have legal title to the assets it says it owns?)
3. business — determining what liabilities the business could face and the viability of opportunities.

Financial due diligence

- Take the amount the vendor tells you they withdraw from the business with a grain of salt.
- The best way to verify the profit-and-loss is by looking at the business's GST returns for the previous two years. Add up the sales. Add up the expenses. Do these amounts match the sales and expenses in the profit-and-loss? If they don't, how much are they out by? Could this be explained by the fixed assets purchased in the balance sheet? If there is no logical explanation for discrepancies then this should set off warning bells.
- The GST returns will also show you if the business is receiving GST refunds. If so, it means that it is cashflow-negative, or running at a cash loss.
- If the number of debtors is high, this means there are a lot of people who owe money to the business, which isn't a particularly good sign. Find out how long an average customer will take to pay.
- What is the shareholders' current account balance? This is money that they have put into the business. If the number keeps going up, then it means the business is actually going backwards. If the shareholders' current account is in the red, it means the shareholders are sucking the business dry. This is a bad sign. Check it against the previous year's balance to see how the situation has changed.
- Make sure the profit is real and tied back to a tax return.
- Always get a second opinion on the business from your accountant and solicitor. Make sure your accountant understands business, though. Too many accountants pigeon-hole themselves as bean counters and don't know how to grow a business.
- Calculate your 'working capital' needs. This is normally three months of trading costs that you will need to have available to you during the first year of business.
- Determine what capital investment could be made, when and the cost. How do you plan to fund this investment?

Legal due diligence

It is important that your solicitor completes a legal due diligence of the business to determine that:

- the assets of the business are legally owned by the vendors
- there are no pending legal disputes

- the terms of trade, employment contracts and client contracts are in order
- key supplier arrangements are tied down.

A solicitor will also review the terms of the lease you will likely be taking over.

They also need to review the sale-and-purchase agreement once it has been presented. This could come prior to the due diligence or after.

Business due diligence

Talk to someone who is in business and understands it to get a better idea of the growth opportunities and potential risks you face. Understand where the business is at in its life cycle and how the industry is generally performing. How long before you need to sell it? Do you have enough energy and resources to grow the business to where it needs to be? What is an achievable business forecast? If you were accountable to someone else, what key performance indicators would you set?

The best business owners run their businesses as if they are working for someone else. They don't think of the business as their own, or take liberties because they own it. Instead, they have a higher expectation of themselves than what they would expect of their staff.

Terms of the contract

So you've completed your due diligence and have been made aware of the business's risks and opportunities. The financials have been verified and you are comfortable with how long it will take you to make your money back (or pay off the investment), despite it being longer that what the vendor suggested. Now it's time to document the terms of the sale in an agreement for the sale and purchase of a business. This agreement will record the purchase price and settlement date, the entity buying the business, whether the purchase is subject to finance, and often a restraint of trade on the vendor (as you don't want them starting up in competition the next day). It will include vendor warranties around the turnover of the business and the level of assistance the vendor will provide.

You can then start on the next part of the equation of taking over the business:
- make a profit
- grow the business

- pay back your investment
- grow the business some more
- sell!

> **Tip:** I own a number of businesses, and I coach many businesses. I also have my own coach. Working with a coach can be a great way to fast-track growth with clear goals, better structure and support. For me, accountability is the key to unlocking faster success.

22. Starting a business

I have seen many businesses through working with my clients. Some people have strived to become self-employed, while others have fallen into or inherited a business.

Some of the businesses I see are a complete waste of time, paying the owner less than the minimum wage. You have to ask why they keep at it; I do ask my clients this, because my fundamental belief is that if you are going to work harder than before, put in your own money, take on more risk than an employee as well as putting relationships under strain, then it has to be worth it, both financially and emotionally. Personally, I don't buy into the idea that being passionate about your business in isolation is justification for continuing it. I stress to clients that passion is irrelevant if you are not making money. *You need to make money.* You need to make more money than you could earn elsewhere, otherwise the hidden cost (or opportunity cost) of being in business is too high.

For the right person, however, being self-employed and building a business is their calling, a way to build a strong income and create something of value that can be sold at a later point.

To start a business from scratch, you need to understand how to run a business and you need to know that your business idea can be taken to the market. Having a good idea does not a business make, but it is definitely a good start.

Starting a business is always trickier than you realise. If you're ready for hard work, some long days and weeks, and initially making little money but you are inspired by your idea or concept, then starting a business could be just what the doctor ordered.

A lot of people think when they start a business that they will fast-forward to business success. While this is possible, few end up there as quickly as they thought they would. Most have to systematically build a business from an idea (which, on its own, isn't really a business), to its infancy (when you have to invest money), to its childhood and right through to its maturity, and this can take years. But if you have it in you, and you do it right, a lot of money can be made, tax efficiencies can be created, and you are in the driver's seat of building an asset that can pay you a salary *and* eventually be sold. For those with the stomach for it, it's an exhilarating ride.

What factors count the most in start-up success?

When it comes to the success of a larger start-up, what makes the most difference? Is it the idea for the product, or does the team you have working for you make more of a difference? Does the team's ability to execute and adapt to being punched in the face by the customer make more impact than the business model? The business model is about having a clear path to generate customer revenues, but if you are too slow to achieve this, does funding play a bigger part in your ability to succeed? Or is it timing: is the idea too early and the world is not ready for it; is it early and you have to educate the world; is it just right; or is it too late and there are now too many competitors? Bill Gross, in his research about why start-ups succeed (summarised in his TED Talk), unpacked these elements across 200 different businesses.

He looked at what factors had the biggest impact between success and failure across all the companies. Airbnb, a wild success, was passed on by many initial investors who thought it crazy that people would rent out their home to a stranger. But the timing of this business was spot on; it launched at the height of the GFC when households needed extra income. Likewise, YouTube happened to launch after broadband penetration crossed 50 per cent in America. YouTube didn't even have a business model when it started, but the timing was perfect. The idea wasn't new but the conditions at launch proved critical.

Gross concluded that, for big start-ups, execution matters a lot, the idea matters, but timing is key. Is the customer ready for your product? Are market conditions ripe for your product? If you can get your timing right, you are more likely to succeed. The other factors rounding out the top five were having a workable business model and adequate funding.

To avoid being a statistic, you also need to know the top causes of business failure, so you can avoid them:
- timing – things don't happen as quickly as you expect and you run out of money waiting for things to pick up
- the market isn't ready for the product and you have to educate them
- using the wrong business model

- insufficient capital to invest
- owner focuses on the wrong things to create wealth
- lack of due diligence (no market for the product)
- not understanding what your life costs are, and making sure the business can cover this — this results in drawing too much out of the business to fund your personal situation
- no real business plan
- personal use of business funds
- poor management of stock
- over-investment in fixed assets
- poor debtor arrangements
- growing too fast or growing too slowly
- competition
- low sales
- lack of experience
- poor location.

How do I move from being self-employed to running a business?

The answer to this is simple: you have to make your business profitable. You need to separate out your personal spending and drawings and give your business a shot at shining. For some reason, the average Kiwi business struggles with this notion. You can be good at a particular skill, but that does not mean that you will be good in business. The two points are unrelated.

To make money in business, you need to be good at business. There is no formal training for this, and your accountant, despite being your natural first port of call, is probably the worst person you could speak to about the practicalities of growing a business.

There are two main steps.

1. Know what your business needs to do to break even — what are your expenses?
2. Know what it needs to do to be profitable — how much do you need to sell to cover your cost of investment and living costs?

You can then work backwards to get a better understanding of the components that make up profit. Remember, *profit* is the output. If you want to change an output, you need to understand how the inputs work together to affect the end game.

In business, you have opportunities to sell your product or service. These opportunities can be called *leads*. You must convert these leads into customers. The ratio of success from lead to customer is your *conversion rate*.

Creating business profit

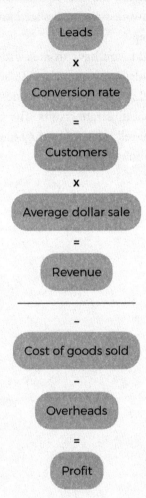

Each *customer* will spend an average amount with you per transaction, or over a period of time, depending on the type of product or service you sell. The *average sale* multiplied by the number of customers translates to your income or *revenue*. Your *profit margin* (profit as a percentage of sales) helps you calculate your profit.

When working with my clients, I break down each component to determine what can be improved and how. The 'how' is often the toughest part. Many people assume that to increase profit you need to sell more or get more customers. But, as you can see from the diagram on the previous page, you have seven broad opportunities to increase your profit, ranging from more effective advertising to better training or incentives for sales staff, to cutting the overhead costs of the business. By the time I have finished with a client's business we have sliced and diced and strategised ways to change its landscape.

No matter what you do, you have to measure your performance. You cannot tweak or tune unless you measure. This is where a lot of small businesses come unstuck: they lack the basics of reporting tools or management accounts that illustrate results. The financial statements they get from their accountant tell them what they have done the year before, not what they need to do going forward.

23. Other investments

While property and businesses are the most popular forms of investment for Kiwis, there are other valid options to understand, as they too have benefits. The key distinction between property and business and the other, more traditional types of investments (managed funds, shares, etc.), is that one usually has to be mortgage-free in order to justify other forms of investment. Because the majority of Kiwis are not in this position, these investments are not on many people's radars. However, after you have killed your mortgage, you will have an opportunity to consider a wider pool of investment options.

KiwiSaver

KiwiSaver is a voluntary, work-based savings scheme set up by the government in July 2007 to encourage New Zealanders to save for their retirement. If you're employed, living in New Zealand and under the age of 65, you can choose to contribute 3, 4, 6, 8 or 10 per cent of your gross (before-tax) wage or salary to your KiwiSaver account. Your employer has to contribute as well — at least 3 per cent of your gross salary. If you are self-employed you can make voluntary contributions.

There are many benefits to being in KiwiSaver:

- If you're employed, your employer has to contribute at least 3 per cent of your gross wage or salary to your KiwiSaver account. That's on top of your own contributions.
- Your funds are locked away until you are 65, which means you can't inadvertently fritter away this money. The exception to this is if you need to withdraw funds to buy your first home or you get into financial hardship.
- It is an enforced savings scheme, with the money deducted from your pay before you even see it.
- The government pays into your KiwiSaver account as well — paying an annual 'member tax credit' (if you are a contributing member aged 18 or over) of up to $521.

- As well as saving for retirement, you can also use KiwiSaver to help you save for your first home through a HomeStart grant and home-purchase withdrawal system.

Choosing a KiwiSaver fund

You can choose the KiwiSaver scheme in which your savings are invested or let your employer or the government choose one for you. KiwiSaver schemes are run by providers such as banks and investment companies.

Most KiwiSaver schemes have several different investment funds into which you can put your money. Each fund has a different mix of things it invests in — such as bank deposits, bonds, shares and property. *KiwiSaver schemes and their investment funds are not guaranteed by the government.* Each fund has a different risk rating (conservative, balance, growth, etc.), and different fee structures and levels of diversification.

KiwiSaver is a great opportunity to jump ahead with your savings. If you can afford to be in it, you should be. However, if you are going backwards, then you might consider opting for a holiday from KiwiSaver in order to channel more income towards clearing debt.

I do not encourage clients to opt out of KiwiSaver lightly, however, as increasing their take-home pay (by not being in KiwiSaver) means their employer is not contributing to the scheme either. Stopping comes at a cost. However, it is sometimes the right thing to do in order to free up funds and tidy up your financial situation. There is no point have money squirrelled away until you are 65 if you are going to go bankrupt tomorrow!

> **Tip:** If you are self-employed, contribute to your KiwiSaver fund up to the level required to qualify for the maximum 'member tax credit'. This works out at around $20 per week for an annual government contribution of $521.

Term deposits

A term deposit is money deposited at a bank that cannot be withdrawn for a fixed period of time or 'term' (unless a penalty is paid or interest is forfeited). When the term is over the money can be withdrawn or it can be held for another term. Generally speaking, the longer you leave the money in the bank, the better the interest rate (yield) offered.

The rate of return is higher for a term deposit than for a standard savings account because the bank is not obliged to return the money to you on demand. Instead, the bank can take the money and invest it elsewhere for a period of time (within the initial term) to gain higher returns than if the money was on call.

Term deposits are typically provided by mainstream banks. They are usually low-risk, because there is a high reliability of the bank paying you the interest when it is due, and repaying the initial investment (term deposit) when you request it. While the expectation remains higher than most investments, it is still not guaranteed. This means that in the event of bank failure, the government isn't obliged to step in to bail out the bank.

Term deposits are simple to set up and have very few conditions attached. That said, you should understand that for the bank to pay you a return on the money held in a term deposit, the bank needs to lend the money out to another party or parties, investing it with the intention of earning a higher interest rate than it is obliged to pay you. The bank lends the money under general lending guidelines; for example, if the bank lends to a developer, it is normal for the bank to take the first mortgage over the developer as a form of security for the investment.

If the entity you have lent the money to is a finance company, they tend to offer higher returns than a mainstream bank. This is usually because the investments they make (with the money you have given them) are riskier because they are lending money to businesses who haven't been able to get their lending from a mainstream bank, and as a result the finance company can't always take as much security in the investment as a mainstream bank. This risk is recognised and they will therefore pay you a higher interest rate.

In a financial crisis, as happened in 2007, if the developer goes under and the finance company ranks second behind a mainstream bank in getting their investment back, it's your invested funds that are lost. Many of us are happy to get a higher return on our investments but are slow to connect the dots that the higher return means higher risk. When the deck of cards falls, as we saw in the Global Financial Crisis, you tend to lose a lot.

The return on a term deposit is generally lower than that of investments in riskier products like stocks or bonds.

At the time of writing, we don't yet have a deposit guarantee scheme in New Zealand. We are the only country in the OECD that doesn't have one. This means that in the event of bank failure, the government isn't obliged to step in to bail out the bank and protect the deposits of customers. There is a proposed scheme put forward in government to protect up to $100,000 of deposits per person with the bank by issuing a type of insurance to deposit holders (that they pay for), but it ensures their savings are protected in the event of bank failure. Consumer NZ suggests this would protect 93 per cent of deposit holders. You may think it's unlikely that a New Zealand bank would need to be bailed out, but as previously noted, BNZ has had to be bailed out twice in its history.

Debentures

Debentures are similar in concept to a term deposit in the sense that you are paid interest over a fixed period and you are supposed to receive your money back at the end of the term. However, unlike a term deposit, debentures can vary in risk. Higher-risk debentures should pay a higher rate of return, although this is not always the case, especially when the finance company wants to downplay the real risk of the investment.

The finance company is free to on-lend the funds, much like a bank, and typically they lend the funds to higher-risk activities. They have terms and conditions that highlight where you rank if the finance company goes under, which means you might not get all your money back if the finance company backs a dodgy investment. Be aware that finance companies are usually smaller outfits than banks and have limited resources if a development they have invested in goes under.

The paperwork will always say if a debenture is secured or unsecured. An unsecured debenture is riskier than a secured debenture, but being secured is a bit misleading because if the finance company goes under the 'security' can count for little.

Bonds

Bonds are a fixed-interest product. You hand over your deposit and collect a payment (in the form of interest or a coupon, which is a certificate giving you the right to receive a payment). Governments, local bodies, state-owned corporations and corporates can all issue bonds. When you buy a bond you are, in effect, lending money to the organisation issuing the bond. In New Zealand, bonds are traded on the New Zealand Debt Market (NZDX).

Governments issue bonds to borrow from the market and fund their day-to-day operations from within their own country or a foreign source. Foreign-currency government debt is also known as sovereign debt.

If you invest in foreign-government bonds, you need to understand what is happening in the country you are investing in, because the quality of the bond you are buying is only as good as the country issuing it (i.e., taking your money). *You should never lend to anyone who cannot afford to pay you back.* The same rule applies whether the borrower is a friend, a company or a government.

Until recently it was assumed that governments of large, stable countries were a relatively low-risk proposition because, like mainstream banks, they have significant resources to call on to honour their debts. However, the GFC highlighted several countries which are less stable than first thought.

Bonds issued by councils, local bodies and state-owned utilities are considered slightly higher risk than a government bond, as they are one stage removed from the government's obligations.

Similarly, bonds issued by corporations can be safe or risky depending on who is issuing them. For example, Whitcoulls is an example of a corporation that issued bonds during the GFC. When the bonds matured, they returned the investment to the bondholders, but two months later the company went into receivership. If this had happened before the bonds had matured, they would not have paid out.

In theory, corporate bonds are considered riskier than most bonds, but this blanket assumption is misleading. Like any investment, the risk is relative. The risk with corporate bonds depends on who the corporation is, where it is and the timing of the bond issue. For example, bonds issued by New Zealand finance companies were great for a long period of time, but in the space of 18 months between 2008 and 2010 most of them stopped trading and defaulted on their obligations. On the other hand, if Apple was to issue bonds they would be one of the safest investments in the world. Also, if it is a good investment, you are first in line to be paid out should the company go under.

Some bonds have an expiry or maturity date which indicates when you will be paid out. Perpetual bonds do not have a maturity date, so you pay once and receive coupons/interest at a set rate, but the issuer is not obliged to return your money at any set point. The coupon rate can be reset periodically and this is the main weakness of a perpetual bond — it may be reset at an unfavourable rate. Then, if you tried to sell it, you might lose money.

Like shares, bonds can be complicated and require detailed and impartial analysis and comparisons of performance and projections. If you do not have the understanding or time to do this, but you still wish to invest in bonds, you should probably have someone manage your bond portfolio for you.

Shares

When you buy a share, you become a shareholder of the company. You are buying a stake in the company, and, in most instances, the company will pay you an annual dividend based on the number of shares you own. This dividend is your share of the company's distributed profit.

Shares are bought and sold on exchanges. To buy and sell shares in New Zealand you could go through a sharebroker (also called a stockbroker), who has access to all the shares listed on the New Zealand Exchange (NZX), or via an online platform like Sharesies. One of the main benefits of online platforms is you can now invest smaller amounts of money (micro investing), making investing far more accessible to many.

Shares go up and down in value, which is all part of the investment journey. If you look at the sharemarket's trajectory since the 1930s (see overleaf), you can see strong overall growth and despite major hurdles like world wars, recessions and oil shocks, markets have rewarded long-term investors.

Although time smooths volatility, while trending up, it also takes some dips along the way. If you zoomed in a bit more, you'd see that the share-market has dropped by more than 15 per cent 15 times during the past 90 years. In 12 of these times, it corrected itself within a year. In the remaining three instances it took more than a year to correct itself, but then recovered strongly. We don't always know when markets will bottom out, but they always do, and the subsequent returns can come very fast. In fact, for every decline greater than 10 per cent since World War II the average historical returns over the subsequent 12, 24 and 36 months has been positive.

The positive news is that the market did correct itself. But, if you had to cash in your shares for genuine reasons, right at the point of the drop, any future correction would be irrelevant. With shares, it's really important to get the timing of when you exit and cash in right. Typically, I try and build in 12 months' grace for any big move (like liquidating an investment). If this buffer was built in from the start, you could pause, catch your breath, and wait for the storm to pass, without having to take a knock on your investment value. Don't underestimate the power of being able to hit the 'pause button'.

Managed funds

When you invest in a managed fund, your money is pooled with other investors' money and spread across different kinds of investments. The range

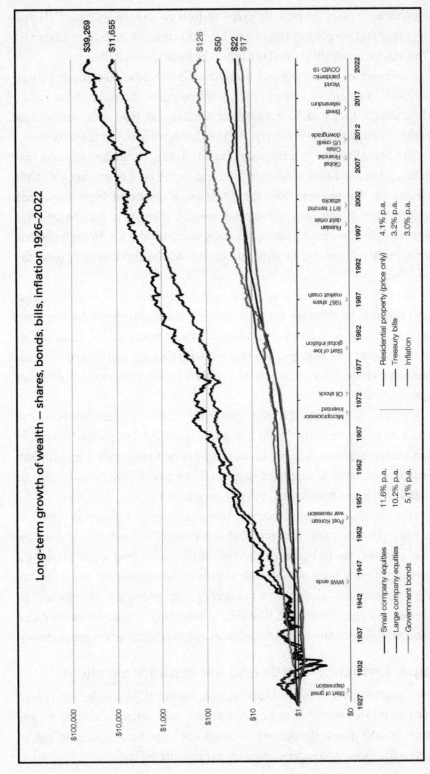

Long-term growth of wealth — shares, bonds, bills, inflation 1926–2022

Small company equities — 11.6% p.a.
Large company equities — 10.2% p.a.
Government bonds — 5.1% p.a.

Residential property (price only) — 4.1% p.a.
Treasury bills — 3.2% p.a.
Inflation — 3.0% p.a.

$39,269
$11,655
$126
$50
$22
$17

Start of great depression
WWII ends
Post Korean war recession
Oil shock
Microprocessor invented
Start of low global inflation
1987 share market crash
Russian debt crisis
9/11 terrorist attacks
Global Financial Crisis
US credit downgrade
Brexit referendum
World pandemic: COVID-19

1927 1932 1937 1942 1947 1952 1957 1962 1967 1972 1977 1982 1987 1992 1997 2002 2007 2012 2017 2022

Source: Consilium Graphica, 2023, Consilium NZ Limited   Always remember that past performance can show us patterns. but is no guarantee of future results.

of investments can include different industries, currencies, asset classes, geography and weighting of equities. This mix of assets is called *diversification*. Typically, the more diversified the fund, the lower its *volatility*.

KiwiSaver is an example of a managed fund. Managed funds can be described as defensive, conservative, balanced, growth or aggressive funds. Alternatively, they can be focused on a particular type of investment or market, such as shares, property, commodities or emerging markets.

You pay someone to administer the fund, choose the investments that make up the fund and rebalance the fund to the type of market you have selected or risk you can tolerate. Their fee is deducted from the fund's performance. If you have a financial advisor, then they will charge a fee to review the fund each year, and ideally compare the fund's performance against other funds, facilitating any change to the fund weighting or the fund itself.

You can earn income from managed funds as well as getting capital gains. Be sure to measure the income after the management fee has been deducted. I have seen some amazing results with managed funds, as well as some amazing fees charged, which counteract a large portion of the gain otherwise made. Fees vary greatly between fund managers and different types of funds.

One of the benefits of a managed fund is that your money is spread across more investments than if you purchased shares or property directly. This means your investment is more diversified than direct investment. This diversification is supposed to give you some comfort, by reducing the volatility (the ups and downs) of your investment.

Like shares, managed funds are not guaranteed to go up in value all the time. In fact, there is a risk that the value of a fund can drop below what you paid for it. However, the risk of this happening is less than with investing directly, because your risk is spread across more than one company or investment. It is likely that a portion of your retirement savings will be invested in a retirement fund. The split of how much should be invested in a managed fund at different phases of retirement is discussed on pages 296–8.

Superannuation funds and life insurance policies

You can also invest in private superannuation funds. Much like KiwiSaver, you pay into a fund that is ring-fenced for your retirement. This means that you can't access the money invested until you reach a certain age — maybe 50, 55, 60 or 65, depending on the specific policy.

Like any investment you need to ask yourself two questions about a superannuation fund.

1. If I am contributing $1 to this investment every month, am I better to keep paying into the fund, or should I invest my dollar elsewhere?
2. If possible, should I cash in my policy and apply the capital to another investment, such as reducing my mortgage, a deposit for an investment property or a managed fund?

The answers to these questions will depend on how well the fund is currently performing and if your employer is making contributions to your fund. Unfortunately, it's likely that the regular statements sent to you will not clearly show fund performance. Often they simply indicate how much you will receive if you withdraw your funds at an attractive and imagined rate of return — without showing the actual rate of return. When I have investigated some funds for my clients I've found that the actual return has been less than 1 per cent for years! If it looks unlikely that the return is going to increase, it might pay to cut your losses and withdraw the funds to invest elsewhere.

Do your homework and always read the investment statements carefully. Has the investment increased in value? If so, what's the rate of increase? What is expected to happen in the next year? How does it rate as an overall investment (what ranking does it have)?

If you're not sure, call the fund manager and keep talking until you understand exactly what is happening to your investment. If the statement omits key performance data, you can usually bet the fund is not performing well.

Which investment is best for you?

In deciding which investment is best for you, you need to ask yourself these six questions:

1. How much of my wealth do I want to put at risk?
2. How much of my money can I afford to invest?
3. What growth rate do I need to achieve?
4. How much volatility in performance can my situation stomach?
5. How long do I have before I need to think about cashing in my investment?
6. How much risk do I want to take?

You won't be able to answer these questions until you can establish what return you need from the money invested to achieve your financial goals.

To determine what risk to take, you need to clarify whether you are on track to achieve your financial goals with savings alone, whether you want to buy a first home or whether you plan for retirement. If there is a shortfall, this will help you calculate the level of return you need in order to grow your wealth to a sufficient level to meet your goal.

It's important that you distinguish between your *tolerance* for risk and your *capacity* for risk. For example, many retired couples had money invested in finance companies before the GFC. They were getting a good return (interest rate) on the money invested but, unfortunately, a great number of those people who had invested their money in high-interest, high-risk investments could not afford to lose the capital they had invested. They have since been left shaking their heads and asking why they exposed their hard-earned money to such risky investments.

> **Tip:** Sometimes the best investments are the ones you *don't* make. Invest only in products you understand and people you know you can trust.

It's important to note here that whether you trust the celebrity who is endorsing a product or not has no relevance. (Personally, I think it is unethical to have any celebrity endorse an investment or finance company unless they started it themselves.) Famous face or not, there's no good reason for investing your hard-earned money in something you do not understand.

I've heard of so many people who invested in finance companies because of the face of the company's advertising campaign, then lost their money. It's sad, but these people took no precautions. They simply wrote out a cheque to someone they didn't know for a product they didn't understand. In all likelihood the famous face probably didn't understand what they were representing either. I've said it before and I'll say it again: the only person who will ever truly care about your money is you. Don't be stupid or reckless, and do not cry foul play when you took no precautions. Stand up and take some responsibility for your investments. Invest on sound principles, understanding the merits of each investment and how it will affect your longer-term goals.

> **Tip:** Always check the investment rating of your investment to understand the level of risk you are taking and how the company's investment stacks up against market comparisons.

Whose advice should you seek?

A lot of advisors specialise in one field. They can give you good advice in that area, but it is given in isolation. For example, they may give good investment advice, but not understand the complexities and nuances of your overall personal situation.

A financial planner will take a look at your wider circumstances, and may do a good job of managing your money to retirement, but may not know much about specific investments outside of managed funds; for example, how to invest in property and whether this is the right thing for your wider situation. The financial planner will not directly manage your funds, instead passing your funds over to a fund manager, who will manage it on your behalf. The fund manager, like the stockbroker, will clip the ticket on the funds invested, irrespective of the results. If your financial behaviour is a problem, neither the financial planner nor a fund manager will have the system to fix it — because changing behaviour requires a degree of accountability and regular check-ins, which is not the core business of someone who wants to invest your money.

An insurance advisor gives advice on insurance policies, but, unless they are qualified to comment beyond that, it's best not to rely on further advice.

Accountants often say they are business advisors, but in a lot of instances they simply complete your tax return and add little value to the day-to-day running of your business.

> **Tip:** Getting advice from the right people is critical to getting ahead, so work out what you need to know and who best can answer your questions.

What investment is best for me?

There is usually a time and a place for all types of investments in your financial journey, but if you invest in the wrong asset at the wrong time it will slow your wealth progress. So when you're just starting out, your investment strategy will be different to those who have money and are already on the property ladder. Similarly, those who don't need to build wealth, but have enough to last through their retirement, will have other investment needs.

When you are just starting out, you typically don't have enough cash for a deposit to buy a property — so your investment options are limited and usually more liquid. Likely investments include term deposits and managed funds.

Once you're on the property ladder with equity, you can start to build your wealth through residential property investment. Once you've grown enough wealth, you can start to diversify your strategy with other assets, then balance liquidity with different asset classes and diversity within each class.

Value of investments	Less than $100,000	$100,000–$1 million	$1 million plus
Stage	Starting out	Building up	Sitting back
Wealth objective	Get onto the property ladder	On the property ladder, need to grow wealth for retirement	Retirement-ready, need to hold investment value
Investment options	Savings Term deposits KiwiSaver Managed funds ETF	Residential investment property to access maximum leverage and pace of wealth creation KiwiSaver	Diversified wealth strategy. Investments could include: — property (residential, commercial, with or without leverage) — managed funds/ETF/shares — alternative investments — term deposits — crypto (but only if you have surplus capital).

PART FOUR
Retirement

24. Retirement planning

> If you can't fly, run; if you can't run, walk;
> if you can't walk, crawl, but, by all means,
> keep moving. —Martin Luther King Jr

If you are going to plan for retirement, you need to know how much it's going to cost. This is perhaps where most of us get stuck, trying to work this out. Of course, the cost of retirement is different for each of us, because we all live our lives differently and each lifestyle has a different cost.

So instead of debating the number you need to save, let's agree first principles — that a good retirement is being able to live the life you are most comfortable with, for as long as possible. This is built into the very definition of financial success:

> **FINANCIAL SUCCESS (NOUN)**
> Living a life you enjoy. In control of your money, with a plan to ensure your retirement is sorted. To be at peace with your finances. To have a shared financial goal with your partner. To have created financially independent children. It is not measured as a specific number or end point. It is ongoing.
> Synonyms: Happy, in control, purposeful.
> Antonyms: Anxious, aimless.

To calculate your retirement number, you have to understand the general formula — then overlay your numbers to help understand what you need to live a comfortable retirement and compare that with what you are likely to have. If there is a gap between the two numbers, then we have a problem — we call this your retirement savings gap. Most Kiwis have a gap, so don't be too concerned if you have one too. The thing we need to be concerned with is the size of the gap, and what wealth strategies and behaviours are going to be effective in closing it.

Remember, we can't go back and change the beginning, but, in the words of C.S. Lewis, you can start where you are and change the ending. So let's go.

How much will I need?

The challenge with retirement planning is that everyone's lifestyle differs in style and cost. There is no universal amount that needs to be saved by the time you hit retirement to ensure you have saved 'enough'. What you need to work out is your 'number' (see Chapter 26). Then you need to determine if you're going to achieve that number or whether there is going to be a shortfall. If there is a shortfall, you need to decide what you are going to do about it.

The rubber hits the road at this point. You can borrow for many things in life — homes, cars, children's educations or university fees — but not retirement. To fund your retirement, you need to have saved enough money or be able to earn enough equity to live the lifestyle you enjoy.

How much you need will depend on the lifestyle you want. Let's keep it simple. Ask yourself the following questions.

- How much does my current lifestyle cost? (see below)
- Do I want to be able to travel when I retire? If so, how often, how far and how much will it cost?
- What one-off costs will I have after I retire? Consider car replacements, holidays, big dentist bills or home renovations. Am I planning on paying off any of my kids' student loans, or helping my family out financially?
- Do I intend to be mortgage-free when I retire?
- Do I plan to downsize my house around the time I retire (to minimise my mortgage outgoings)?
- Do I have a superannuation policy or KiwiSaver balance? If so, how much am I likely to receive when I retire?
- Am I likely to get an inheritance?
- Do I plan on working past 65?

What does your lifestyle cost?

Let's not overthink this.

Starting at the beginning: how much are you paid each year, after tax, and how much did you save? The difference is what your life costs.

Example: You are paid $2,000 per week from your employer. This is your after-tax pay, or net pay. If you annualised it, it would be $100,000.

You managed to save $10,000 last year – so that suggests that your lifestyle costs $90,000. Of course, you might be able to reduce this amount, but for now let's assume you don't need to.

So that's pretty easy. Now we need to work out whether there are any costs you are paying now that won't be a cost for you in retirement. The most obvious example is a mortgage. Ideally you will have paid this off by retirement. That's the hope — but that is also the next thing you need to check. When are you likely to pay your mortgage off, based on how you're tracking now?

For the example above, let's assume that you pay $30,000 a year in mortgage payments, and as luck would have it you're going to be mortgage-free at age 64. So your lifestyle from that point should cost you $60,000 ($90,000 less $30,000). Another cost you might hope to reduce are kids' costs, although this is a bit harder to determine. Although your dependants might have flown the nest, if you are now a grandparent you will want to spend money on the grandkids and help out financially wherever you can. For that reason, many of my clients keep kids/family costs in their budget even if their children will be adults when my clients are retired.

Downsizing your home and receiving an inheritance both provide one-off income, but it can be tricky to rely on these strategies in retirement planning, because you don't have control over the first and the second has wider consequences to work through.

Annual deficit

The annual deficit is the income you expect to receive in retirement, less the cost of your lifestyle.

At this stage we are expecting you might get a pension — so let's say that is $20,000 per annum. If your lifestyle costs $60,000, then you'll have a shortfall of $40,000 per annum.

Annual deficit = $40,000

Years in retirement

The definition of retirement can differ from person to person. Not all of us stop working at 65. Some people keep working, some move to smaller roles, part-time roles or volunteer roles. For many people, working keeps them feeling young.

For financial purposes, we're trying to get a sense of how many years you will be retired. The usual goal is to be able to fund your retirement until the age at which you are likely to die, based on general statistics and family history. This can be anything from 65 to 100! As a placeholder, let's assume you'll be retired for 25 years (for most people that will get them to age 90). Some people think they won't live that long, and maybe they won't. But we definitely don't want it to be a financial problem if they do.

Years living in retirement = 25 years

One-off costs

These are the less frequent costs that you might have during your 25 years of retirement, such as car replacements, big holidays, renovations, transferring money to family, or paying off children's student loans. You are not usually obliged to incur any of these costs, but it's important to allow for them if they're important to you.

In this example, let's assume you want to go on a big European holiday for $50,000 and upgrade your car one last time, costing $60,000.

Total one-off costs = $110,000

Cash injections

This covers inheritances or big inflows of money that are not connected to you having to sell assets or trade in investments. We do include those types of assets, including downsizing your home, below. But for now we're trying to work out what your retirement will cost you, not how you could fund it. Funding your retirement is the second part of the equation.

Retirement cost equation

Annual deficit	×	Years living in retirement	+	One-off costs	−	One-off cash injections	=	What your retirement will cost
$40,000	×	25	+	$110,000	−	0	=	$1.1 million

Complete the calculation above to work out what your retirement will cost you. For the example we are using, it suggests that retirement will cost $1.1 million. Ouch.

Now we need to look at how much wealth you will build between now and retirement in order to work out your retirement gap, and timeframes of when the money runs out.

Retirement gap calculation

Your retirement gap is your retirement cost ($1.1 million in our example), less the amount of wealth you have to fund it.

Existing wealth

Your existing wealth includes your future KiwiSaver balance, savings, investments, properties you could sell, and your ability to downsize your home. I prefer to keep downsizing your home out of the mix where possible. This is your 'get out of jail free' card — which of course you can play whenever you need or want to — but I prefer that you keep this up your sleeve, rather than build it into the wealth plan. That said, if we are desperate, we will factor it in — it all depends on the size of the savings you need to bridge your retirement gap.

Building on the example above, let's assume that your KiwiSaver will be paid out, and we expect the balance to be $400,000.

Retirement cost	−	Existing wealth (excl. home)	=	Savings needed
$1.1 million	−	$400,000	=	$700,000

The size of your retirement gap (extra savings needed)

If your gap is greater than $300,000, then you are going to need to consider using leverage to grow wealth. It's not that you couldn't consider other investments, but at face value they're unlikely to close the gap.

As a rough rule of thumb, if I buy an investment property, I expect to earn $300,000–$500,000 per property. So, based on the retirement gap of $700,000 above, this suggests that you would need at least one investment property. The intention usually isn't to hold the property indefinitely, but instead to realise or borrow against the capital gain and bring this gain back into the pot of money you are going to live off.

Impacting your retirement gap

Before we focus on refining your wealth strategy, you still have levers you could pull to reduce the gap. You could work for longer, spend a bit less, or downsize the home. Equally, there are things that might make the gap bigger, like helping your kids onto the property ladder or being in a position to leave money to charity. Of course, you want to be able to do this without jeopardising your own retirement — put on your own oxygen mask first.

The power of savings

Never underestimate the power of saving a smidge more, or spending a smidge less. It can translate to a lot of money, provided you keep it up. For example: if you spend $10,000 less each year of retirement, this will lower your annual deficit by $10,000. If you continue to do this for the full 25 years, you will lower your savings gap by $250,000.

Which brings me to costs in retirement. A lot of people assume that their living costs will drop significantly when they retire. They don't tend to, at least certainly not for the first seven years of retirement, when you are likely to take up hobbies, go on that big holiday, or tick off the things you want to get done on the bucket list, which all come at a cost. Also, remember that your fixed living costs don't change when you retire. You still have to pay the bills, buy food, maintain the house, go to the doctor and stay fit. In spite of that, your discretionary spending might still drop because you don't need to buy as many clothes or go to as many cafés, although some of these savings might be offset by higher medical and insurance costs.

Paid work after 65

The longer you can work, the better it's going to be for your retirement. If you want to work, or are happy to work, then this further reduces your retirement gap. My observation, however, is that just because you want to work, it doesn't mean there will be work for you. And if there is sufficient work, you might not want to work as for as long as you had thought. For these two reasons, I prefer to ignore this bonus income from my retirement calculations, and instead link it to something fun, like a bucket-list holiday. So if you do work, then great — you get the reward! But if you decide not to, your plan isn't compromised. It's weirdly freeing knowing you don't have to do something, and often has the perverse outcome of you wanting to do it.

Downsizing your home

Yes, you could downsize your family home as part of your plan. Please don't overstate what this will release, because it seldom eventuates as you expect. Again, I try and keep this out of the mix at this point, because we don't yet know whether the next 20 or so years are going to be good or bad. Ideally, downsizing your home should remain a contingency in case you get a bad run. Typically downsizing the home replaces three years of annual deficit, or buys you another three years in retirement.

Helping your kids out

Most of my clients who have children want to be able to help them onto the property ladder if they can. There are a few ways to go about this, depending on how old my clients are when they decide this is one of their goals. If they are young enough, we might look to buy a second investment property and earmark this for the kids. The kids probably won't live in it, but you can hold it until its value increases by $300,000–$400,000 then sell it so you have the funds to help your kids with their future home deposit. You don't need to tell the kids you are doing this, just in case you decide not to give them the money! But in my experience this is one of the more motivating financial goals you can have.

Hope for the good, plan for the bad

The trick to a good plan is to first plan for what's plausible, then to be aware that things can go wrong. Your income might drop earlier than you expected, you might get sick and can't work for a time, the house might need random repairs, or your relationship might take a pause. These are life's realities. We can't know what the future holds. Of course, there are also opportunities that we can't plan for either, such as receiving an inheritance earlier than expected, or being offered paid work doing something you love that wasn't otherwise factored into the plan.

Then you have the economic bad day. A recession strikes so your KiwiSaver or investments lose value, right when you need to withdraw them. Perhaps we're hit with unprecedented and prolonged inflation, or a capital gains tax is introduced, the pension age is extended or removed all together. All of these things could happen — because 25 years is a long time to plan for.

Neither you nor I can control some of these things, but I know the best way to buffer yourself from the shock of a bad day, bad year, or just a bad time is to have more than you need. This provides a shield to protect you from the onslaught of bad luck or bad timing.

Clients who appear to have more than enough to see them right might ask why I still want them to grow wealth. My reply is: you have enough wealth to last you on a good day. But on a bad day you don't. All we are doing is getting your money working harder so that you feel good on both good and bad days. This is also why I like to keep the capital from downsizing your home up your sleeve — it can be a much-needed cushion to get you through that potential bad day.

Case study

I have two clients, a couple both aged 45. They have a combined income of approximately $160,000, a daughter, a home worth $1.2 million and a mortgage of $300,000, payable over 25 years. Their daughter is planning to go to university, and plans to get a student loan. They each contribute 3 per cent of their income to KiwiSaver. They want to retire at 65 and they want to keep their current lifestyle in retirement. They want to know whether this is a realistic goal, or whether they need to get used to the idea of working for longer or spending less in retirement.

Before working with me, they were spending all the money they earned, so I could confidently say that if they kept up their current spending and saving habits, they would run out of money in retirement. With no changes they should have been mortgage-free at retirement and they would have cashed in their KiwiSaver at that point — but their KiwiSaver was only going to fund about 40 per cent of their retirement needs (excluding holidays and car replacements). So they had a gap.

However, they were capable of saving. They just needed to remove the inefficiencies from their spending, get clear on their goals, and have clear targets, better systems and a whole lot of accountability. Within three months of working with me, we achieved annualised savings of $25,000. These savings then became their engine room for progress. Even with car replacements and the trip to Europe, you can see from the graph on the following page that they should be mortgage-free in 10 years. This will save them $215,000 of interest, which is helpful, because the money that was getting paid on the mortgage can now be saved and channelled into their retirement savings earlier. Once mortgage-free, their living costs drop due to no mortgage payments.

The outside line on the graph shows their current mortgage of $300,000 and the number of years before they would be mortgage-free if they stuck to their current arrangement with the bank. However, by working to a plan and using their cash surplus they can repay their mortgage faster, as shown by the inside line.

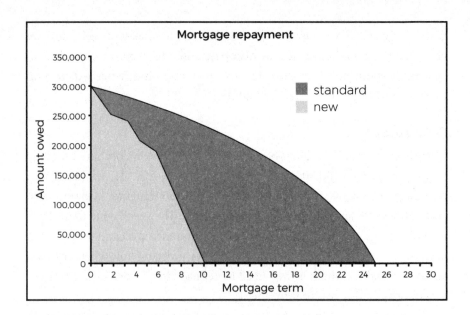

Mortgage repayment

While it's preferable to channel all funds into repaying your mortgage as fast as you can, one-off costs such as car replacements and overseas holidays need to be funded from your cash surplus, which means that, in the years these events occur, the mortgage will not reduce at the same rate. You can see this by the bumps in the graph above. Overall, though, factoring in the things they want to do, they are still in a position to be mortgage-free in 10 years instead of 25, which is a fantastic result.

After 10 years, or once they are mortgage-free — whichever is sooner — the money that was going to repay the mortgage can be saved in cold hard cash. So not only do they save the interest they won't have to pay to the bank because they are mortgage-free, but they also save their fixed mortgage payments which previously cost them $25,000 per annum. So in 10 years' time, once mortgage-free, their cash surplus doubles to $50,000 once they are not making mortgage payments — and that's excluding pay rises and bonuses. It's a double whammy.

If this surplus goes into a savings account, even earning just 1 per cent interest after tax and inflation, they should have $500,000 available before retirement. These funds, when added to their KiwiSaver, form their retirement pot, which they will live off until aged 80. How they should invest this pot of money is discussed in Chapter 27.

Their retirement pot, coupled with the current pension, would allow them to maintain their current lifestyle for as long as possible, but based on my calculation could stretch until age 80.

To get them to 90, we might need another $300,000. This is their retirement savings gap. It is at this point that we consider their options to close the gap further — could they:

- work beyond 65?
- downsize their home?
- spend less before and during retirement?
- grow their wealth by $300,000?

Because the plan covers 45 years (from age 45 to 90), which is a heck of a long time, my preference will always be to grow wealth in addition to any other concession the client might want to make. If we adopted a wealth strategy while paying off the mortgage, to get them mortgage-free earlier again, this could solve their long-term savings gap. To get them mortgage-free in six years, say, I would need to grow $200,000 of wealth that could be cashed in and applied to their mortgage in year six. This one-off income, combined with the preceding five years of effort would get them mortgage-free. Working backwards, the only wealth option that can be adopted without slowing the mortgage repayment plan (of 10 years initially) is an investment property. Not every property can achieve this outcome, but if I set the right criteria for this property, balancing the gain needed within the timeframes and cashflow constraints of the client's situation, we can achieve incredible progress. So even if they were open to downsizing their home by $300,000, I would be reluctant to call it a day without investigating other options for them.

25. Will the government help you?

Consistent with other OECD countries, New Zealand has an ageing population. Although exacerbated by the numbers of post-war baby boomers (people born between 1946 and 1965), our ageing population is considered a permanent change in our population demographic, caused by people living for longer and having fewer children.

New Zealand currently has roughly 850,000 people over the age of 65. This figure is expected to more or less double over the next 50 years (it will hit 1 million by 2028), with people over 65 making up more than one-quarter of New Zealand residents in 2073. The number of people living beyond 85 is expected to quadruple.

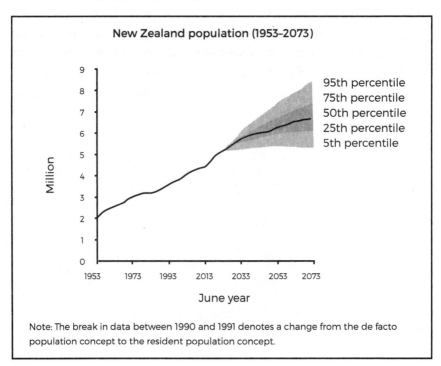

New Zealand population (1953–2073)

95th percentile
75th percentile
50th percentile
25th percentile
5th percentile

Million

June year

Note: The break in data between 1990 and 1991 denotes a change from the de facto population concept to the resident population concept.

Source: Stats NZ

The fact that people are living longer means they are likely to spend more time in retirement, which creates a rapidly growing pension cost for the government. In 1970, people were expected to live on average another 13 years (male) or 17 years (female) after age 65. Now, life expectancy has increased to 20 years beyond 65 (male) and 23 years (female), with the next generation of kids likely to live a further five years again.

While on one level this is an achievement, fiscally it is a problem, with the New Zealand Superannuation Fund (NZ Super Fund) having to support people for far longer than was originally intended when introduced in the 1970s. Internationally, more than half of the OECD countries have responded to this by increasing the age at which people are entitled to pensions to 67.

Retirement Commissioner Diane Maxwell, in her report to the government in December 2013, suggested increasing the pension age to 67 by 2017, with a 10-year notice period before it came into effect. This would effectively mean that, by 2027, the retirement age would have increased to 67, with an ongoing 'schedule and review' of the pension age and forecasted life expectancy. Among other things, the objective is to give transparent and adequate notice of age-of-eligibility changes. The core principle is to ensure that each resident enjoys the same proportion of their life receiving government superannuation.

In her report, Maxwell also suggested a longer-term schedule for eligibility increases and the year in which they would take effect. Personally, I think the government should just raise it in one go and get it sorted out so people can better plan for their financial future.

Eligibility age	66	67	68
Proposed year for new age to be in place	2036	2046	2056

Other suggested changes include changing the index to calculate the pension entitlement (that is, if 32 per cent of a person's life after the age of 20 should be funded by a pension, the age at which this entitlement starts would rise as life expectancies rise), changing the entitlement depending on when a person uses their super (meaning they would receive less when they first retire, then an increasing amount as their ability to work decreases) and means-testing. In my view it's unlikely means-testing will be used, as it can be seen as punishing savings behaviour and might discourage people from working longer or act as an incentive for them to hide their wealth.

Of course, none of these recommendations have been enacted, but that isn't to say they can't or won't be in the future. As it stands our economy is already struggling to pay its pensions, and with an expected 1.6 million people over the age of 65 (by 2073), we have a problem that will need to be addressed at some stage. Whether it is addressed by the time I hit 65 (most likely), or my kids hit retirement age (certainly), a change will happen.

What could that mean for you?

Practically, the pension pays a superannuitant roughly $500,000 in pension payments. If the pension was removed, that would mean you'd need to come up with another $500,000 of wealth to bridge the gap. I'm not interested in debating whether the pension should be changed or removed, I just need to build in a contingency of another $500,000 into my clients' financial plans.

Helping ourselves

It's no real surprise to learn that New Zealanders have not, and probably have never, saved enough for their retirement. Fun fact: we track to the bottom quartile of savings compared to other OECD countries. This is slightly embarrassing, but let's move on.

If you didn't work out your retirement number, there are some hacks you could use. For example, according to a 2023 Massey University report, a one-person household would need a lump sum of $355,000 for the most basic (100 per cent 'no frills') lifestyle. This assumes living costs of around $830 per week. The numbers change around if you are a couple wanting to live provincially or in our larger cities.

No frills means just that. No frills, no fun and almost no food. Not quite, but you won't be eating too much meat or dairy, that much we know — because your budget can't afford it. You won't be travelling or buying a weekly coffee. The silver lining of this number is that the amount you need to save is lower, and therefore more achievable.

If you want a bit more choice with how you spend your money and the occasional treat, then the 'choices' lifestyle is going to cost you more. If a one-person household, you will need to save $717,000, or closer to $1 million ($969,000) if you are a couple. For this little bit of extra choice, you are going to need to save quite a lot more — roughly $500,000–$700,000, depending on whether you are a one- or two-person household and are living in a metropolitan or a provincial area.

Most of my clients want a bit more from their retirement than a basic living standard, which is why our default target savings for a two-person household living in the city is usually $1 million–$1.5 million, before we do detailed cashflow modelling. This is based on spending $100,000 annually for 25 years ($2.5 million), less the pension ($500,000 per person, $1 million for a couple). The client can deduct their KiwiSaver balances and other investments from the savings gap of $1 million–1.5 million — but in most instances there is still going to be quite a big savings gap remaining. The size of this gap is what feeds into the wealth strategy that will be right for you.

The hardest thing about determining how much you need for retirement is understanding how much you need to be happy now, and balancing that with what you need to be happy in the future. This is subjective and differs for each person. But let's assume you know what you need to be happy now and you're working on a plan in order to get to your goal as fast as possible.

26. What to do with your retirement savings

We spent a lot of time in Chapter 24 trying to understand your retirement shortfall, so we could work out which wealth-creation strategy will be appropriate for your situation, whether you need to use leverage, and how soon you need to get started on the wealth strategy.

What we glossed over is what you do with the savings you make until you retire, and how you structure these once you are in retirement. This is your investment plan. Your investment plan is a subset of your overarching wealth strategy and feeds into your retirement plan.

Assuming you can get mortgage-free before retirement, you are likely to have a chunk of savings that needs to be put to work. Leaving the money in the bank or under your mattress isn't going to cut it in retirement, so now we need to overlay some smart thinking.

For example, you are 55 and you're now mortgage-free. You were saving $25,000 per annum when you had a mortgage. Now that you are mortgage-free, you can save $50,000 per annum. What do you do with the $50,000 that is accumulating each year?

If you had an investment property as part of your wealth strategy, I would encourage you to repay a portion of the debt, to lower the interest cost so the rent covers the outgoings. As a rough rule of thumb, you need to reduce the debt to 65 per cent of the original purchase price for the rent to cover all property costs. This assumes the property is yielding 4 per cent.

For example, if you purchased a property for $700,000 and borrowed 100 per cent of the purchase price at the time, you will need to reduce the lending to $455,000 (so the loan is 65 per cent of the original purchase price). Lowering the mortgage balance will lower the interest cost enough for the rent to cover the interest and the property-related costs, no longer requiring a weekly top-up. Paying off the mortgage to $455,000 is a repayment of $245,000. If you were repaying $50,000 a year, it would take you five years to lower the mortgage enough for the property to no longer require a weekly top-up. You would have then made the property cash-neutral, which is the best hold strategy you can adopt, because now you can hold it for as long as you need to in order to get the capital gain you require without creating any downward pressure on your own cashflow.

As you repay the investment property mortgage, structure the repayment via a line of credit (revolving credit) so you can re-access the money applied to the debt in the case of an emergency. In repaying the mortgage by $245,000 you have de-risked your ability to get the capital gain. Well done! That said, it's taken you five years to do it, so now you are aged 60.

Let's assume you keep up the savings rate. Between the ages of 60 and 65, you will have saved another $250,000 ($50,000 per annum x five years). With that money we need to set up an investment fund (managed fund), and start channelling your savings into this fund, monthly as your cash surplus builds.

If you didn't have an investment property to de-risk, and you had access to a line of credit on your mortgage, then you could fast-track your investment into a managed fund when you were mortgage-free (aged 55). On this basis, you should have contributed $500,000 towards the managed fund by retirement.

Calculating your lifetime cashflow

When I am trying to determine how to invest a client's retirement savings, I pay attention to how much they will need each year, and when I think the funds will run out.

If you are trying to gauge where you might end up, you need to first calculate how long it will be before you are mortgage-free. Then you can multiply your annual cash surplus at the point of being mortgage-free by the number of years you will have left until retirement. This becomes the start of your *lifetime cashflow*.

Next, deduct any extra one-off costs (big holidays, renovations, car replacements, etc.) you are expecting between now and retirement, and add in your KiwiSaver balance.

The result is your total cash inflow or *accumulated savings*. At 65 or 70 (or whenever you are planning on retiring), your savings should be at their maximum, as this is what will fund you in retirement. We call this your retirement pot. How we invest your pot is covered overleaf. But before we can work out the right investment strategy, we need to work out when the money is likely to run out.

What is your annual deficit (see page 266)? Divide your retirement pot by your annual deficit to give you an indication of how many years your pot will last. If your annual deficit was $40,000 and your one-off costs were $80,000, you could say that your one-off costs are two years' worth of your annual deficit. So if you were going to run out of money at age 75, before your one-off costs, this would now suggest you would run out of money at age 73.

As you know, we multiply the annual deficit by 25 to work out what you should need for retirement, and then we subtract what you are likely to have. The difference, which is usually a shortfall, is the wealth problem to solve. Before we can narrow down the right investment strategy, we need to know the size of the problem (retirement gap), and how long before we must plug it. This is your retirement runway.

Retirement runway

How long before the money will run out? You need to know this number before you start to narrow down the right investment strategy for you. Your investment strategy will differ if your money runs out in the next five, eight, 10 or 15 years. Timing matters more in retirement planning than you might think.

Depending on the timing, we can apply different investment strategies. For planning purposes, I tend to group the time into buckets, with each bucket having different options.

When will you need to access your retirement pot?	Investment options
0–3 years	Term deposits, conservative managed funds. Could also work for longer, spend less, delay or reduce one-off costs
3–5 years	Managed funds (conservative, balanced), term deposits, sale of business, downsize home
6–10 years	Investment property using leverage, managed funds (balanced, growth), shares, sale of business, downsize home
11–15 years	Investment property with or without leverage, managed funds (growth), shares, sale of business, downsize home, reverse mortgage

What type of fund should you invest in?

Funds are divided into five main categories, based on a fund's exposure to equities (shares). A managed fund has a mixture of different asset types, including cash, property, bonds, commodities and equities. These come together within the one fund as a way of diversifying the overarching investment. Investment in equities is what creates the volatility and growth of the fund. So the less the fund is invested in shares, the more reliable the return will be, but also the lower the return.

When we read of the different fund types — defensive, conservative, balanced, growth and aggressive — this is telling us the weighting the fund has towards shares. For example, a conservative fund is 2 per cent weighted to shares, and an aggressive fund is 98 per cent weighted to shares.

This graph shows the types of asset that make up a typical balanced fund, with 40 per cent weighted towards equities and 60 per cent weighted to other investments. The weightings can move around depending on the fund you have chosen and how the fund is rebalanced over time. The average range of each weighting is shown below.

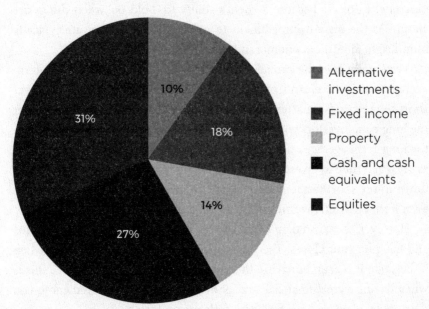

10%
31%
18%
14%
27%

- Alternative investments
- Fixed income
- Property
- Cash and cash equivalents
- Equities

Source: Alpha Wealth Funds

Fund type	Exposure to equities (%)	Historic average growth rate (and range) (%)	Volatility (%)
Conservative	20	6.86 (-9.08 – 16.2)	2.88
Balanced	50	7.94 (-9.5 – 21.95)	5.02
Growth	80	8.82 (-23.02 – 39.24)	9.73
Aggressive	98	9.28 (-29.04 – 49.38)	11.95

Source: Consilium NZ Limited

This table shows the highest and lowest returns of the different portfolios over a recent year, and the average return during that period of time. The volatility of a return (standard deviation) is how much it can jump around over a 12-month period, on average. The greater the volatility the higher the return, on balance, over time. For funds with a greater weighting to equities, typically their return is higher but their predictability of outcome from week to week is much lower.

A portfolio weighted highly in equities tends to experience high highs and low lows. While your wealth plan may require a higher return, whether you can stomach the rollercoaster ride to get there is another thing entirely. When I am designing a portfolio for a client, I pay attention to the return needed, and try and take the course with the least volatility to achieve the outcome. I do this because a client's ability to 'hold on' when things are choppy is the biggest impediment to getting the gains that are typically found right after the economic storm.

Very rarely does the annual return of an investment equal its long-term average, nor is its return from quarter to quarter predictable. In fact, over short time periods, quarterly returns can be highly volatile. However, over the long run, investors who accept short-term volatility are rewarded with the long-term average return. If you are a long-term investor, there's never really a bad time to invest. Even though markets may swing sharply up and down in the short term, over the long run investors are well compensated even if they started investing at the worst of times.

However, there can definitely be a bad time to cash in your investments and hang up your gloves. The key is being able to stay in the market when it feels like it is crumbling and the media are talking up a collapse. This is when having a great financial advisor becomes the secret ingredient to you doing what is needed, even when it feels uncomfortable.

Which fund provider should you go with?

New Zealand has heaps of fund providers, each offering their own version of a conservative, balanced or growth fund. Some perform well, some don't. What I do know is that there isn't one fund provider that has the top-performing funds across all fund types. So, you might spread your investments across different providers if you are seeking to get the best performance for each. This is where it gets complicated, and I cannot stress enough the importance of getting independent financial advice. Please work with an advisor who is not limited to one fund (their employer's fund), but can get access to all funds across the market to broker the best option for you.

Detailed retirement planning

To work out which type of asset class you should be investing in, you need to look at the timing of cashflows more closely. Let's say you are going to save $500,000 before you retire; how long would that last you in retirement?

How far the funds will stretch will depend on your annual deficit each year in retirement. Let's say you want to spend $80,000 per annum in retirement. The pension will give you about $20,000 of this ($40,000 if you are a couple). So, you would need to be able to access $60,000 of your investments each year. This means you don't need to access the money for 10 or more years, and when you do access it, you will draw down $60,000 from the funds each year.

Things that might further delay your need to access the funds

If you are going to downsize the home at some point, the sale proceeds will be added to your retirement pot — but think of them as a third layer of retirement savings.

Savings between now and retirement are the first tranche of your retirement pot. Invest these for the longest term. Your KiwiSaver is the second tranche that adds into your retirement pot. As a starter, assume you will live off the KiwiSaver investments first before tapping into your other investments.

Let's say your KiwiSaver balance allows an annual cash drawdown for four years. If you are 55 now, you can save for 10 years, and then live off your KiwiSaver for four years, so you won't need to access your investment pot for 15 years. This allows you to take a longer-term perspective on how hard your money can work for you.

Downsizing your home could be another asset that would emerge in the next 15 years, bringing in another tranche of funds to live off, to avoid having to access tranche 1 of your investments.

Case studies

Case study 1: couple in their thirties

My clients were a couple in their late thirties with two young children when they first contacted me. They had a mortgage of $510,000. Initially they weren't saving; in fact, they were trying to find enough money to cover their ballooning daycare costs, which became their excuse for their lack of progress. When I started to work with them they were frittering in excess of $20,000 per annum, in spite of their daycare bill.

Our first job was to find this fritter money and redirect it to debt repayment. We also needed to restructure their mortgage to repay their debt faster. Working to this plan they are now on track to be mortgage-free in just over 10 years, when they will be in their late forties.

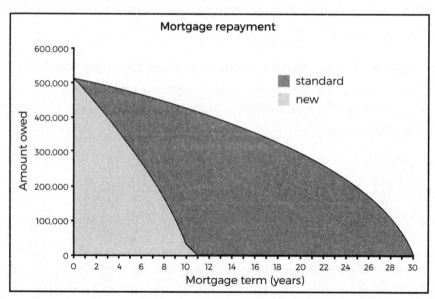

Barring any major curve balls, once mortgage-free, we can then assume that the money that was going into repaying their mortgage will then go into a savings account (while we work out the right investment strategy for them). This will continue to grow until they retire, at which point their KiwiSaver will be paid out to them. Assuming this is added to their savings, they would have approximately $1.3 million in their retirement pot.

Once retired, they would start to eat into their savings balance, until the funds are exhausted when they are in their late eighties. Of course, this doesn't factor in home upgrades, helping the kids onto the property ladder or any negative curve balls (e.g. sickness, redundancy, separation, or political changes like a capital gains tax being introduced or the pension rules changed). But it is a poster child for starting early to give yourself more options in the future.

Their cashflow projections do not factor in downsizing their home or any inheritances received. The trick for this couple is to continue to find the money that is being lost and start to more aggressively pay off their mortgage. Although my preference is for them to grow wealth *while* paying off their mortgage, instead of waiting another 10 years to get started.

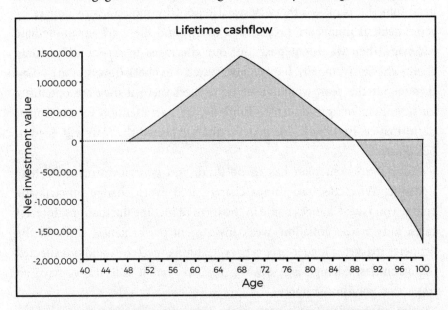

Tip: When calculating life expectancy, use 90 years.

So, if this couple starts now, assuming they don't get any almighty curve balls (like separation, redundancy or prolonged support of their kids), and the economy or government don't change the rules on superannuation or capital gains tax, then they should be OK. But if anything changed for the worse, they might not be. This is one of the reasons why I aim to grow more wealth than they appear to need — because I want to know that on a bad day, they are still going to be OK.

The key is how they track against these projections. Their ability to execute this plan becomes the single greatest definer to success. This is where it is so important to check your progress regularly. Measure, compare, reset. Your ability to hold your course through changing conditions is critical. Small degrees of slippage create a disproportionate negative impact on the plan. A weekly $100 difference in spending feels like nothing, but over 25 years, it is $125,000 of difference to what we could have saved. If you don't feel like you are a seasoned navigator, or you can't afford to miss a blind spot, then this would be the time to work with a financial advisor, or financial personal trainer.

With my clients, I tend to check in quarterly. This seems to be long enough between drinks to make sure we aren't too slow to reset if things aren't tracking as they need to. Small inefficiencies can't be allowed to creep back into the plan — otherwise we'll be out by thousands of dollars by retirement. If things are progressing nicely, and there are no immediate red flags, then we might push out our check-ins to six-monthly. Some clients check in annually, but we have systems to check how they are going throughout the year, which allow us to alert them if they are operating outside their 'margin of error'. Similarly, we pay attention to investment performance, because if this is lower than expected the plan will need to be adjusted.

Your retirement plan has to be fluid, and your investment strategy dynamic. Why? Because things change, and every change impacts the course you take. Changes come in the form of income fluctuations, interest rates, kids' needs, inflation, weak investment performance, shifts in the property market, a longer property cycle, unplanned costs and unexpected opportunities. Change isn't always negative, but it will always have an impact on your investments.

Not all people start planning for their retirement in their thirties, especially if they are trying to survive the challenges of having a young family. Most people start in their forties or fifties. If the clients in this example delayed working on their plan until their late forties, and all other constraints are held constant, they would run out of money at age 74, with a $1,025,000 shortfall for retirement. Their options for bridging this would be to work longer, earn more, spend less, downsize their house and invest in an investment property sooner. They might need to consider purchasing two properties over time, or hold the properties for up to two property cycles.

Case study 2: couple in their early fifties

This couple, in their early fifties, had a goal of getting in control of their money and sorting their retirement. They had a small mortgage of $20,000, and around $250,000 in pensions earned in the UK.

They felt they had left their run late. Initially they were going backwards financially, using their revolving-credit facility to absorb their overspending. We stopped this but could only create a small cash surplus on a week-by-week basis, as their fixed costs were disproportionately high. This was an annual improvement of $25,000, although it created only a moderate cash surplus of $19,000 as a chunk of this money was needed to stop them going backwards. However, it was enough to pay off their mortgage in a little over 12 months.

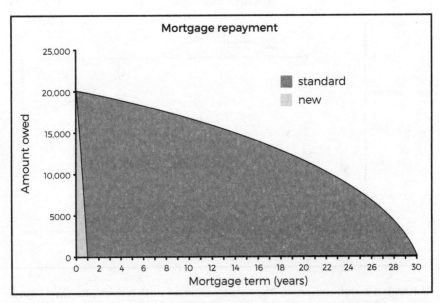

Based on their improved situation, if they were mortgage-free in 12 months, then their cash surplus of $19,000 plus their mortgage repayments of $1,500 per annum could be combined and saved for the next 13 years. They would have saved in excess of $300,000 by the time they hit retirement, at which point their pension of $250,000 would be paid out and added to their savings.

If we assumed their discretionary spending was cut back by $10,000 when they retired, then their funds would last until they were aged 76.

If these clients were prepared to work until the age of 68, however, saving at the same rate, they could fund their retirement until they were aged 82. While it is easy to suggest they should work until 68, they would need to work for an employer where this is possible. Based on this scenario, we estimated that their shortfall in retirement (up to the age of 90) would be $465,000. They had five options for bridging the gap.

1. Earn more money, either through pay increases beyond inflation, or by working for longer.
2. Spend less — before and during retirement.
3. Invest their savings well.
4. Downsize their home before they run out of money.
5. Use the equity in their home to buy another property, but they would need to do this soon as the bank's willingness to lend them money starts to reduce as they get older.

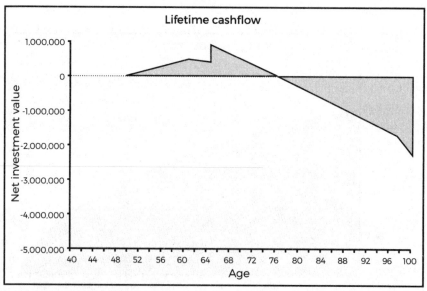

Through a combination of higher income and cost reductions they could increase their annual cash surplus before retirement by approximately $27,400 per annum. However, this might come at the cost of not enjoying their lifestyle or, worse, deterioration in health due to overwork. As such, I was reluctant to push too hard on this option, preferring to get their money working harder for them.

Using the equity in their home as security for an investment property would be a good option, provided the property they purchased fit very specific criteria, as we have a very specific problem to solve. That is a $465,000 retirement gap, and a runway of almost 15 years until retirement and a further nine years until they were going to run out of money and need to access the gain from the investment property.

If they purchased a property, we would need to adjust the projections to reflect that they might not be able to save as much ahead of retirement as they thought, because they would be topping up the rental and paying down some of the mortgage on it, if their situation required this. This means they would run out of money sooner (because they have saved less), which would require them to sell the investment property within around 15 years to close out the savings gap in time.

> Tip: If increasing your cash surplus is an option, then go for it. If downsizing your home is an option, then do it. But if in exhausting these options you realise there is still little room to move, you need to consider leveraging your equity to grow your savings faster, or lower your expectations for retirement.

Case study 3: couple in their early fifties with a large mortgage

Kim and Tom, a couple in their early fifties, had a mortgage of $300,000, which was on a 25-year term. They did not have a cash surplus, but were able to meet their mortgage payments each month. Based on this, they would be on track to repay their mortgage by the time they were in their mid-seventies, assuming they could earn at the same level until that age. However, they planned to stop working at 65.

Keeping their mortgage payments static, and making no changes to their finances, in order to be mortgage-free by the age of 65 they would have to downsize their home by $300,000. They did not want to do this, which meant they had to get serious about their situation and develop a plan to improve it. They frittered away $30,000 per annum. We found this and put them on a plan to kill their mortgage in seven years. This goal factored in a $10,000 annual holiday and car replacements.

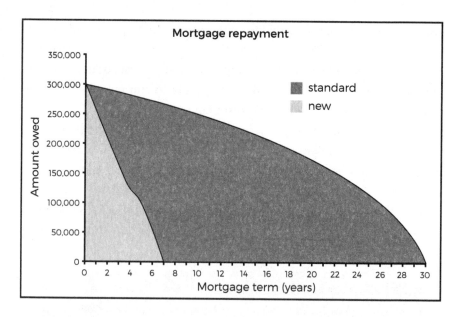

We then had to work on a strategy to prepare for retirement. They had eight years to save for retirement once they were mortgage-free. Based on the assumption they would channel their cash surplus, including what was being put on the mortgage, into savings, they would have saved $415,000 for retirement. These savings, combined with their KiwiSaver balances, meant that they would have a total of $590,000 to live off. From the graph below, you can see that this will fund their lifestyle until they are aged 92 without having to downsize their home.

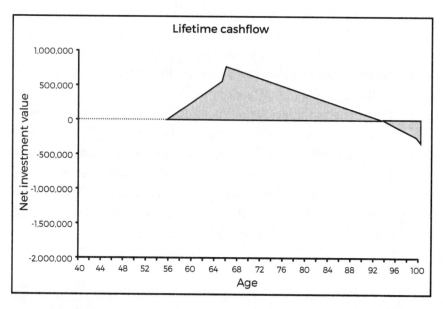

Case study 4: couple in their early fifties, on an average income

This couple were aged 50 and 52, with a combined after-tax income of $98,000 when they first came to me. They were contributing to their employers' superannuation schemes at 4 per cent, and these contributions were being matched by their employers. Their home was worth $800,000 and they were partway through a renovation, with a further $20,000 to spend. They had a $224,000 mortgage. They also had other debts, including for the purchase of $20,000 boat.

They said their situation was stagnant, but I would have described it as going backwards and about to sink. Their annual cash surplus was $10,000, but this was a false reading because they had $20,000 in consumer debt. They had a revolving-credit mortgage without a savings plan — which is a recipe for disaster, as it disguises the lack of financial progress. Both enjoyed gambling, smoking and drinking. They felt they worked hard and should be able to play hard — and play hard they did. Nonetheless, the fact that their goals seemed unattainable was dragging them down. He desperately wanted a bigger boat and she wanted the renovations done. They both wanted to get set up financially for their retirement and to be able to lend a financial hand to their children. None of this seemed likely. They did not feel in control and they did not understand how their mortgage worked. Instead, they continued to hope that going to work every day would provide them with a comfortable retirement.

After our first meeting, my assessment showed their mortgage would not be repaid by retirement age, nor would there be any additional money to fund their retirement. A bigger boat was certainly not possible and the renovation was off the cards. They had no inclination to change their lifestyle, so any plan would need to factor in their vices. The best plans make allowances for natural tendencies and non-negotiables!

Their mortgage rate was high given the type of property they owned and because of how their bank had structured it. We were able to refinance with another bank that viewed their property more favourably, reducing the interest rate and allowing a much-needed top-up to clear their debts and fund the last of the renovations. Time was not on their side — their retirement was less than 15 years away.

If they'd kept doing what they'd been doing they would have been mortgage-free in 20 years, but that meant working for another 20 years (until aged 70) and they would still feel weighed down by their finances and not in any position to help their family. After factoring in their goals and working backwards to establish what needed to be adjusted, we were able to build a plan that not only had their mortgage repaid in seven years but also allowed for the bigger boat and opened the door for them to have the choice of retiring at 62 (without giving up their vices).

Three years later they have completed their renovations and bought the bigger boat. They are $3,300 ahead of schedule, and projecting forward at that rate of progress they will be mortgage-free in less than three years, which is much better than what was initially projected. After that point, the mortgage-repayment money can be saved too, putting them even further ahead of their plan.

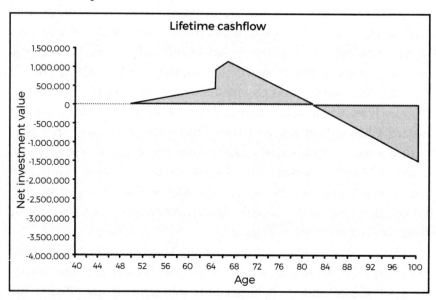

If they continue to stick to this plan until they are aged 62, they will be able to fund their retirement until they are 81 — assuming they receive a government pension at age 65. If they get a pay rise above inflation during this period, they could extend the time over which they could fund their lifestyle in retirement or even decide to retire sooner.

As a further step, the couple have decided to acquire an investment property for their children to live in. The children will pay market rent and this will be sufficient to cover the mortgage, so the parents are not topping up the property. However, the main objective of this purchase is to make a capital gain on the property, which the entire family will benefit from in the long term. This is a great example of using family resources to everyone's advantage.

Fun fact: they named their new boat *EnableMe*.

Case study 5: single woman turning 60, with a mortgage

This client had just turned 60 and was single (having been widowed three years earlier) with two adult children when she first came to me. She worked as a human resources advisor and had a before-tax salary of $90,000 per annum. She had just started contributing to KiwiSaver at a rate of 3 per cent. She'd had a stroke approximately 12 months before coming to see me.

She owned a property worth $700,000 that was next door to her daughter's property, and had a $250,000 mortgage. There was a large home and a minor dwelling on her property; my client lived in the minor dwelling and rented out the main house for $600 per week.

The mortgage on her property had 17 years to run. She thought she was operating her finances to break even. However, if she had factored in the biennial trips overseas she enjoyed, she would have seen that she was going backwards. Because of the support she received from her daughter living next door she didn't want to move, nor did she want to give up her overseas travel. She was happy to work for another eight years.

The stroke was a reality check, and immediately afterwards her primary focus was on being able to return to work at full capacity. After that, her concerns focused on her financial future, particularly looking forward to her retirement. Having no partner, and not wanting to burden her children with her finances, her resources were limited. Being single, she knew it was up to her to make sure she was on track.

She realised that, although she had equity in her property, her cashflow was tight. If she continued paying her mortgage as it was currently structured it was going to take her 17 years to pay off, assuming she was able to keep up her mortgage repayments after her retirement in eight years' time.

Living in the minor dwelling was a good idea and suited her fine, but it wasn't enough to solve the problem of having to work until the mortgage was paid off, by which time she would have been celebrating her seventy-eighth birthday!

My client had made some good decisions, but these decisions in isolation were still not enough to give her a good retirement fund. She needed to make a number of tweaks across the board to have the retirement she wanted. A plan would give her clarity about what she needed to spend to maintain her current lifestyle, and to reassure her she would still have a cash surplus. This meant restructuring her mortgage to allow her to build up a surplus and reduce her debt faster, and to save on interest. She also needed to maximise her tax deductions. Executed correctly, these simple changes were enough to achieve her goals, including her overseas travel.

When we started working together, we projected she would be mortgage-free in eight years. After three years she is on track to achieve this. She has also enjoyed a lovely trip to Spain and is planning a trip to Alaska next year. If my client can continue this plan until she is 68 she will have paid off her entire mortgage and be able to retire much earlier than she originally planned. The rental income she receives from her former home, combined with the government pension, will sustain her lifestyle indefinitely.

27. Spending your retirement pot

Once you're mortgage-free, redirect your new-found savings (the annual surplus) into a savings account while you work out the right investment plan for you. Usually you can't afford to keep your savings in the bank for any significant length of time, as the bank's savings rates or term-deposit rates are lower than inflation, and we need your money to be growing, rather than shrinking. This will usually mean that you must set up an investment account, or a managed fund.

The right managed fund for you will be determined by the return you need to get (after fees), the volatility you can stomach, when you need to access the fund, and the level of diversification within the fund. I strongly recommend you engage an expert financial advisor at this point. Ideally you don't want them to be aligned to any product provider, as you need them to canvas the market before narrowing down your options. The advisor and product provider will charge a fee, so make sure that the numbers feeding into your plan are the return from the investment after all fees. If you don't have a financial advisor, now would be the time to get one.

The Special Offers chapter on page 331 includes a discount code if you want to have an initial session with my team.

Living off your pot of money

Firstly, never underestimate how jarring it is to move from accumulating savings or a nest-egg, to then eating into it. It stands to reason this will feel strange; after working towards a milestone for so long, to arrive and have to switch your mindset from accumulation to decumulation is not an easy transition. Few people navigate this smoothly, but it's a lot easier to manage if you have a plan. Your investments also need to have their own plan for decumulation, because as you eat into your retirement pot, your mix of investments will change. Best you are equipped for this.

How to invest for the different retirement phases?

This is quite a complex topic, so I recommend enlisting a great financial advisor to help you. But in broad brushes, let me cover the basics of how you should invest your retirement pot.

I like to have different buckets of money for the different phases of retirement, as each phase can be invested for a different timeframe and be given a different risk weighting.

Emergency fund

Set aside $50,000–$100,000 in a term deposit or a line of credit on a mortgage.

Living fund

Pop one year's worth of your annual deficit into an oncall savings account, and another 12 months into a term deposit. You will draw from the oncall account each week to top up the pension in order to cover your living costs. This fund will be depleted, but we will look to reinstate it from your term deposit over the course of the year. The idea is that you should always have two years of living costs accessible to you.

Investment fund

Tally up three years of annual deficit. This amount should be invested in a low-risk fund. Together with your living fund, this would cover you for the next five years of retirement.

Now tally up five years of annual surplus and the one-off costs that will likely be incurred between years five to 10 of your retirement. This should be invested in a balanced fund.

Lastly, whatever is left over could be invested in property or in a growth fund.

While you could literally invest each bucket separately, with a different fund and even a different provider, this would significantly increase your management fees. Instead, your advisor should work out the weighted average return of your fund and invest accordingly, moving money down to your living fund from the pot of investments as needed.

What to include in your investment fund

Your retirement pot can include all tradeable investments, including savings, shares, managed funds, KiwiSaver funds, property, digital currency, metals, etc. It does not include the family home or your bach, which are considered lifestyle assets.

Your retirement pot should have an investment property in it wherever possible. An investment property can help to diversify your retirement pot, and if you're using leverage you can still grow wealth.

The weighting between property and non-property assets in your retirement pot will change as you move from growing wealth, to holding value, to starting to sell down.

In the years leading up until retirement 75–100 per cent of your investment assets will be tied up with property. This is so you can benefit from maximum leverage/capital gain and get your retirement pot as full as possible before you retire.

Once you have closed your retirement gap, and your retirement pot is full, we shouldn't need as much leverage (or mortgage). Now we need to change the mix of assets. If you have two properties, this might be when you sell one down to repay the mortgage on the other. Or you might sell a property to pop more money into a managed fund. Property as a rule is the least volatile of all asset classes. Its income (rent) is consistent, which helps supplement living costs in retirement. The capital gain comes in cycles, so the timing of the sell-down will be important to get right.

Liquidity is key

As your retirement pot depletes, you will slowly liquidate non-liquid assets (investment properties first, then the home via downsizing). These assets often have a higher value than other investments. As you sell down property, you are likely to invest these proceeds in conservative managed funds and term deposits as you are unlikely to have the stomach for much volatility. You will live off these funds before you start to draw against your other more liquid investments, such as managed funds, which may have been invested with a longer-term outlook.

Build a plan to consider how you will draw down your capital to provide cashflow to you. Yes, you are eating into your capital, but at this point that's what it's for. To be able to live solely off income earned from your investments, you'd need to have a whole lot more saved by retirement, which isn't possible for most.

First 5–10 years of retirement	Active, bucket list, travelling, higher expenses	First five years of funds need to be accessible, so invest in low-risk investment. The second five years can afford to have moderate risk.
Next 10 years of retirement	Less active, rising health and fixed costs	You don't need these funds for a while, so invest in income and growth.
Final years of retirement	Highest health needs, considering a legacy	Minimum 15-year horizon can be in growth assets and include property (leaning towards commercial rather than residential, as we will need a higher cashflow).

When you are thinking about your investment assets (property/equities/ managed funds/savings/KiwiSaver), the mix of assets changes as you move through the stages of retirement.

When you need to close the retirement gap, and bring leverage into your wealth strategy, around 75 per cent of your investment assets will usually need to be leveraged against property. As you close this savings gap, you will need less leverage for your own retirement, although you still may want to help your kids onto the property ladder, which might require the use of leverage for a little bit longer. Within the first five years of retirement, I would expect some property assets to be sold to help repay the debt on the remaining property assets, so the remaining investment property starts to pay you an income. Within 10 years of retirement, I would expect your investments to be weighted more towards liquidity (managed funds), with only 25 per cent of your investments tied up in property or illiquid assets. The only exception to this is if you have excess wealth for retirement. Liquidity becomes less of an issue when you have too much.

Reviewing your investment strategy

Work with your advisor to proactively review your entire investment portfolio annually. This includes an assessment of each asset's performance and whether a change of strategy is needed.

The advisor should also look at any changes to your personal situation, which might also cause a reset of the investment strategy. This could include changes in your spending levels or new priorities.

Reviewing your portfolio should include deciding whether to sell any of your investments:

- Assess each investment's growth rate compared to similar investments.

- Compare hold costs.
- Are you throwing good money after bad?
- Will you lock in your losses if you sell now?
- Should you liquidate your assets to put towards something better?

28. It's time for action

'You can't go back and change the
beginning but you can start where you are
and change the ending.' —C.S. Lewis

Winston Churchill said that continuous effort, not strength or intelligence, is the key to unlocking our potential. I agree. But for effort to be continuous any reasonable person will need to see results. You need to know that you are making the progress you need to make for the goal to be achieved.

To see progress, you need a plan that highlights where you are starting from, what the destination is, and clarity around how to get there. Clarity is the output of a better framework and structure to work within. Clarity gives focus. Focus creates propulsion. Propulsion gives progress. Progress builds confidence, which enhances momentum.

Understand where you are starting from. Don't misdiagnose your starting point or exaggerate the tools you have to work with. If you aren't saving, it's because you have the wrong money habits. If your money isn't growing, it's because you have the wrong wealth strategy.

If you misdiagnose your starting point, you will miscalculate the speed at which you will get ahead. Some set their goals too low, underselling themselves, while others are too lofty in their financial ambitions, setting themselves up for failure. We all know that if you are on a diet or trying to get fit, and you are following a regimen, you expect it to work. You expect to see results if you have followed the plan. If you don't, then you're likely to fall off the wagon. That's a normal response, and it applies to money planning too. If you don't see the expected results within the agreed timeframe, you'll lose heart, which is quickly followed by a loss of focus and clarity.

But this is avoidable. You want to know that you are on track, or what you need to do to get on track. Knowledge is power, and power is control. The beauty of managing your finances without emotion is that the outcome is a mathematical certainty. If you follow the plan you will get the results.

Once you get started, you will build some momentum by initially moving in the right direction. But you need to build this up as fast as possible if you want to get results quickly. Give yourself 12 weeks to crush it. If you haven't achieved in that timeframe, then enlist help.

In my opinion, being accountable to someone outside of your relationship is key to getting an accurate diagnosis of your starting point and determining what you are capable of, but most importantly to keep you honest and working to your plan. *Do not let your genetics determine your financial potential.* Understand your money personality and the role money plays (or doesn't play) in your relationship to increase your chances of success.

Follow these steps to ensure you make progress fast:
1. Understand your psychology of spending.
2. Create a cash surplus.
3. Make a plan.
4. Stick to your plan.
5. Buy a property (most likely to live in).
6. Buy an investment property (using equity).
7. Pay off the mortgage on your home.
8. Save (and invest the savings well).
9. Retire!

Remember, where you are starting from is irrelevant. We face towards the sun, and we move forward.

Starting is important. Finishing is key. Arriving at your destination early is even better.

Perseverance is key. Getting the right results time and time again is what creates the best outcomes. There are no short cuts.

> **Nothing in the world can take the place of persistence. Talent will not; nothing is more common than unsuccessful men with talent. Genius will not; unrewarded genius is almost a proverb. Education will not; the world is full of educated derelicts. Persistence and determination alone are omnipotent.**
> **—Calvin Coolidge, the thirtieth president of the United States**

Keeping motivated

The most effective motivator for any behaviour change is getting results, fast. Anyone would be prepared to make a concession on a day-to-day basis if they could see the benefits immediately. Likewise, there is nothing more demoralising than trying hard but not seeing a result.

The beauty about managing your money without emotion and following a plan exactly as it is set out is that the results become a mathematical certainty — you simply can't stop yourself from getting ahead faster. The plan must be the perfect balance of stretching you to your capability without compromising your ability to achieve.

To do this you need to optimise all aspects of your financial life — that means every aspect of your finances, including your mortgage, bill payments, any investments you may have and your discretionary spending — to make sure they are working together to get the best possible results for you.

When all the elements of a plan are working together well, your past behaviour will not dictate your capability. But don't leave anything to chance. For something to be sustainable, the change has to be minute, but the impact huge.

The certainty of results

It's comforting to be able to rely wholly on an outcome, leaving nothing to chance. Promised results provide comfort and confidence. Equally, the surprise of an unexpected outcome, especially a negative one, creates confusion and despondency.

Nothing demonstrates this better than trying to lose weight. I know when I go on a strict diet and follow it to the letter — drinking eight glasses of water and exercising — but hop on the scales at the end of the week to find that I haven't lost any weight, the despair is overwhelming. This is the same feeling many people get when they make a concession in one area of their spending or receive a pay rise only to find their circumstances don't improve.

That said, positive outcomes, like a pay rise or an unexpected bonus, must be captured and put to work. This extra income doesn't naturally ring-fence itself, and instead will most likely slip through the cracks, unnoticed.

There are other parallels between trying to lose weight and trying to get ahead financially. This is one of the reasons I call myself a financial personal trainer! As I said above, if you've tried to lose weight one week and not achieved anything — or even worse, put on weight — this can be a trigger to fall off the wagon well and truly. Instead of hitting the gym with more force, many simply feel demoralised — and open (and finish) a packet of Tim Tams. It's emotional and illogical, but it still happens.

Similar emotions affect people who've experienced a setback with money. If they feel like they have tried to stick to a budget but their circumstances do not seem any better or they are not seeing their debt reduce, then they get frustrated and demoralised. Instead of trying to save more, they hit the shops and splurge in frustration. This reaction, while emotional, is fairly common.

The key to combating this is to ensure you get the results you expect and for those results to be sustainable.

Gaining momentum

Forward momentum is one of the greatest financial weapons you can have. Forward momentum allows you to maximise growing your wealth. To gain momentum you need to be on the move. With a good plan in place you'll start to move in the right direction, and that is when you want to gain momentum — not when you are going backwards! Remember these three steps for gaining and building momentum to achieve your goals.

1. A good plan creates forward movement.
2. Movement builds momentum.
3. Momentum gets you to your goals.

In the beginning, moving in the right direction is the goal. After that, look to build speed. The first 12 weeks of any plan are the most critical. You have to get some runs on the board during this first quarter, otherwise you'll lose interest.

In building momentum, it's important to create an environment that empowers you and encourages you to behave the way you know you should. If you need to be accountable to someone in order to reach your potential, find a reliable advisor whom you trust and get on with it.

Personally, I check in with my financial coach every 12 weeks, as I have a way of rationalising anything and everything to myself, and I still sometimes lose sight of my longer-term goals.

Sticking to your plan

To stick to a long-term financial plan, you need five things to be operating in unison:

1. You can't feel deprived.

2. You need a regular, independent assessment of your potential as your circumstances change.
3. You need to get results.
4. You need to be accountable for the results you get.
5. You need to reset quickly as your situation changes.

Being accountable

Fact: being accountable to someone qualified and impartial increases the chances that you will reach your goals faster. Many people happily use personal trainers and sports coaches to improve their performance on the sports field or to improve their day-to-day lives. Whether you are a couch potato or an elite athlete, the support and guidance of a coach or personal trainer can help you do things better and faster. They help to remove imaginary limitations, including self-doubt, and to overcome real obstacles. They motivate you and keep emotion out of the equation. They show you better techniques, and help stretch you. For the same reasons, you should seek assistance with managing your finances. Good financial coaches can dance between the dynamics of different money personalities and different financial goals to get the best results for you.

A financial personal trainer is there to quantify your potential, down to the last dollar. If you are time-poor, their expertise can fast-track your progress. Not only will you get ahead faster, but you will also have a sounding board for all your financial decisions — having someone impartial to discuss your finances with allows you to mitigate the effects of the money dynamic in your relationships and helps you suppress any irrational behaviour you may have around money. A financial personal trainer will also help you master any negative natural tendencies by cutting to the chase without emotion. They'll keep you on track to achieve your goals as quickly as your circumstances allow.

> Getting ahead faster is not reserved for the financially successful; it is an entitlement for all.

If you don't want to work with a financial personal trainer, you have to have the ability to be honest and open about your finances. You could sit down with friends and set goals and check in with each other to make sure you're on track to achieve them. Have a budget party! Just remember that if you're struggling it can often pay to speak to someone who is qualified and independent. You need to know your capability, and self-diagnosis often sets the bar too low.

Even though I have written a comprehensive and effective programme to help people get ahead faster, I still apply the same principles to myself. My husband and I have paid off three mortgages, and own a number of investment properties and other assets. But I still check in with my coach to make sure that we are living to our potential. Some of the stuff he tells me I already know, and some of it I know but am not doing. Someone emotionally disconnected from my situation can see things that I can't because I'm too close to see the wood for the trees — even though I'm the financial equivalent of an arborist. I also like someone telling my husband what to do.

> **Tip:** It's important that your coach is independent of any product promotion. Conflicts of interest are rife in the world of finance, so be sure to ask any advisor directly if they know of any conflict of interest they may have.

Remember, entering retirement is stressful. You go from a lifetime of building assets to decumulation, overnight. It's a jarring transition. If you don't know when your money will run out, you'll feel anxious spending money and there'll be little joy entering the next phase of your life. You can turn this around by making a robust financial plan.

PART FIVE

Other factors

29. Helping your children — a hand-up, not a hand-out

As you get older, the two most common and costly risks to your retirement goals are your adult children and a relationship breakdown (see Chapter 30).

It's natural to want to help your children. In fact, helping your children is one of the top goals for my clients with kids. Usually, they want to help them onto the property ladder at some point in the future, and they want this factored into the plan. While I am all for this, I am conscious that some gifts can encourage independence, and others a dependency.

So, how can you support your kids to achieve their financial potential without undermining the necessary life skill of money management? How can we make sure the money scripts our kids are exposed to will help not hinder them? I personally believe it's a parent's job to train their kids in the skills needed to grow wealth. If the parent doesn't excel in this regard, or if the kids won't listen, then bring in a money coach to deliver the right messages. I encourage my clients to bring their kids to our meetings. If nothing else, the kid clocks that getting ahead requires planning; that it's OK to get help to be better with money; that working with someone else can help you get better results than what you could have managed yourself; or that Mum and Dad take this whole 'retirement' thing pretty seriously. Each child catches different lessons — but all lessons feel like a positive money script.

I'm not suggesting that you shouldn't be generous with your children. If you're going to be generous, though — and even if you aren't — bear in mind that as a parent you play a huge part in the financial makeup and ongoing success of your children. A hand-up is always better than a hand-out.

The first step is to be a good example. Get your finances in order and start living within your means with a strategy to own a house, kill the mortgage and sort your retirement, or at the very least to get ahead financially. Then you need to teach your children. This is where most people fall short. They are their children's worst enemy when it comes to financial fitness.

Being generous with your kids can be just what they need to reach their potential. But, in most instances, this will become the very thing that derails their financial growth. I see more and more children enabled by their parents to under-achieve financially, whether the parents have wealth to spare or not.

Research and common sense confirm that children given too much too soon tend to develop a distorted sense of entitlement, which makes it difficult to cope with the rollercoaster of life.

The financial environment you provide for your child while they are growing up will be one of the most important influences in their financial fate. This is a huge responsibility for parents who also lack the necessary life skills of successful money management.

The behaviour you instil in your children will stay with them long after they leave home, so there is a pressure to get it right. However, competing with this pressure is a common pull towards generosity and ensuring they don't go without.

As a parent, you need to make sure your children know how to:

- save
- spend wisely
- earn money
- talk about money
- invest
- benefit from leverage.

The parents of daughters need to take greater care to discharge this responsibility, as too many adult women are still dependent on their partner to create financial success.

Reality-check: Over-indulging your child with material possessions will almost certainly seal their fate as shoppers and make it very difficult for them to cope with instances of delayed gratification.

Children tend to be disconnected from the reality of their family's financial situation, usually because parents enable this — often because the parents are also disconnected. For all the families I work with, I encourage age-appropriate honesty with the kids. If the money is running out, explain this and explain what you as a family need to do to fix it, the reasons why and the rewards at the end. *Don't devalue this critical learning experience.*

We teach our children to try their very best at everything they do. But what if they lose? What if they are aiming to be top and they fail? Learning to work through failure constructively is just as important as learning to be a humble winner. Financial failings are some of the best learning experiences for everyone, including our children.

Some parents don't want to share their financial situation with their kids because they are embarrassed. Yet, because of that, you should. We are accountable to our children. They are trusting us to do the right thing by them — socially, physically and financially. If things are tight, demonstrate this to your kids. Show them that when the money runs out it is gone. Teach them that credit is not their friend. Get your house in order. The happy side-effect of teaching your kids good money habits is that you, as their parent, will need to lift your game to lead by example. Everyone wins!

What to tell our girls

In my day job, I meet many smart women who have accomplished so much. As a social class, we would all agree that women have made huge inroads. But the painful truth is that for all the advancements women have made, too little has changed in the way women deal with money and the share of the load at home. What goes on behind closed doors is still 'old school' and not transferrable to the environment our daughters will need to survive in.

This wouldn't be too much of an issue if women could bank on relationships sticking and their life partner doing what was needed to ensure the family unit ends up where it needs to be. But for our daughters, this is more of an issue, because the reliance on security from a partner has eroded further. Being a working mum will be the norm, as most families will not be able to afford to have one parent staying at home (well, not if they want to own the home they live in).

This is not to say that females should expect the worst, but on some level we resign ourselves to accepting average when it comes to our financial wellbeing. Too many women do not take control of their financial status. All too often, I see broken relationships where the woman is not able to do what is needed because their financial status and position is too weak.

Many women in second marriages, or with significantly more assets than their spouse, are not protecting the wealth they bring to the relationship. Females are more likely than males to intermingle inheritances into the family finances, and lose it to relationship property claims. I can't count the number of times I have seen this, and it breaks my heart. These women feel uncomfortable discussing money issues with their new partners.

Too often I see intelligent women turning a blind eye to the financial inequality of a relationship in the name of keeping the peace. I understand that it is ultimately their decision, but what message is this showing their children, especially their daughters? It's dysfunctional and damaging. How is this teaching our sons to respect women as equals when this financial disparity exists at home?

With the challenges that our children are likely to face, and the lack of security being offered to females, the need to teach our daughters and equip them with the tools for success is crucial, to attempt to make the playing field more even. And if they have no point of reference to be financially strong for themselves, where are they supposed to learn this? To protect themselves, they need to learn these skills well before they might need to put them into practice. They need to learn these skills from their parents, while at home, to avoid developing a dysfunctional relationship with money.

To nurture others and to give of ourselves are two wonderful traits that come more naturally to some than to others, and, it seems, often come more naturally to females than to males. If giving is something you wish to encourage in your children, then make sure the lesson is tempered with examples of how to give successfully and not at the expense of your own financial wellbeing. Your daughters will most likely face more financial challenges than your sons, so prepare them for this. Get them ready through conversation, by sharing the workload at home fairly, by giving equal pay for chores, and equal opportunity to complete different jobs. Take the time to explain and illustrate how financial success can be achieved without a future partner, and how, once it's achieved, it must be protected. Equip your children for success by helping them to identify the challenges they are likely to face and how to push through them, with their health, relationship and finances still intact.

Teaching your kids about money

First things first: teach your children that income less expenses equals surplus or deficit. Surplus equals choices or options. Deficit equals problems.

A tangible example is the most effective way of showing this. Gather the family round the kitchen table and show them, using real money, what is coming in and what is going out.

- Withdraw your entire monthly income after tax in cash (in $50, $20, $10 and $5 notes).
- Print out your bills (utilities, mortgage, etc.). Show receipts of your car bills, groceries, school costs, hobbies, etc.
- Put all the money you make on the table. Tell your kids that this is what you earn every month. They can touch it, count it, hold it, but the point is that there is a fixed amount of money coming into the household every month. It can seem like a lot initially.
- Next, ask your kids what the costs are for running the household. Get them to call out suggestions, such as mortgage or rent, electricity, phone, food and school costs. Get them to write these things in a list.
- Check off their list against your list, getting them to add the expenses they missed to their list.
- Beside each expense, get them to write down the monthly cost. Show them the bill so they can see how much it is. After they have written the amount down, have someone remove that money from the middle of the table.
- Continue writing down expenses and removing money from the table until you are left with an amount which represents how much money you have left over to spend on discretionary items.

This exercise is a very effective way of engaging the family with the reality of your financial position. When working with my clients, I encourage them to bring their children to our meetings so they start to understand how financial discussions should be handled, and what obstacles Mum and Dad are facing and how they are choosing to navigate them. It is a powerful learning exercise that can make the parents a little uncomfortable, but is enlightening for their kids.

Pocket money and allowances

Sound financial parenting begins with pocket money. It is fixed and regular, and is the most effective tool for teaching your children about money management.

The amount you should pay varies according to your children's ages. I advise one dollar weekly for every year of age up to the teenage years, when you need to take a different approach. You need to increase the child's responsibility as they get older, increasing the allowance and stretching out the frequency of payment from weekly to monthly once they hit high school. Too many adults struggle to budget if they are not paid weekly or if their pay cycle is out of alignment with bill payment deadlines. Adjusting the frequency of your child's allowance helps them to develop this skill.

People often ask me when is an appropriate time to start paying your child an allowance. Realistically, an allowance needs to be introduced when the child is asking to buy things like clothes, travel and technology.

From the age of around five or six, the general principle of an allowance should be introduced. Discuss with your children what the allowance can be used for — and what it can't. An allowance should be used to cover specific costs such as clothing, mobile phones and entertainment — things that children can control and choose to spend money on.

By the age of seven or eight, children could be required to do basic chores, such as making their bed each morning, setting the table and tidying their rooms every night. A child could be made to do chores to earn 'pocket money'. Pocket money is different to an allowance. An allowance is a set figure attributed to specific costs that the child is made responsible for managing. For example: as a parent you may choose to give your child $600 per annum to spend on clothes. This is the budget for clothes and the child is responsible for managing this budget/allowance. The allowance stands apart from pocket money, which is an incentive to earn more money.

By the age of 10 or 11 kids will have developed maths skills that you can put to work. Give them a list of everything they need for school and an allocated budget. Give them the money to pay for it, and let them keep the change.

Between the ages of 12 and 13 you could be adding money to their allowance for clothes purchases. Excluding big-ticket items (coats, shoes, etc.), let your child choose where the money goes and make their own mistakes.

> **Tip:** Do not top up your child's allowance if they run out of cash before their next allowance is due. Give them the option of trying to sell some of their stuff (preferably not to you) or doing more jobs (refer them to the list of special jobs on the fridge).

Introducing EFTPOS

- Give your kids an EFTPOS card, but encourage them to check their balance and to withdraw cash to make purchases instead of using EFTPOS.

- Do not give your child access to your EFTPOS card.
- *Do not give them your credit card!*
- If your child wants something expensive (like going on a school trip), ask what they are going to do to contribute to it, what they will give up and why the thing they want is important (what they are going to get from it).

Pocket money guidelines

- Give $1 weekly for every year of the child's age (e.g., a six-year-old is given $6 a week).
- Give the money to them in cash. Encourage them to physically bank the money or to put it into a money jar.
- You are trying to teach your children that the money received is not simply for them to spend on their wants. It is to teach them to plan for the future, to enjoy their purchases, to give and, most importantly, to save.
- For the first two years of pocket money (from the age of six or seven) give your child three piggy-banks. Label them:
  - Fun money (45%) — for something they want to buy
  - Giving (10%) — for charity
  - Saving (45%) — for something that lasts, an asset or something they need.
- So, of the $6 given to a six-year-old, for example, allocate $2.50 to fun, $1 to giving and $2.50 to saving.
- Let your children research the charity they want to give money to and take them to visit the charity with their donation, so they can make a physical payment and see first-hand what they are supporting.
- Start bringing their financial decisions to life. Show them how their financial actions have consequences. Let them experience the joy of giving and the excitement of saving for something.

The great thing about allowances or pocket money is that you can teach your children in a safe environment the difference between want and need.

Fun money is to be spent on doing things they want and love — things like buying an ice cream, going to the movies or buying a kids' magazine or book.

Savings are a way for them to get what they want or need. Naturally, items that need to be saved for tend to be more costly and are supposed to have a lasting benefit. Things kids might put their savings towards could include buying sports equipment or more expensive books or games. When it comes to savings, encourage your children to think about what they want to buy. They might not know initially, and in the absence of a specific goal encourage them to keep growing their little nest egg.

Sit down and help them with the maths so they have an idea of what they could afford if they saved for a longer period of time. Based on the numbers above, my five-year-old would save $2 per week, so over the course of a year he would build up $100. He could grow it faster by doing extra jobs.

Show them that they could grow their savings even faster if they saved some of their fun money as well. They will determine something they want to save for once they have some financial boundaries.

Once they select their savings goal, get them to cut or print out a picture of their goal and glue it to the savings jar or piggy-bank. A bit of positive visualisation is never a bad thing.

More tips

- Encourage your teenager to get a part-time or holiday job — the more mundane and boring the better! It teaches them to suit up and show up every day, to get on with others, and to realise that if they don't want to work in this type of job for the rest of their lives then they need to apply themselves.
- Teach your children the value of a purchase. When buying something, get them to go through the process of determining if they need it right now, or if it can wait a week, or what could be substituted for it.
- Teach your children to always turn the lights off when they leave the room. Assign someone the task of being the household 'energy saver'.
- Talk to your children about money. It shows you respect them.

Building financially independent kids

Developing your child's financial literacy and confidence requires consistent effort. You must assume responsibility for this. Help your child to build age-appropriate financial skills beyond budgeting and delayed gratification.

Younger kids: 5–9 years

The best financial foundation to give your child is that money is not to be feared or revered, it just needs to be mastered.

Learning goals
- Know where money comes from (and that the supply is limited).
- Understand that money is earned.
- Know what it means to consciously/mindfully spend.
- Begin to practise delayed gratification.
- Understand concept of giving to others.
- With money we must think about today, the future, and other people.

Key conversations
- Money is not magic — talk about how it's earned and where it comes from.
- Options with our money — to share, save, and spend (jam jars appropriate in this early stage).
- We don't just save money, we also save clothes, toys, books, etc.

Key milestones
- Determine value-based jobs where kids can earn money.
- Start paying pocket money for regular (being part of the family) jobs.

Tweens and young teenagers: 10–13 years

Begin to take the theory of money and putting this into real-world application.

Learning goals
- Understand why we need a plan for our money.
- Understand why we set spending limits.
- Understand the concept of compounding interest.
- Understand the concept of credit and paying interest.
- Have a sense of what entrepreneurial spirit means.

Key conversations
- Why do we earn money?

- Why is thinking and planning for the future important?
- Different money personalities (spender, saver, shopper).
- What is credit (credit cards, store cards, Afterpay, pay-day loans) and interest.
- The difference between debit and credit cards.

Key milestones
- Have a short-term savings goal.
- Learn about spending limits — take over the family grocery budget for two weeks.
- Start receiving a living allowance, not linked to jobs.

Older teenagers: 14–16 years

If your kids can create positive attitudes and behaviours towards money early on, these will stick with them throughout their life and get them on the inside lane, quicker.

Learning goals
- Connect money with the role it plays for the future you.
- Understand the relationship between time and money.
- Have a basic understanding of investment and building wealth.
- Understand the opportunity cost of spending.
- Be able to read and understand a bank statement.
- Understand where their talents lie.
- Know life costs for their current lifestyle and how much money is spent on the family.
- Link life costs to what you need to earn.

Key conversations
- Money gives you choices and you need to plan for those choices.
- Money doesn't make you happy, but money and happiness are linked.
- Parent's money story — explain where your lessons about money came from.
- Talk about your biggest money regret.
- Call out the difference between a hobby and career.
- Explain how advertising and marketing tactics encourage unconscious/mindless spending.

- Discuss wealth-creation strategies you are using and why having a wealth-creation plan is important.
- Talk about trade-offs you are making to grow wealth.

Key milestones
- Get a part-time job.
- Create a spending plan.
- Have a savings goal.
- Manage an allowance that covers haircuts, phone and clothes.
- Negotiate a better deal on one of the family bills.
- Take over the holiday budget for a short family holiday.
- Join you at an enable.me meeting to see how you set a budget, measure your progress and be accountable.

Young adults: 17–19 years

Give your kids the tools they need to survive the financial landscape they are entering. Empower them to get in control of their money so they can design the life they want and have a strong sense of control.

Learning goals
- Know the key paths to growing wealth.
- Understand what to think about before investing.
- Understand KiwiSaver basics.
- Understand taxes and what they are paid for.
- Introduce property and leverage.
- Know the difference between good and bad debt.
- Know that everyone has failures, and that's OK.
- Understand the implications of student debt.

Key conversations
- Outline your financial situation: how much you earn, how quickly you got there and how much money is leftover each month.
- Explain credit cards and how to use them.
- Explain why women are more exposed financially than men.
- Talk about the differences between working for someone else and working for yourself.
- Discuss the habits of successful and effective people.
- Talk about time vs money and how it impacts debt.

- Decide if they are going to complete tertiary study after high school.
- Talk about the financial cost of further study and options of how they will cover this.
- Set key milestones.
- Have a long-term savings goal.
- Have a reference from their job.
- Research different jobs and their pay.

Loans

If you loan your adult child money, be sure to document this as a loan that has to be repaid on demand. If your child is in a relationship with someone, make sure you lend the money to both of them (with a loan agreement), because, in the event of their relationship ending, you want to make sure that the money owed to you is part of the relationship settlement. Obviously you could forgive your child's portion (post-settlement) or reimburse this to them once you have been repaid.

I have seen several instances where parents loaned money to their child to buy a home with their partner, only for the relationship to end and the ex-partner to take no responsibility for repaying the loan back to the parents. This could have been avoided if things were better documented (see Chapter 30).

Using the equity in your home can be a way to help out your kids, as well as being a great opportunity to leverage to buy a second property for yourself. Obviously this comes with some risk. Losing money is an unacceptable outcome when your home is exposed.

To limit risk, I suggest you borrow 20 per cent of the value of the investment property against your home from your existing bank. For the mortgage for the investment property, go to another bank, and use your 20 per cent deposit to obtain funding for the remaining 80 per cent. This way, you have limited the exposure against your home to 20 per cent of the investment-property value.

> **Tip:** Your bank will always try and cross-secure your properties, but often they don't have to, and you don't need to in order to get the finance.

Leaving a legacy

Retirement planning requires you to fit your own oxygen mask first before contemplating helping the kids. However, if your kids are not financially secure, this will become your problem too.

One of the most effective legacies you could give your kids is a deposit onto the property ladder, to help them buy their first home or investment property. This might be from $100,000 to $300,000. Most of my clients are unlikely to save this in addition to their own retirement savings needs, so we have to get creative.

If your goal is to help the kids, we will likely need a second investment property earmarked for the kids. The first one is for you and your retirement, the second is for them. The capital gain on this second property is ring-fenced for the kids in the future and will provide the deposit they will eventually need.

If it's important to you, include an inheritance for your children in your wealth-building plan. I find that for at least one parent, fulfilling this goal will be what energises them to stick to a plan. If the goal resonates with you, it unlocks motivation and focus.

If the goal is to help the kids onto the ladder, then let's name that very early on, and build a retirement plan to facilitate it. Set the expectation with your children early, too, so they are on the same page about their likely inheritance.

One of life's greatest joys is to be able to help your kids in a meaningful way, while you are young enough to bear witness to it.

30. Relationship property

With relationships breaking down in record numbers, many people are having to start again both financially and emotionally later in life. On the one hand, this can be seen as an opportunity for a new start in both life and love, but on the other, you could be exposing yourself to the risk of further diluting your wealth should that relationship fail too.

Few people can afford to lose their assets, so you need to protect them and understand that you could lose key components of your wealth unless you take time to protect yourself — from both your partner and yourself.

Generally all property acquired after a relationship begins is relationship property pursuant to the terms of the Property (Relationships) Act 1976. However, there are exceptions to this, one of which is the ability to acquire separate property during the course of a relationship even though that relationship may have existed for several years. This is particularly relevant to receiving an inheritance.

What is relationship property and separate property?

Under the Property (Relationships) Act, 'relationship property' is usually shared equally and includes:

- the family home
- cars
- household furniture
- all property acquired while you are together, irrespective of whose name is on the title to those assets.

All property that is not relationship property is called 'separate property'. Most property owned by one person before the start of the marriage, civil union or de facto relationship is separate property, excluding the relationship property described above.

The Act provides that some limited forms of property acquired from third parties during the course of a relationship can be held as separate property. In particular, the following, if acquired from a third party (i.e., not the other spouse/partner), are separate property:

- property acquired by inheritance or gift
- property acquired because the person receiving the property is a beneficiary under a trust (which has been settled by a third person).

The Act also provides that property acquired as above will remain separate property unless:

- with the express or implied consent of the spouse/partner who received it, it becomes relationship property, or
- that property (or the proceeds from the sale of that property) has been so intermingled with other relationship property that it becomes unreasonable or impracticable to regard that property (or the proceeds) as separate property.

A common example is where one spouse/partner receives an inheritance. If that inheritance is then banked into a joint bank account (for example, by transfer from a solicitor's trust account), then, depending on what happens with the funds in that account, an intermingling argument could arise.

It's possible to protect an inheritance from intermingling by banking it into an account in the sole name of the person receiving the inheritance. However, this then prevents the free use of those funds, as the receiving spouse/partner will always need to be aware of not using the funds in such a way as to suggest they have been intermingled. For example, it may prevent them from using those funds to reduce the mortgage on the family home. If the inheritance is property or personal chattels, and that property becomes the family home or family chattels, then it is deemed relationship property unless both parties enter into a contracting-out agreement (see page 322). To get around this, the spouse/partner receiving the inheritance could:

- transfer the funds into an inheritance trust, or
- enter into a contracting-out agreement to protect that asset from an intermingling argument.

If the relationship ends, assets are divided. They are either divided as agreed between the parties, or in line with a contracting-out agreement. Where no contracting-out agreement is in place, and no agreement can be reached, the assets are split under the rules of the Property (Relationships) Act.

Debts are also separated into personal debts and relationship debts.

Relationship debts are taken into account when dividing the joint assets. Personal debts usually remain the responsibility of the person who incurred them.

Protect what you have

If there is an uneven split of wealth between spouses when entering a relationship (either getting married or becoming de facto), then you need to protect yourself. (In New Zealand a relationship becomes de facto for relationship property matters after three years of living together as a couple.) It's not particularly romantic, but you need to ensure that if the relationship goes south you walk away with what you brought to the table. Whether you draw up a contracting-out agreement or put your property into a trust, take precautions.

When advising clients, I tend to take a simple view: what you bring to the relationship should remain separate property and what you amass in the relationship can become joint property. This is particularly relevant if you have children from a previous relationship. You need to make sure you are all protected.

> **Tip:** No reasonable person should take offence at you wanting to ring-fence your wealth built up before the relationship started. If they take offence, this may be a 'red flag'.

Contracting-out agreements

If you agree to divide your property differently to how the Property (Relationships) Act would split it, you can contract out of the Act by entering into a contracting-out agreement. This agreement acts in a similar way to a pre-nuptial agreement (pre-nup), but it can be entered into before, during or after you split up.

For the agreement to be legally binding, you must ensure:
- the agreement is in writing and signed by both partners
- each partner gets independent legal advice before signing
- each partner's signature is witnessed by his or her lawyer, who must also certify that the lawyer has explained the effect and implications to that partner.

> The High Court can cancel a contracting-out agreement if the agreement is so one-sided it could be considered a 'serious injustice'.

Receiving inheritances

If you receive an inheritance from a family member or friend, *please do not intermingle it with relationship property*, because if you separate from your partner at a later date you could lose half of it.

I recently had a female client who had inherited $200,000 and wanted to use this money towards home renovations. She was in a relationship which was a bit rocky. She did want to protect her inheritance, but she did not take any precautions and spent the money on the family home, which she owned jointly with her then-husband. The money spent increased the value of the house. They later split. Her husband got access to half the value of the house, which was inflated by her inheritance.

Inheritances are supposed to be sacred, in the sense that if you were to separate from your spouse or de facto partner tomorrow, and had received a lump of money, they should have no claim to it. The problem, though, is that ignorance can inadvertently jeopardise everything.

You need to understand what triggers an inheritance becoming relationship property so you can ensure you do not fall prey to this. If you use the inheritance for general living costs, then it could be said that you have intermingled it, therefore making it joint. If you share it with your spouse or apply it to joint assets, this could inadvertently taint it too.

To avoid this, you need to transfer the inheritance into a separate trust before it is used for any purpose. *Do not spend a dollar of it before doing this.* Ideally you would have the trust formed prior to receiving the inheritance, so that the inheritance bypasses any personal bank account altogether, but this is not always possible, especially when an inheritance is unexpected. At the very least, make sure the bank account the inheritance is being paid into is at a separate bank from your joint banking and is an account in your name only.

Transferring the money into a trust means that you no longer hold the inheritance; the trust does. This is a pertinent point in the case of a relationship break-up. If you do not own the property/wealth, then it cannot form part of the relationship property pool of assets for joint splitting.

If you want to use the inheritance to improve the joint family home, or within your relationship generally, then be sure to document the transfer as a loan to be repaid back to your trust on separation. If you want to use the inheritance for personal enjoyment, like a family holiday, you will need to advance the funds to yourself as a beneficiary of the trust, as opposed to linking the trust to your joint finances.

Take steps to protect the wealth your family has amassed and gifted to you. All too often it is the spouse of the beneficiary who has the most to say about the inheritance they are not entitled to. I have seen families torn apart by the spouse who has too much to say about something not directly related to them.

> **Tip:** Do not think your relationship is sacred and therefore you don't need to take measures to protect your inheritance. It's not, and you do.

Insurances

I don't really like insurance companies. But insurance should play a big part in de-risking any financial plan. This is because the biggest contributor to the plan is you. It is your income that allows you to pay the mortgage off faster, and your ability to keep earning that allows you to save for retirement. It stands to reason that the biggest risk to the entire plan is you and your ability to earn income.

If you can, I recommend you have adequate insurance in place to protect this income from sickness and trauma, so the plan can keep functioning even if you are unable to work. But what is adequate for me is probably a whole lot less cover than your insurance broker wants to sell you. This is where your financial plan should dictate what is needed, and this should change each year based on the progress that has been made. For example, if you pay $50,000 off your mortgage one year, then this should reduce your life insurance needs by $50,000 the following year. A reduction in cover should translate to lower insurance premiums.

So yes, we need insurance, but you want the right amount, and to reduce the cover each year. Your insurance plan should be dynamic, adjusting quickly as progress is banked. Be sure to work with a great insurance broker to help you navigate this. If you can afford it, then I would also recommend medical insurance and pet insurance (if you have pets).

The reason I recommend you use a broker is that policy wordings can change dramatically between different insurance companies. It is impossible for you to make an informed decision as to which policy is going to be better for your current circumstances.

Don't over-insure, as that is a waste of money. Instead, take out the right amount of insurance to de-risk your plan.

31. What happens when you die?

I always ask my clients if their wills are up to date. In more than 80 per cent of cases, they are not. In fact, many people don't even have a will, and, frighteningly, most of the people without a will also have children.

Everyone plans to get around to it eventually, and it's never in the urgent pile of things to do — but it should be, as a messy estate is awful to work through and places unnecessary stress on an already grieving family. Even a strong and close family can be destroyed through a lack of estate planning or a poorly executed will.

They say that weddings bring out the worst in people, but I would disagree. Death brings out the worst in people. It brings out greed and hurt. What astonishes me most is that the greed isn't usually from the direct family, but from their spouses and the wider family. The easiest way to avoid this happening to your family is to have an up-to-date will.

Wills

You can form, revoke or change a will at any time during your lifetime as long as you have the mental capacity (i.e., you are of sound mind) to do this. You should review your will annually and make changes as laws or circumstances change. If you have separated, married, have had more children or grandchildren, or someone named in your will has died, then your will needs to be adjusted to reflect this.

What some people do not realise is that your will is automatically cancelled when you marry or enter into a civil union. The only exception to this is if you specifically state in the will that the will is written in contemplation of your marriage. Similarly, if your marriage is ended by a dissolution order, any benefits given to your ex-spouse under the will are cancelled. But be careful — if there is no dissolution order (i.e., you don't formally separate), then unless you change your will to say differently your ex-spouse will continue to inherit.

What if you don't have a will?

If you die without a will, or your will is invalid, you are said to be intestate. If you die intestate, your property is distributed according to the Administration Act 1969, where an order of priority of distribution is in place. The basic order is:

- your spouse, civil-union partner or de facto partner (of more than three years)
- your children
- your parents
- your siblings
- your grandparents
- your uncles and aunts.

Under the rules of intestacy the estate is totalled and divided as follows:

- your spouse takes all personal chattels, $155,000 and one-third of the balance of the estate, and
- your children take the other two-thirds, divided evenly.

If there is no spouse, the children take the entire estate, split equally. If there is no spouse or children, the parents take everything. If there is no spouse, children or parents, the siblings take everything in equal shares, and so forth.

> Money is contentious at the best of times, and even more so at death. Sort out your affairs while you are living to avoid a nightmare for those who are left behind.

The Special Offers chapter on page 331 includes a discount on preparing your own digital will.

A final note

Understanding money fundamentals, and managing your money and mortgage well, are the cornerstones of financial health. When I am working with my clients I take the time to get each core building block working well before I start building onto of the foundation they provide.

Make sure you understand these fundamental money principles:

- The stronger the foundation, the faster and bigger you can build.
- You can't start planning your retirement until you know what you need, and whether you will have enough.
- If you aren't going to have enough, then you need to grow wealth.
- If you're going to grow wealth, you need the right strategy and mix of leverage and diversification.
- If you're going to use leverage, you need equity.
- To have equity, you usually need to be on the property ladder.
- The more equity you have, the more wealth you can create.
- The faster you repay your mortgage, the more equity you create.
- The more you save, the faster you can pay off your mortgage.
- The better your money habits, the faster you save.
- The stronger your money belief, the clearer your goals, the better your spending structure, then the easier and faster you'll see results, improve money behaviours and set better habits.

These steps are all interlinked, and in mastering each component you master money.

Planning retirement: Retirement strategy · Estate planning · Wealth distribution · Asset class management · Liquidity management

Growing wealth: Retirement projections · Wealth strategy · Leverage · Property investing · Investment planning · Diversification

Managing finances: Cashflow management · Debt repayment · Financial resilience · Saving strategy · Mortgage repayment · Insurance and wills · KiwiSaver

Money fundamentals: Money beliefs · Money habits · Money mindset · Setting financial goals · Spending and saving behaviour

In my day job, I take each component and design a plan to help my clients unlock their financial capability, save more, move forward faster and get their money working harder. The best plans need to be executed well, and my team support clients to clinically execute on their plan. The plans are agile and adaptable as circumstances do change (whether it's curve balls or Mack Trucks). Support with accountability is the sweet spot for ongoing success.

What do I want you to take away from this book?

- You need to save. If you don't, or if you need to save more, then you need to change your money habits.
- Changing behaviour is hard. It can be made easier with clear goals, targets, better systems, accountability and, most importantly, results.
- If you want to fast-track change, increase the odds of change, or super-charge progress, engage a financial personal trainer. See the Special Offers chapter (on page 331) for a discount code for enable. me.
- Financial success favours the brave and those who have a well-thought-out plan.
- For a financial plan to work, you must understand your psychology of spending, and learn how to budget effectively, how to save for a property and how to navigate the many financial curve balls life will throw at you.
- Target saving a minimum of 20 per cent of your after-tax (take-home) pay. Some will be starting from 0 per cent, others higher.
- Once you have maximised your cash surplus, it's time to get your money working harder. This is when you need a clear wealth strategy. This is where you will benefit from some expert advice.
- If you have a mortgage, you must learn how to kill it. Could you get rid of it in 10 years? That should be your target.
- Do not be naïve enough to think the bank is your friend.
- Do not be silly enough to think that a celebrity endorsing an investment makes it a good investment.
- Paying your mortgage off is a strategic step towards financial progress, but this in isolation will not achieve a comfortable retirement.
- You will probably need to use the equity in your home to purchase an investment property. But the right property for you will depend

on the problem you need to solve. Setting the property criteria is tricky. Engage an expert. Don't assume all properties are created equal, because they aren't.

- If you can't afford to buy in the area you want to live in, then buy an investment property and rent in your preferred area.
- Learn what you need for your retirement and work out your options for achieving it.
- Understand how much time you have before retirement and the investment constraints you must work within.
- Review your KiwiSaver fund and provider. Even if you are in a good fund, it won't be the best fund forever, so canvas the market each year, or outsource this to an advisor who has access to multiple KiwiSaver products.
- Being the underdog simply means you have to get creative, and get moving.
- Don't buckle under the pressure. Ever. Never give up. There are more opportunities than obstacles, but you usually need to be trained in how to spot them.
- Retirement is not bigger than you. You've got this.

Anyone approaching retirement has a financial place to be and a deadline to get there by. Some of you will be ready to push forward and take more purposeful steps on an already long-planned journey, but many of you will be starting off on the back foot.

Irrespective of where you sit on the financial spectrum, to achieve financial success you need 80 per cent clarity, 10 per cent confidence and 10 per cent competence. If you are serious about arriving at your financial destination within an allocated timeframe, then you need a plan to get you there, with executable steps and measurable progress. Then you go for it.

My favourite Māori proverb sums it up beautifully:

**Te tiro atu tō kanohi ki tairāwhiti ana tērā whiti
te rā kite ataata ka hinga ki muri kia koe.**

**Turn your face to the sun, and the
shadows will fall behind you.**

Financial success is no accident. Good luck!

Special offers

I would like to offer a discounted first meeting with an enable.me financial personal trainer to anyone who would like help to get ahead faster after reading this book. In that meeting, one of my team will work with you to ascertain where you are at financially, where you want to be and whether it is possible to reach your goals faster. It will then be up to you whether you decide to work with us from that point. Either way, the outcome of your first meeting will be that you will know your capability and your next step will be to unlock it.

> Visit enable.me to request a consultation with one of my amazing financial advisors (and financial personal trainers), and be sure to mention this book. You will get a $250 discount off the initial meeting (normally $400). If you sign up for a coached programme, you will receive a 5% discount off the programme cost.

If you have short-term debt, register for my masterclass — Debt-Free Me — and qualify for a 50 per cent discount. Go to www.enableme.co.nz or www.moneyfit.me to find out more.

If you need a will, go to www.advicefirst.co.nz/digital-wills/ and get a 25 per cent discount by mentioning this book.

If you are just starting out, and know you would benefit from working with a financial personal trainer but don't have much money to invest, then go to www.moneyfit.me for an initial consultation with one of our money coaches. The initial session will be discounted if you mention this book, and if you decide to work with them on a six-month coaching programme, you will qualify for a 5 per cent discount.

* Note all offers are valid until December 2025

Good Shepherd

If you want to do some good, there's no better place to go than Good Shepherd. This book is aimed at people who are in a position to help themselves. But some of us aren't. Some of our more vulnerable have been subject to economic harm and financial hardship. Good Shepherd is an amazing organisation that delivers effective support to women, girls and their families to overcome their setbacks and move forward. They deliver services that support in a holistic and meaningful way, such as:

- advocating with creditors to resolve debt issues for their clients
- negotiating debt balances to be reduced, and penalties and interest waived
- offering loans with no interest or fees to help someone on the brink reset and move forward with dignity.

Good Shepherd helps people find their path to long-term financial wellbeing. Their no-fee, no-interest Good Loans can be used to purchase essential items and consolidate harmful debt. Their specialist coaches provide advocacy, information and options that respond to people's experiences and strengths. They are incredible. Being being a not-for-profit, they need our support. If you want to donate, or if your employer takes pride in their employees' financial wellbeing, then hook them up with Good Shepherd to create positive change for those without a voice.

To donate or find out more, go to www.goodshepherd.org.nz

Resources

Articles and books

Acuff, Jon. *Do Over: Make today the first day of your new career.* Penguin, 2017.

Ariely, D., and Kreisler, J. *Dollars and Sense: Money mishaps and how to avoid them.* Boxtree, 2017.

Chammas, H.J., *Millionaire Mindset and Success Habits: How to overcome your own limiting beliefs that make you stand in your own way to becoming financially free.* Independently published, 2021.

Clear, James. *Atomic Habits: An easy and proven way to build good habits and break bad ones.* Avery, 2018.

George, Vishal. *Money Mindsets: Science-based stories to rewire your money beliefs, goals and habits.* Behavioural by Design, 2023.

Grant, Adam. *Hidden Potential: The science of achieving greater things.* Viking, 2023.

Klontz, Brad, Klontz, Ted, and Kahler, Rick. *Wired for Wealth: Change the money mindsets that keep you trapped and unleash your wealth potential.* Simon & Schuster, 2010.

McChesney, C., Huling, J., and Covey, S. *The 4 Disciplines of Execution: Achieving your wildly important goals.* Free Press, 2021.

McKeown, Greg. *Essentialism: The disciplined pursuit of less.* Penguin, 2021.

Rick, Scott, Cryder, Cynthia, and Loewenstein, George. 'Tightwads and Spendthrifts'. *Journal of Consumer Research* vol. 34, issue 6 (April 2008).

Rohn, Jim. *The Art of Exceptional Living.* Sound Wisdom, 2022.

Rohn, Jim. *The Power of Ambition: Awakening the powerful force within you.* Sound Wisdom, 2022.

Rohn, Jim. *The Seasons of Life.* Jim Rohn International, 1981.

Zellermayer, O. *The Pain of Paying* (doctoral dissertation). Department of Social and Decision Sciences, Carnegie Mellon University, 1996.

Podcasts

Huberman, A. 'The science of setting and achieving goals', 2022.

Videos

Ariely, D. 'How to change your behavior for the better'. TED Talk, 2020. www.youtube.com/watch?v=tPBFVIxnbDw

Ariely, D. 'The pain of paying: The psychology of money'. YouTube, 2013. www.youtube.com/watch?v=PCujWv7Mc8o

Gross, B. 'The single biggest reason why start-ups succeed'. TED Talk, 2015. www.youtube.com/watch?v=bNpx7gpSqbY

Acknowledgements

This book is the result of so much effort and support from so many people. Firstly I must mention the Allen & Unwin team. It has been a pleasure to work with such a passionate and competent group of people. I would like to make special mention of Jenny, Tracey and Kate. I also want to thank Ben from Consilium NZ Limited for sharing incredible data and insights around the sharemarket and other investment alternatives, their historical performance and patterns.

At enable.me, more recently a division of AdviceFirst Limited, I work with an amazing group of people who share my vision of improving the financial future of Kiwis by providing practical advice and support using a proven methodology to create positive change in our clients' lives. The enable.me team are fighting to create a better future for us all. I am flattered I can help lead such an inspiring group of people, and I consider you my 'comrades in arms'.

To the working mums everywhere — you all deserve a hug. No one understands the balls you juggle, apart from other working mums. I salute you all.

To Mum, Dad and Kui, thank you for your continual support. Being able to call for a chat, have a good laugh together, draw from your wisdom and rely on your help with the children is invaluable to me and my family. To Billy, the guy I married at 18, who still selflessly supports my pursuit of excellence, thank you. Knowing then what I know now, you would still be my first choice. I don't mention God often — likely because I don't know how to describe my relationship with Him — but He is steadfast to me. In those dark and quiet moments, knowing I can pray to Him and He hears me calms my soul. Lastly, to my darling (and sometimes annoying) children, Cameron and Madison: I do it all for you.

May the Lord bless you and keep you, may His face shine upon you. May He be gracious to you. —Numbers 6:24-25

Appendix I: The 10-step programme

Becoming financially successful is as simple as following these steps.

1. Understand your psychology of spending.
2. Become financially literate.
3. Make a plan.
4. Stick to your plan.
5. Buy a house.
6. Kill your mortgage!
7. Save or leverage.
8. Invest.
9. Retire.
10. Enjoy your retirement!

Understand your psychology of spending

Don't let your genetics determine your financial potential. Understand your money personality (see Chapter 2) and figure out how to work with it to increase your chances of success. If you are in a relationship and you understand your partner's spending and your partner understands yours, and you work together to mitigate any conflict around money issues, it should be impossible for you to fail.

Become financially literate

Learn the rules of money and apply them to your unique circumstances to get ahead faster. Sadly, New Zealand has one of the lowest levels of financial literacy in the developed world. Even many of our successful businesspeople don't know how to manage their personal money.

Make a plan

Develop a plan to make sure you are doing things smarter — as smartly as you possibly can. I believe that if I cannot radically improve the financial position of a client from when I first meet you, then either you have missed something or you are not trying hard enough.

I aim to optimise people's positions and empower them to stretch themselves to reach for and achieve goals that would have seemed impossible before we began working together.

The key to every successful financial plan is spending less than you earn so that you can repay any debt you have as quickly as possible.

Stick to your plan

It's important to continually review your circumstances. If you don't have time to do this — and it does take time — get someone impartial to do it for you. Small slippages can add up to big numbers over time if left unchecked.

Once you have a written plan, be accountable to it. Make it fluid enough that curve balls can be absorbed and the numbers can change as circumstances change; for example, if you get a pay rise. Be accountable to someone, somewhere, who is qualified to comment and will challenge you and your assumptions.

Buy a house

You need to be on the property ladder, as this has historically been one of the better-performing asset classes. Psychologically it is easier to pay off debt than to save. Be sure to buy in an area where capital gain is expected. Rent and own an investment property over home ownership if you have the choice (see Chapter 9).

Kill your mortgage!

Once you have your property, you need to attack the mortgage, as the total cost of having a mortgage for 30 years can be up to three times what you initially borrowed. Channel all surplus funds into the mortgage.

Save or leverage

Once you've paid off your mortgage, focus on saving for retirement. If it's unlikely that you will save enough, you need to think about what you are investing your funds in, and whether a better return can be achieved without exposing yourself to unnecessary risk. Alternatively, use the equity in your home to borrow money and invest in another property.

Invest

If you are able to leverage off your equity, buy an investment property in an area that is going to have high demand and therefore strong capital-gain prospects. This property needs to be as close to cash-neutral as possible. The capital gain less the holding costs is what is going to help cover your retirement shortfall.

If you have saved enough funds, these can be put into myriad investments. Remember that your appetite for risk needs to be curtailed by your situation. If you are approaching retirement, don't invest big, because you will probably not be able to afford to lose big.

Retire/enjoy your retirement!

Once you have retired, you will need a new plan to follow as your capital will likely reduce over the next 25 years. This decrease in capital is needed to fund your lifestyle but, unless it's built into a clear plan, you will not feel you have permission to enjoy the money you are spending. Get a plan, get perspective and stay in control.

Enjoy your retirement — you've earned it!

Appendix II: Financial compatibility questionnaire

Money is one of the most common sources of tension in relationships. If this is true for you and your relationship, the first thing you need to do is talk to your partner. To see where the greatest problems lie, complete this financial compatibility questionnaire.

For each question below, grade your answer from 1 to 5.

5 = strongly agree

4 = agree

3 = don't feel strongly either way

2 = disagree

1 = strongly disagree

	Question	You	Partner
1.	I think it's important to make compulsory savings every month, even if the amount saved is small.		
2.	Life is short. If you work hard, you should be able to spend what you earn when you want to.		
3.	Couples should keep their finances separate, and only share finances for costs that are equally split (such as rent, power, phone).		
4.	Couples should have a budget that they stick to every week.		
5.	I prefer to save up for things, rather than use credit cards or hire purchase.		
6.	I always pay off my credit card in full at the end of the month.		
7.	If I get a build-up of debt on my credit cards I consolidate it all into one low-interest credit card or loan.		
8.	I spend more on holidays each year than I did the previous year.		

9.	Having the latest gadgets is important to me and part of the image I want to project.		
10.	If we can't afford it I would rather not go on holiday, however much I need a break.		
11.	I plan to retire early by making as much money as possible and living to a financial plan.		
12.	If one of us brings in more money, then the other should compensate by taking over more of the household chores.		
13.	When my parents die, I am expecting an inheritance. I believe that this is my property and will not be intermingled with my relationship finances in any way.		
14.	I am a feel-good spender and get a kick from buying things, even if they are small and inexpensive. I have also been known to buy things when I can't necessarily afford them.		
15.	I expect my partner to contribute equally to the costs of our living expenses.		
16.	If I earn more than my partner, I should be able to spend more on myself as I feel I have worked harder for it.		
17.	I think that whatever money comes into the partnership, regardless of where it comes from, should be shared equally. We are a team, after all.		
18.	I prefer to spend spare money on property or investments, rather than stuff like cars, holidays, clothes or shoes.		
19.	If we were to split up I think the person who has earned most should be entitled to most of the possessions.		
20.	I sometimes hide the fact that I have spent money, by hiding purchases or saying things cost less than they did.		
21.	I think my partner wastes money on some things and can be too generous with family and friends.		
22.	I think my partner is over-careful with money and I am sometimes embarrassed by their stinginess, especially if it means someone else is forced to pay due to their meanness.		
23.	I am afraid to discuss money issues with my partner, as it tends to get personal and usually ends in a disagreement.		

24.	I would like to know more about what is happening to our money but my partner controls the day-to-day finances.		
25.	We often disagree on what we should spend our money on.		
26.	I don't understand finance in general; it intimidates me, so I choose to ignore it and bury my head in the sand.		
27.	I think it is OK if one partner wants to handle all the money affairs, provided they are actually in control of the money.		

Interpreting your result

It's important to interpret your scores in two ways: first focus on your overall compatibility by looking at your overall score difference, then concentrate on the results of the questions where you have the highest points of difference.

An overall score difference of 0 means that you are perfectly compatible on every aspect of money management and are unlikely to have conflicts around money. Be aware, though, that compatibility does not necessarily translate to increased capability.

An overall score difference of 1–24 means that you are compatible on most things but may have one or two areas to discuss and work through.

An overall score difference of 25–49 indicates that you have different attitudes regarding money management in a number of areas, and this is likely to create some tensions in your relationship. While you should sit down and discuss these issues, the discussion could become heated and personal. You might need to engage an impartial third party if you are committed to working towards a better end game and do not want emotional baggage and conflict to interfere with it.

An overall score difference of 50–74 clearly highlights that you have significant differences in your attitudes to money which will inevitably put a strain on your relationship. Remember, money is indirectly linked to most areas of life, so if you do not have a healthy synergy the impact will be far-reaching. Money is important and you must set aside some specific time to work through these issues. You may also wish to consider getting some relationship coaching to help you through this. While you may be coming at the issues from different perspectives, it usually pays to focus on your common goals. Once you agree what you are working towards and your individual requirements, a good financial coach can help you to tailor a plan so that everyone gets what they need individually and less emphasis is placed on each other's behaviour.

An overall score difference of 75+ means that you have totally different attitudes and behaviour in relation to money and you are likely to need to really focus on this area in order to resolve conflict in your relationship. Consider whether you tackle this together, for the sake of the relationship. If that is not the best approach, you may need some professional help. I have worked with many couples, some of whom were polar opposites. Their coping mechanisms were either serious conflict or disengaging themselves from reality. Neither option will work in the long term. If you are committed to the relationship, keep working on these issues, otherwise they might tear your relationship apart.

Appendix III: Financial assessment template

Use these templates to figure out where you are financially at the present time. Part 1 will help you understand the money you have coming in; Part 2 breaks down your current assets and liabilities; and Part 3 is a spending analysis that you can use to figure out where your money's going, and where you can make changes to start getting ahead.

Part 1 — Your income
Income

Net per annum

Name | [   ]

Annual $
(after tax)

Source of income

Type of income

Total _____

Name | [   ]

Type of income

Total _____

Income totals

Net per annum

Person 1

Person 2

Joint TOTAL

Part 2 – Your financial position (net worth)
Assets — Property

Property address	Owned by	Purchased when	For how much	Current value

Total property assets			Current value total:	$

Current mortgage structure

Which bank	Fixed or floating/for how long	Comes off fixed rate when	At what interest rate	Monthly repayment	Current balance

Total mortgage debt

Current debt total: $

Net property assets (current value total LESS current debt total)

$

Other assets

	Value
Car (1)	
Car (2)	
Motorbike	
Caravan	
Boat	
Savings	
Superannuation	
KiwiSaver	
Shares	
Bonus bonds	
Investments	
Term deposits	
Other	
TOTAL OTHER ASSETS	$

Other liabilities

Details (e.g., credit cards, hire-purchase car loan)	Interest rate	Card limit	Monthly payment	Amount owing
TOTAL AMOUNT OWING				$

Total other assets from p. 347 $

Total amount owing   – $

Total net other assets
(other assets LESS
amount owing)   = $

Total net property assets
(from p. 346) $

Total net other assets
(from above)   + $

Sum = total wealth   = $

Part 3 — Your outgoings

	Monthly amount	Current annual
Accommodation		
Cleaner	x 12	
Furniture and homewares	x 12	
Gardening (lawns, garden bin)	x 12	
House maintenance	x 12	
Landscaping	x 12	
Mortgage	x 12	
Rates (water, land, regional)	x 12	
Rent	x 12	
White goods and electrical	x 12	
Other (e.g., body corporate fees)	x 12	
	Subtotal 1	
Basic living costs		
Clothes, shoes (including dry-cleaning)	x 12	
Electricity/gas	x 12	
Food and household shopping	x 12	
Internet	x 12	
Mobile phones	x 12	
Alarm	x 12	
Firewood	x 12	
	Subtotal 2	
Children, education, family costs		
Daycare	x 12	
Babysitting	x 12	
Children's clothes	x 12	
School extras (trips, etc.)	x 12	
School fees	x 12	
School uniforms	x 12	
Tertiary education fees	x 12	
Text books, stationery	x 12	

Tuition/activities	x 12
Contributions to other family	x 12
Kids' activities	
	Subtotal 3 _____

Car, vehicle expenses

Boat/campervan	x 12
Boat/campervan insurance	x 12
Boat/campervan maintenance	x 12
Maintenance	x 12
Parking	x 12
Petrol	x 12
Registration and WOF	x 12
Taxis, public transport	x 12
Tyre replacement	x 12
AA membership	x 12
Road user charges	
	Subtotal 4 _____

Financial

Bank fees	x 12
Car insurance	x 12
Child support payments	x 12
Contents insurance	x 12
Credit-card repayments	x 12
House & contents insurance	x 12
Investment/savings	x 12
Life, income protection & trauma insurance	x 12
Medical insurance	x 12
Pet insurance	x 12
Other (e.g., professional fees)	x 12
Other (e.g., property top-up)	x 12
	Subtotal 5 _____

Medical

Chemist and prescriptions	x 12
Dentist	x 12
Doctor	x 12
Optometrist	x 12
Podiatrist	x 12
Naturopath	x 12
Massage	
Specialist	
Supplements	
	Subtotal 6

Discretionary

Alcohol	x 12
Annual holidays	x 12
Bars, clubs, pubs	x 12
Birthday presents and gifts	x 12
Books and magazines	x 12
Christmas presents	x 12
Church, tithing	x 12
Cigarettes/vaping	x 12
Donations	x 12
Entertainment	x 12
Easter	x 12
Hairdresser	x 12
Hobbies	x 12
Makeup, toiletries	x 12
Memberships (e.g., gym)	x 12
Online subscriptions	x 12
Restaurants and cafés	x 12
Short breaks/weekends	x 12
Special events/outings	x 12
Sports	x 12
TAB, casino, Lotto	x 12

Takeaways	x 12	
Pet and vet	x 12	
Work lunch	x 12	
Coffees	x 12	
Other	x 12	
	Subtotal 7	
Total expenses	Add subtotals 1–7	$
Total net income (from page 344)		$
Total expenses (from above)	–	$
Initial surplus / deficit	(Total net income LESS total expenses) =	$

If your total net income is greater than your total expenses, you have a surplus.

If your total expenses are greater than your total net income, you have a deficit.